Lecture Notes in Computer Science   6626

Commenced Publication in 1973
Founding and Former Series Editors:
Gerhard Goos, Juris Hartmanis, and Jan van

Raimondo Schettini   Shoji Tominaga
Alain Trémeau (Eds.)

Computational Color Imaging

Third International Workshop, CCIW 2011
Milan, Italy, April 20-21, 2011
Proceedings

 Springer

Volume Editors

Raimondo Schettini
Università degli Studi di Milano-Bicocca
Dipartimento di Informatica Sistemistica e Comunicazione
Viale Sarca 336, U14, 20126 Milano, Italy
E-mail: schettini@disco.unimib.it

Shoji Tominaga
Chiba University, Graduate School of Advanced Integration Science
1-33, Yayoi-cho, Inage-ku, Chiba-shi, Chiba, 263-8522, Japan
E-mail: shoji@faculty.chiba-u.jp

Alain Trémeau
Université Jean Monnet, Laboratoire Hubert Curien UMR CNRS 5516
18 rue Benoit Lauras, 42000 Saint-Etienne, France
E-mail: alain.tremeau@univ-st-etienne.fr

ISSN 0302-9743   e-ISSN 1611-3349
ISBN 978-3-642-20403-6   e-ISBN 978-3-642-20404-3
DOI 10.1007/978-3-642-20404-3
Springer Heidelberg Dordrecht London New York

Library of Congress Control Number: 2011924494

CR Subject Classification (1998): I.4, I.3, I.5, I.2.10, F.2.2

LNCS Sublibrary: SL 6 – Image Processing, Computer Vision, Pattern Recognition,
and Graphics

Typesetting: Camera-ready by author, data conversion by Scientific Publishing Services, Chennai, India

Printed on acid-free paper

Springer is part of Springer Science+Business Media (www.springer.com)

Preface

We would like to welcome you to the proceedings of CCIW 2011, the Computational Color Imaging Workshop, held in Milan, Italy, April 20-21, 2011. This, the third CCIW, was organized by the University of Milano-Bicocca with the endorsement of the International Association for Pattern Recognition (IAPR), the Group of Italian Researchers on Pattern Recognition (GIRPR) affiliated with IAPR, and the Italian *Gruppo del Colore* (GdC).

The second CCIW was organized by the University Jean Monnet and the Laboratoire Hubert Curien UMR 5516 (Saint-Etienne, France) with the endorsement of the International Association for Pattern Recognition (IAPR), the French Association for Pattern Recognition and Interpretation (AFRIF) affiliated with IAPR, and the *Groupe Franais de l'Imagerie Numrique Couleur* (GFINC).

Our first goal, since we began the planning of the workshop, was to bring together engineers and scientists from various imaging companies and from technical communities all over the world to discuss diverse aspects of their latest work, ranging from theoretical developments to practical applications in the field of color imaging, color image processing and analysis. The workshop was therefore intended for researchers and practitioners in the fields of digital imaging, multimedia, visual communications, computer vision, and consumer electronic industry, who are interested in the fundamentals of color image processing and its emerging applications. We received many excellent submissions. Each paper was peer reviewed and then the General Chairs carefully selected only 16 papers in order to achieve a high scientific level at the workshop. The final decisions were based on the criticisms and recommendations of the reviewers and the relevance of papers to the goal of the workshop. In order to have an overview of current research directions in computational color imaging, four different sessions were organized:

- Computational photography
- Color and perception
- Color imaging
- Computational imaging

In addition to the contributed papers, four distinguished researchers were invited to this third CCIW to deliver keynote speeches on current research directions in hot topics on computational color imaging:

- Gaurav Sharma, on "Imaging Arithmetic: Physics U Math > Physics + Math"
- Maria Vanrell, on "Perception-Based Representations for Computational Color"
- Erik Reinhard, on "Color Spaces for Color Transfer"
- Keigo Hirakawa, on "Spectral Filter Array Design for Multispectral Image Recovery"

There are many organizations and people to thank for their various contributions to the planning of this meeting. We are pleased to acknowledge the generous support of the Chiba University, the University of Saint Etienne, the Dipartimento di Informatica Sistemistica e Comunicazione, Universitá degli Studi di Milano-Bicocca, and Gruppo del Colore. Special thanks also go to Francesca Gasparini, Gianluigi Ciocca and to all our colleagues on the Conference Committee for their dedication and work, without which this workshop would not have been possible. Finally, we envision the continuation of this unique event, and we are already making plans for organizing the next CCIW workshop in 2013.

April 2011   Raimondo Schettini
                                                                  Shoji Tominaga
                                                                  Alain Trémeau

Organization

CCIW 2011 was organized by the University of Milano-Bicocca, Italy, in cooperation with the University of Saint Etienne, France, and the Chiba University, Japan.

Executive Committee

Conference Chairs   Raimondo Schettini
      (University of Milano-Bicocca, Milan, Italy)
    Shoji Tominaga (Chiba University, Japan)
    Alain Trémeau (Université Jean Monnet,
      Saint-Etienne, France)

Program Committee

James Archibald (USA)
Sebastiano Battiato (Italy)
Simone Bianco (Italy)
Cheng-Chin Chiang (Taiwan)
Bibhas Chandra Dhara (India)
Gianluigi Ciocca (Italy)
Brian Funt (Canada)
Francesca Gasparini (Italy)
Theo Gevers (The Netherlands)
Yeong-Ho Ha (Korea)
Patrick Lambert (France)
Peihua Li (China)
Hubert Konik (France)

Lizhuang Ma (China)
Ludovic Macaire (France)
Yoshitsugu Manabe (Japan)
Jussi Parkkinen (Finland)
Maurizio Rossi (Italy)
Ishwar K. Sethi (USA)
Gerald Schaefer (UK)
Bogdan Smolka (Poland)
Sabine Susstrunk (Switzerland)
Johji Tajima (Japan)
Joost Van de Weijer (Spain)
Maria Vanrell Martorell (Spain)
Xiangyang Xue (China)

Sponsoring Institutions

University of Milano-Bicocca, Milan, Italy
Chiba University, Japan
Laboratoire Hubert Curien, Saint-Etienne, France
Université Jean Monnet, Saint-Etienne, France
Gruppo del Colore, Italy

Table of Contents

Color Imaging

Computational Imaging

Colour Spaces for Colour Transfer

Erik Reinhard and Tania Pouli

University of Bristol, Dept. of Computer Science
{reinhard,pouli}@cs.bris.ac.uk

Abstract. Colour transfer algorithms aim to apply a colour palette, mood or style from one image to another, operating either in a three-dimensional colour space, or splitting the problem into three simpler one-dimensional problems. The latter class of algorithms simply treats each of the three dimensions independently, whether justified or not. Although they rarely introduce spatial artefacts, the quality of the results depends on how the problem was split into three sub-problems, i.e. which colour space was chosen. Generally, the assumption is made that a decorrelated colour space would perform best, as decorrelation makes the three colour channels semi-independent (decorrelation is a weaker property than independence). However, such spaces are only decorrelated for well-chosen image ensembles. For individual images, this property may not hold. In this work, the connection between the natural statistics of colour images and the ability of existing colour transfer algorithms to produce plausible results is investigated. This work aims to provide a better understanding of the performance of different colour spaces in the context of colour transfer.

Keywords: Colour Transfer, Colour Spaces, Correlation.

1 Introduction

Colour is one of the main image attributes used in art, photography and visualisation for relaying information, or for conveying a specific mood. Tools available to alter and manipulate the colour content of images tend to require extensive user input or simply do not offer sufficient control over the result. This leaves many such tools out of reach of untrained users. Considering such users, colour transfer forms a class of techniques that allow the colour palette of an image to be altered using a second image as a reference. The task is then to select a reference image whose colours are preferred. Subsequently the algorithm will modify the original image such that it acquires the palette of that reference.

In essence this operation can be seen as a function that, given two images, produces a third that has maintained the semantic content of the one while acquiring the colours of the second. This of course can be achieved in many different ways, using different descriptors for the image content, or operating in different colour spaces, leading to an extensive collection of colour transfer techniques.

R. Schettini, S. Tominaga, and A. Trémeau (Eds.): CCIW 2011, LNCS 6626, pp. 1–15, 2011.
© Springer-Verlag Berlin Heidelberg 2011

This set of techniques can be broadly categorised into two classes, namely those that treat colour transfer as a 3D problem, and those that decompose the problem into a set of three 1D problems. The latter class is the focus of this paper, and relies on an important insight from the area of natural image statistics.

Natural image statistics is the study of statistical regularities in images, and usually aims to help understand how the human visual system operates. The argument is that human vision has evolved in the presence of a natural environment, and is therefore in some sense specialised to observe and interpret natural images. Such images are normally taken to be those that occur in nature, and for instance do not contain man-made structures.

In the context of human vision, Ruderman et al tested this hypothesis. They converted a set of spectral natural images to LMS cones space, a colour space that resembles the responses of the L, M and S cones in the human retina (the letters stand for Long, Medium and Short wavelength, respectively, indicating the peak sensitivity of each cone type). This image ensemble was then subjected to Principal Component Analysis (PCA), showing that the three principal components obtained closely correspond to the opponent colour channels found in the human visual system, in particular in the retina [23]. As PCA yields components that are maximally decorrelated, we can infer that the human retina aims to decorrelate its input. While formally PCA only decorrelates, it was found that transforming natural images according to this colour space, termed $L\alpha\beta$, yields channels that are close to independent.

By producing a decorrelated image signal, and for natural images largely independent signal, the efficiency of transmitting information through the optic nerve is increased, especially considering that the optic nerve constitutes a bottleneck in terms of transmission bandwidth. On the other hand, it is now possible to use this knowledge for computational tasks. The observation is that if the three colour channels of an image can be made independent, then image processing can take place in each of the three channels independently [19].

This has led to an early colour transfer algorithm which essentially matches means and standard deviations between a pair of images [19]. It can be shown that the choice of colour space is important, i.e. that decorrelation matters. An example is given in Figure 1, where the RGB colour space does not lead to an effective transfer of the colour palette, while the $L\alpha\beta$ space produces a much more plausible result.

Although $L\alpha\beta$ has been adopted as the space of choice for several colour transfer algorithms [19,5,25,34,11,33,26,12,35,32,30], related spaces such as CIELAB are also used [4,28,18]. Other colour spaces implicated in colour transfer are CIE LCh* [14], YC_bC_r [9], Yuv [10,27], as well as colour appearance models [13]. On the other hand, several authors suggest to compute a dedicated colour space for each transfer, based on PCA [8,1,7,31,2].

We argue that the choice of colour space is important, especially for the class of algorithms that decompose the problem into a set of three 1D problems. To test this hypothesis, we present a pilot study for which we collected a small set of images, and divided them into four distinct image sets, containing natural

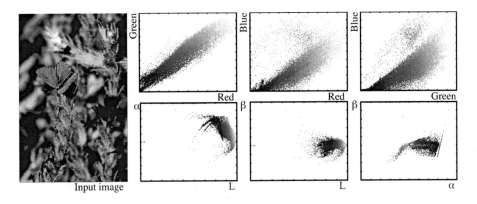

Fig. 1. Decorrelation properties of colour spaces. The top row shows pixel values for pairs of channels in an RGB colour space, taken from the image at the top left. The bottom row shows the same pixels plotted in pairs of channels from the $L\alpha\beta$ space instead. Values in channel in RGB spaces tend to be good predictors of other channels, resulting in an almost diagonal distribution.

scenes, manmade scenes, indoor scenes and night-time scenes. We first measure how well different colour spaces decorrelate each category, predicting how well we expect these spaces to perform for each image category. We then apply the colour transfer algorithm to pairs of images within each image category in each colour space to assess our predictions. We hope the insights presented in this paper provide a useful background for future developments in colour transfer.

2   Previous Work

One of the earliest colour transfer algorithms matches means and standard deviations in the $L\alpha\beta$ colour space that is decorrelated for natural images [19,20]. To achieve a more complete transfer, histogram matching can be used to transfer the distributions of images [14,32]. Some argue that a post-processing step to preserve gradient magnitudes is desirable [32]. A more refined approach sits in-between Reinhard's original technique and full histogram matching, allowing histograms to be partially matched in a controllable manner [17,18].

Recognising that no single colour space may suit all occasions, some authors propose to apply Principal Components Analysis to individual images, creating a dedicated colour space for each transfer [8,1,7,31,2]. To a greater degree this can also be achieved by means of Independent Components Analysis [6].

Most of these methods treat the three colour channels independently, meaning that the choice of colour space as well as the choice of source and target images determine the visual quality of the transfer. Alternatively, it is possible to carry out the colour transfer in 3D colour space, for instance by transferring probability distributions from one image to another [15,16], or by employing Gaussian Mixture Models [24,33,30]. A further technique aims to minimise artefacts by limiting transfers to remain within colour naming categories [4]. Some techniques allow stroke-based user input to define target colours [10] or to define corresponding regions [28,3].

3   Method

An important aspect both in colour processing in the human visual system and in many colour transfer algorithms is the decorrelation of the input. This can only be assessed relative to a set of images. In this section we discuss the data sets that we captured, the colour spaces that we test, as well as the colour transfer algorithm employed. Sections 4 and 5 then present our results, followed by a discussion in Section 6.

3.1   Image Ensembles

To analyse the ability of existing colour spaces to decorrelate different scene categories as well as to evaluate the different colour spaces resulting from these scene categories we analyse several image databases. For this work, we focus both on different scene categories:

- **ND - Natural Day:** contains 95 day-time images shot outdoors in natural locations, without manmade structures. A variety of landscapes and weather conditions are included.
- **MD - Manmade Day:** contains 100 day-time images shot outdoors in manmade locations. These include urban landscapes as well as constructions and monuments from different eras.
- **IN - Indoors:** contains 100 images shot in indoors locations, such as rooms, offices or shops. In many scenes, artificial and natural light sources may be visible, including windows.
- **MN - Night:** contains 52 images shot at dusk or night, in urban locations. Many contain light sources visible within the scene such as street lights.

For the purpose of creating PCA-based colour spaces for each category, we use all the images in each category. When assessing the plausibility of colour transfer, we use a random subset of 6 images from each category (11 from the natural day ensemble).

3.2   Colour Spaces

A set of candidate spaces was selected based on the colour spaces seen in use in colour transfer research. The chosen colour spaces are $L\alpha\beta$, CIELAB (using both D65 and E illuminants), Yxy, Yuv, Yu'v', XYZ, RGB and HSV [22]. We have also computed a dedicated colour space for each of the image ensembles using PCA. Although most colour spaces are well known, the $L\alpha\beta$ space is perhaps least known, and is therefore described in more detail here.

To transform the images to $L\alpha\beta$ space, the input sRGB values are first converted to the device independent XYZ space:

$$\begin{bmatrix} X \\ Y \\ Z \end{bmatrix} = \begin{bmatrix} 0.4124 & 0.3576 & 0.1805 \\ 0.2126 & 0.7152 & 0.0722 \\ 0.0193 & 0.1192 & 0.9505 \end{bmatrix} \begin{bmatrix} R \\ G \\ B \end{bmatrix} \tag{1}$$

After the RGB to XYZ conversion, values are further converted to the LMS cone space to prepare them for the final transform into the $L\alpha\beta$ space:

$$\begin{bmatrix} L \\ M \\ S \end{bmatrix} = \begin{bmatrix} 0.3897 & 0.6890 & -0.0787 \\ -0.2298 & 1.1834 & 0.0464 \\ 0.0000 & 0.0000 & 1.0000 \end{bmatrix} \begin{bmatrix} X \\ Y \\ Z \end{bmatrix} \tag{2}$$

Following Ruderman et al. [23], the LMS values are logarithmically compressed to reduce skew in the data before applying the linear transform to $L\alpha\beta$:

$$\begin{bmatrix} L \\ \alpha \\ \beta \end{bmatrix} = \mathrm{diag} \left(\frac{1}{\sqrt{3}} \; \frac{1}{\sqrt{6}} \; \frac{1}{\sqrt{2}} \right) \begin{bmatrix} 1 & 1 & 1 \\ 1 & 1 & -2 \\ 1 & -1 & 0 \end{bmatrix} \begin{bmatrix} \log L \\ \log M \\ \log S \end{bmatrix} \tag{3}$$

This colour space is characterised by a luminance channel L and two opponent colour channels α and β, which encode yellow-blue and red-green chromaticities. The space is derived from Principal Components Analysis of natural images, and is therefore expected to be a good candidate for colour transfer algorithms, a hypothesis tested in this paper.

3.3 Ensemble-Based Colour Spaces

For each of our image ensembles we compute dedicated colour spaces following a process similar to the one described in [23]. More specifically, the following steps result in a 3x3 matrix conversion matrix, converting between LMS cone space and a space which is decorrelated with respect to a specific image ensemble. Each of the rows of the matrix correspond to a principal component and therefore an axis of the ensemble-specific colour space.

A square patch of 128×128 pixels is selected from each of the images in an ensemble. These patches are then converted to LMS cone space. The patches are logarithmically compressed, and the data in each channel is mean centred, simulating a simplified Von Kries adaptation step [29]. Finally Principal Component Analysis (PCA) is performed on the $N \times 3$ matrix which results from concatenating the scanlines of all image patches. This produces a set of 3 components (eigenvectors) sorted according to their respective eigenvalues. For each of our four image ensembles, this leads to a colour space which in the PCA sense would be more decorrelated than any of the standard colour spaces.

3.4 Colour Transfer

In its simplest form, the algorithm proposed by Reinhard et al. [19,21] shifts and scales the pixel values of the source image to match the mean and standard deviation of the target:

$$L_o = \frac{\sigma_{t,l}}{\sigma_{s,l}} (L_s - \mu_s) + \mu_t \tag{4}$$

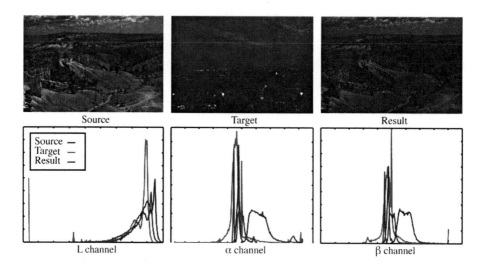

Fig. 2. An example pair of source and target images as well as their resulting output after using the colour transfer technique by Reinhard et al. [19] are shown in the top row. The corresponding histograms are shown at the bottom for the three channels of the $L\alpha\beta$ colour space.

Here, the subscripts s, t and o correspond to the source, target and output images and μ and σ are their respective means and standard deviations. Equation 4 describes the distribution transfer between source and target for the luminance channel only. The same process is repeated for the two opponent channels of the $L\alpha\beta$ space to complete the colour transfer. Figure 2 shows an example pair of source and target images as well as their corresponding histograms before and after transferring the colours between them. Rather than employ the $L\alpha\beta$ space, in the following experiments we operate this procedure in a variety of different spaces to assess their viability.

4   Correlation Analysis

To analyse the extent to which a colour space decorrelates its colour channels for a specific image ensemble, we use a procedure based on measuring the covariance between channels. First, each of our image sets is converted to the different spaces that we wish to compare. Following these conversions, the centre patch of 128 × 128 pixels is selected from each image, arranged to form an N × 3 vector. From this vector a 3-by-3 covariance matrix can be computed, containing the covariance between pairs of channels in the off-diagonal elements and the channel variance on the diagonal elements.

To make the covariance values comparable between colour spaces, we normalise the data used to compute the covariances. This is not straightforward as each colour space has different ranges and possibly different ratios between its

Table 1. The volumes of different colour spaces, approximated by a cuboid

Colour Space	Volume	Colour Space	Volume
$La\beta$	6.4480	YUV'	0.1318
CIELab (E)	6.0447e+03	HSV	0.8333
CIELab (D65)	8.8841e+03	XYZ	1.0351
Yxy	0.2646	RGB	1.0000
YUV	0.0879		

channels. Simply normalising the data by its maximum – whether per channel or per set – is not sufficient as this would potentially change the relations between the three channels of each space and would not necessarily ensure that the results are comparable.

For our analysis, we choose to normalise the different colour spaces according to their volume. Each space is defined by 3 axes, with different ranges and ratios between them. To approximate the volume of each colour space, the maximum and minimum achievable values for each channel are determined. In some colour spaces, such as RGB, these are well defined. In cases such as CIELAB however, values may not be explicitly constrained. Instead, we constrain the input to our analysis such that the initial RGB values are normalised between 0 and 1. Using a simple 3-channel image containing all permutations of 0 and 1, we can determine the minimum and maximum values that can be achieved in each channel for each of the colour spaces that we are examining. These values are then used to compute the volumes of the spaces, shown in Table 1. Since the RGB input is normalised, the RGB space already has unit volume. The normalisation procedure then consists of scaling the image values by the cube root of the colour space's volume, which is sufficient to allow comparisons between them.

4.1 Standard Colour Spaces

Tables 2 and 3 show the resulting covariance matrices for each colour space and for each of our image ensembles.

From these covariance matrices, we take the off-axis elements and average their absolute values, leading to an average covariance for each colour space. We then use these numbers to rank each colour space, leading to the orderings shown in Table 4. The first colour space is thus the most effective at decomposing the specified category of images to decorrelated components.

The first observation is that for all image ensembles CIELAB with illuminant E decorrelates the data more effectively than all other colour spaces. Especially for day-time images, both natural and artificial, this space decorrelates significantly better than the second best colour spaces. Surprisingly, CIELAB with illuminant D65 does not decorrelate well. On the other hand, we see that RGB and XYZ are significantly worse than all other colour spaces. Finally, we note that the ranking is mostly consistent across image ensembles. We expect that this measure of correlation is indicative for the performance of these colour spaces in colour transfer tasks.

Table 2. Covariance matrices for the Natural and Manmade Day ensembles

	Natural Day				Manmade Day		
$L\alpha\beta$	0.0462	-0.0059	-0.0002	$L\alpha\beta$	0.0611	-0.0051	-0.0004
	-0.0059	0.0025	0.0001		-0.0051	0.0027	0.0002
	-0.0002	0.0001	0.0000		-0.0004	0.0002	0.0000
CIELab (E)	0.0062	-0.0016	-0.0002	CIELab (E)	0.0057	-0.0016	0.0003
	-0.0016	0.0009	-0.0002		-0.0016	0.0009	0.0002
	-0.0002	-0.0002	0.0013		0.0003	0.0002	0.0018
CIELab (D65)	0.0048	-0.0030	-0.0107	CIELab (D65)	0.0044	-0.0028	-0.0099
	-0.0030	0.0022	0.0061		-0.0028	0.0021	0.0065
	-0.0107	0.0061	0.0287		-0.0099	0.0065	0.0278
Yxy	0.0616	-0.0027	-0.0041	Yxy	0.0567	-0.0031	-0.0025
	-0.0027	0.0010	0.0008		-0.0031	0.0015	0.0010
	-0.0041	0.0008	0.0016		-0.0025	0.0010	0.0013
YUV	0.1286	-0.0007	-0.0030	YUV	0.1183	-0.0024	-0.0021
	-0.0007	0.0005	0.0001		-0.0024	0.0007	0.0002
	-0.0030	0.0001	0.0004		-0.0021	0.0002	0.0004
YUV'	0.0981	-0.0005	-0.0035	YUV'	0.0903	-0.0018	-0.0024
	-0.0005	0.0004	0.0001		-0.0018	0.0006	0.0002
	-0.0035	0.0001	0.0006		-0.0024	0.0002	0.0007
HSV	0.0075	-0.0019	0.0019	HSV	0.0142	-0.0029	0.0018
	-0.0019	0.0264	-0.0146		-0.0029	0.0262	-0.0077
	0.0019	-0.0146	0.0303		0.0018	-0.0077	0.0311
XYZ	0.0221	0.0234	0.0240	XYZ	0.0201	0.0214	0.0207
	0.0234	0.0248	0.0253		0.0214	0.0228	0.0223
	0.0240	0.0253	0.0276		0.0207	0.0223	0.0241
RGB	0.0269	0.0254	0.0232	RGB	0.0260	0.0234	0.0190
	0.0254	0.0258	0.0236		0.0234	0.0239	0.0209
	0.0232	0.0236	0.0238		0.0190	0.0209	0.0208

4.2 Ensemble-Specific Colour Spaces

We compute dedicated colour spaces for each of the four image ensembles. For comparison, we note that the $L\alpha\beta$ colour space, derived from 12 spectral images of natural environments, takes the form of 3 approximately orthonormal principal axes [23]:

$$L = (\log L + \log M + \log S)/\sqrt{3} \tag{5a}$$

$$\alpha = (\log L + \log M - 2\log S)/\sqrt{6} \tag{5b}$$

$$\beta = (\log L + \log M)/\sqrt{2} \tag{5c}$$

For comparison, the precise components for this colour space are replicated in Table 5. We find that these axes closely approximate the actual components resulting from our principal component analysis, which are shown with their corresponding eigenvalues λ in Table 6.

Table 3. Covariance matrices for the Indoors and Night ensembles

Indoors				Manmade Night			
$L\alpha\beta$	0.1153	-0.0081	-0.0005	$L\alpha\beta$	0.0688	-0.0045	-0.0008
	-0.0081	0.0052	0.0003		-0.0045	0.0054	0.0004
	-0.0005	0.0003	0.0001		-0.0008	0.0004	0.0001
CIELab (E)	0.0088	-0.0024	0.0018	CIELab (E)	0.0058	-0.0016	0.0019
	-0.0024	0.0016	-0.0005		-0.0016	0.0018	-0.0005
	0.0018	-0.0005	0.0028		0.0019	-0.0005	0.0045
CIELab (D65)	0.0068	-0.0043	-0.0126	CIELab (D65)	0.0045	-0.0029	-0.0067
	-0.0043	0.0033	0.0080		-0.0029	0.0027	0.0043
	-0.0126	0.0080	0.0323		-0.0067	0.0043	0.0223
Yxy	0.0865	-0.0040	-0.0036	Yxy	0.0575	-0.0036	0.0001
	-0.0040	0.0025	0.0016		-0.0036	0.0029	0.0010
	-0.0036	0.0016	0.0025		0.0001	0.0010	0.0018
YUV	0.1803	-0.0028	-0.0028	YUV	0.1200	-0.0052	-0.0006
	-0.0028	0.0014	0.0003		-0.0052	0.0024	0.0003
	-0.0028	0.0003	0.0008		-0.0006	0.0003	0.0005
YUV'	0.1376	-0.0022	-0.0032	YUV'	0.0915	-0.0039	-0.0007
	-0.0022	0.0010	0.0004		-0.0039	0.0018	0.0003
	-0.0032	0.0004	0.0013		-0.0007	0.0003	0.0009
HSV	0.0145	0.0039	0.0023	HSV	0.0263	0.0009	0.0051
	0.0039	0.0422	-0.0095		0.0009	0.0282	-0.0021
	0.0023	-0.0095	0.0494		0.0051	-0.0021	0.0388
XYZ	0.0306	0.0326	0.0287	XYZ	0.0205	0.0216	0.0175
	0.0326	0.0348	0.0307		0.0216	0.0232	0.0188
	0.0287	0.0307	0.0303		0.0175	0.0188	0.0204
RGB	0.0424	0.0371	0.0275	RGB	0.0324	0.0248	0.0153
	0.0371	0.0363	0.0281		0.0248	0.0242	0.0170
	0.0275	0.0281	0.0254		0.0153	0.0170	0.0177

Table 4. Colour space rankings according to average covariance ($\times$ 10^{-3}). *E* and *D65* indicate the CIELAB colour space using illuminants E and D65 respectively.

Rank	Natural Day Space	Corr.	Manmade Day Space	Corr.	Indoors Space	Corr.	Night Space	Corr.
1	E	0.7	E	0.7	E	1.6	E	1.4
2	Yuv	1.3	Yu'v'	1.5	Yu'v'	1.9	Yxy	1.6
3	Yu'v'	1.4	Yuv	1.6	Yuv	2.0	Yu'v'	1.7
4	$L\alpha\beta$	2.1	$L\alpha\beta$	1.9	$L\alpha\beta$	3.0	$L\alpha\beta$	1.9
5	Yxy	2.6	Yxy	2.2	Yxy	3.1	Yuv	2.0
6	HSV	6.1	HSV	4.1	HSV	5.2	HSV	2.7
7	D65	6.6	D65	6.4	D65	8.3	D65	4.6
8	RGB	24.1	RGB	21.1	XYZ	30.6	RGB	19.0
9	XYZ	24.2	XYZ	21.4	RGB	30.9	XYZ	19.3

Table 5. The three component axes of the $L\alpha\beta$ colour space and their corresponding standard deviations [23]

Vector	L	M	S	σ
$\frac{1}{\sqrt{3}}L$	1.004	1.005	0.991	0.353
$\frac{1}{\sqrt{6}}\alpha$	1.014	0.968	-2.009	0.0732
$\frac{1}{\sqrt{2}}\beta$	0.993	-1.007	0.016	0.00745

Table 6. The three axes and their corresponding standard deviations for each of the image ensembles

Manmade Day					Natural Day				
Vector	L	M	S	σ	Vector	L	M	S	σ
$\frac{1}{\sqrt{3}}L_{MD}^\star$	0.9619	0.9749	1.0603	0.9174	$\frac{1}{\sqrt{3}}L_{ND}^\star$	0.9449	0.9510	1.0966	0.8354
$\frac{1}{\sqrt{6}}\alpha_{MD}^\star$	1.2488	0.8600	-1.9238	0.1241	$\frac{1}{\sqrt{6}}\alpha_{ND}^\star$	1.2116	0.9771	-1.8914	0.1032
$\frac{1}{\sqrt{2}}\beta_{MD}^\star$	0.9291	-1.0582	0.1301	0.0178	$\frac{1}{\sqrt{2}}\beta_{ND}^\star$	0.9568	-1.0386	0.0763	0.0159
Manmade Night					Manmade Indoors				
Vector	L	M	S	σ	Vector	L	M	S	σ
$\frac{1}{\sqrt{3}}L_{MN}^\star$	0.9871	1.0012	1.0115	0.9928	$\frac{1}{\sqrt{3}}L_{IN}^\star$	0.9796	0.9854	1.0341	1.2813
$\frac{1}{\sqrt{6}}\alpha_{MN}^\star$	1.2466	0.7585	-1.9674	0.1432	$\frac{1}{\sqrt{6}}\alpha_{IN}^\star$	1.2310	0.8236	-1.9510	0.1567
$\frac{1}{\sqrt{2}}\beta_{MN}^\star$	0.9123	-1.0677	0.1664	0.0230	$\frac{1}{\sqrt{2}}\beta_{IN}^\star$	0.9247	-1.0614	0.1354	0.0220

To simplify comparisons between the dedicated colour spaces computed through our analysis and $L\alpha\beta$, we will refer to the resulting axes as $L_{ens}^\star$, $\alpha_{ens}^\star$ and $\beta_{ens}^\star$ in decreasing eigenvalue order, with $ens \in \{ND, MD, IN, MN\}$. The component with the largest eigenvalue for the Manmade Day set for instance will be referred to as $L_{MD}^\star$. The resulting spaces are listed in Table 6.

The relations between the colour channels resulting from this analysis are similar to the ones in the $L\alpha\beta$ colour space. Specifically, the first channel in all cases, $L^\star$, is approximately equal to $L + M + S$, effectively encoding luminance information. The second channel, $\alpha^\star$, is close to $L+M-2S$, encoding information along a blueish-yellowish axis, while finally the third channel, $\beta^\star$, is close to $L - M$, encoding information along a reddish-greenish axis. Unsurprisingly, each of these colour spaces is therefore approximately an opponent space.

Nonetheless, there are individual differences between the various scene categories that merit further exploration. First, the colour spaces resulting from the natural ensemble (ND) have a larger L contribution in the $\alpha^\star$ channel compared to the α channel in $L\alpha\beta$. Second, the L contribution in the same channel is even larger for the MD ensemble, with values for M being smaller to their equivalent in $L\alpha\beta$. In fact, this trend continues in the Indoors and Night datasets. As we explore less 'natural' image classes, the $\alpha^\star$ channel becomes increasingly skewed, containing a larger contribution from L and a smaller contribution from M. Effectively, the yellow-blue axis in $L\alpha\beta$ space becomes more akin to an orange-blue axis.

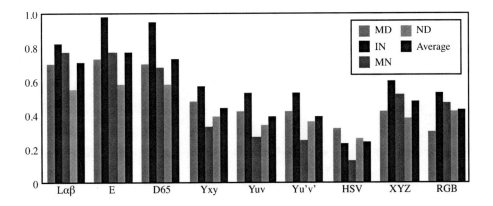

Fig. 3. Percentage of successful colour transfers for each colour space for each of the ensembles, as well as averaged over all four image ensembles. *E* and *D65* refer to CIELAB with illuminants E and D65 respectively.

Further, as we move to less natural sets, a second trend appears. In the third channel, $\beta^{\star}$, the S component contributes more than in typical opponent spaces, essentially replacing the red-green axis in $L\alpha\beta$ with an axis resembling purple-green. Although still significantly smaller compared to the L and M contributions, this cannot be discounted.

5   Colour Transfer

To understand whether these results can be used to inform the utility of colour spaces in the area of colour transfer, we have taken a subset of six images from each of the four image ensembles. Each combination of pairs was used to transfer colours from one image to the other. In this pilot experiment, we have counted the number of images for each colour space and image ensemble that we deem to be plausible results. This approach will only allow us to draw informal conclusions, as a definite result would require both more images as well as a full psychophysical experiment. However, we think that this informal experiment is useful as it may show a trend, and may steer a future validation study.

Figure 3 shows the percentage of successful colour transfers for each of the image ensembles, as well as averaged for all images in all ensembles. These percentages were computed by first running the colour transfer algorithm for all combinations of images within each ensemble (36 for the three manmade ensembles and 121 for the natural day ensemble). Both authors have independently observed each combination, assessing whether the colour transfer could be deemed successful. The criteria were deliberately kept informal, rejecting all cases where the palette was not transferred sufficiently, and all cases which have created obvious gamut problems. The results shown in the figure are averaged over the two sets generated by each author.

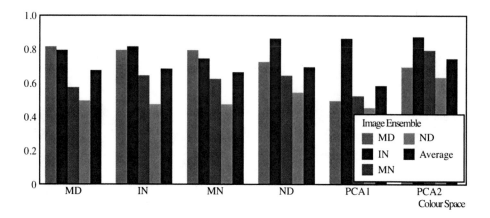

Fig. 4. Percentage of successful colour transfers for each ensemble-specific colour space for each of the ensembles, as well as averaged over all four image ensembles. We also show results for per-image PCA, carried out in the colour space derived from the source image (PCA1) and the target image (PCA2).

We see that both CIELAB variants as well as the $L\alpha\beta$ space tend to perform well, in particular for the indoors ensemble. A peculiar observation is that colour transfer for natural images appears to be a more difficult problem than for any of the other ensembles. This, however, may be attributed to the relatively small number of images involved in this experiment.

Further, the three spaces that have luminance-chrominance channel (Yxy, Yuv and Yu'v') as well as HSV do not perform well. This is predominantly due to the fact that the colour transfer algorithm produces out-of-gamut values that lead to visible artefacts. The RGB and XYZ spaces do not typically produce artefacts, but the transfer of colour tends to be too subtle.

Next, we analyse the ensemble-specific colour spaces that were created by computing PCA on each of our ensembles. By design, this means that colour transfer should be most effective when applied to images with their corresponding ensemble colour space. However, Figure 4 shows that this is not the case. Instead, it appears that the manmade day and indoor datasets have given rise to colour spaces that are effective for transfers in all four image ensembles. A further surprising result is that the natural day colour space is less effective than any of the other three colour spaces.

We have also tested whether ensemble statistics are fine-grained enough, or whether it would be advantageous to compute a separate colour space for each colour transfer. To this end, we have run PCA on the source images only, converting both source and target image to the resulting colour space, and applied the colour transfer algorithm in that space (PCA1). Conversely, we have done the same, instead running PCA on the target image (PCA2). The results are shown in Figure 4. We note that deriving a colour space from the target image is significantly more successful than doing the same on the source image. In fact, this leads to a higher success rate than for any of the ensemble-specific colour spaces.

Comparing Figures 3 and 4 we note that the four most successful colour spaces are CIELAB (E) with a 77% overall success rate, followed by PCA2 (75% success), CIELAB (D65; 73% success) and $L\alpha\beta$ (71%) success. After that the ensemble-specific colour spaces perform reasonably well (67% - 70%). All other colour spaces do not perform acceptably well on our datasets.

Although one may argue that decorrelating individual images would be the most fine-grained approach to colour transfer, we find that similarly excellent results can be obtained by simply choosing the CIELAB space. Thus, it does not appear to be necessary to expend computational resources to deriving either category-based colour spaces or image-specific colour spaces for the purpose of colour transfer.

Finally, we ask whether these results are predicted by the covariance measures that we computed in the preceding section. Comparing Table 4 with Figure 3, it is clear that the average absolute covariance is a reasonable indicator of whether a colour space is suitable for colour transfer tasks. However, this measure does not take into account gamut issues that may arrise. Such problems are more prevalent in some colour spaces than others. In particular, the Yxy, Yuv, Yu'v' and HSV spaces lead to many out-of-gamut pixels, and therefore perform worse than may be expected on the grounds of their covariance statistics.

6   Conclusions

On the basis of four image ensembles we present an assessment of the viability of different colour spaces in the context of colour transfer. First, we find that a space's covariance with respect to each image ensemble is a good measure of how well such a space is likely to perform for colour transfer.

Second, we ask if one space could be found that is universally suitable. To this end we compare the performance of colour spaces derived for single images, those derived for our four image ensembles, and a set of general colour spaces. Surprisingly, we find that CIELAB, if used with illuminant E as the white point leads on average to the best performance, yielding a plausible colour transfer in 77% of all cases tested. This is slightly more than could be obtained with per-image PCA. CIELAB (E) also outperforms all other generic as well as ensemble-specific colour spaces. We therefore conclude that one space indeed fits all.

References

1. Abadpour, A., Kasaei, S.: A fast and efficient fuzzy color transfer method. In: Proceedings of the 4th IEEE International Symposium on Signal Processing and Information Technology, pp. 491–494 (2004)
2. Abadpour, A., Kasaei, S.: An efficient PCA-based color transfer method. Journal of Visual Communication and Image Representation 18, 15–34 (2007)
3. An, X., Pellacini, F.: User controllable color transfer. Computer Graphics Forum 29, 263–271 (2010)

4. Chang, Y., Uchikawa, K., Saito, S.: Example-based color stylization based on categorical perception. In: Proceedings of the 1st Symposium on Applied Perception in Graphics and Visualization (APGV 2004), pp. 91–98 (2004)

5. Greenfield, G., House, D.: Image recoloring induced by palette color associations. Journal of WSCG 11(1), 189–196 (2003)

6. Grundland, M., Dodgson, N.: The decolorize algorithm for contrast enhancing, color to grayscale conversion. Tech. Rep. UCAM-CL-TR-649, University of Cambridge (2005)

7. Kotera, H.: A scene-referred color transfer for pleasant imaging on display. In: IEEE International Conference on Image Processing, vol. 2, pp. 5–8 (2005)

8. Kotera, H., Morimoto, T., Saito, R.: Object-oriented color matching by image clustering. In: Proceedings of the 6th Color Imaging Conference, pp. 154–158 (1998)

9. Kumar, R., Mitra, S.K.: Motion estimation based color transfer and its application to color video compression. Pattern Analysis and Applications 11(2), 131–139 (2007)

10. Levin, A., Lischinski, D., Weiss, Y.: Colorization using optimization. ACM Transactions on Graphics 24(3), 689–694 (2004)

11. Li, Z., Jing, Z., Yang, X., Sun, S.: Color transfer based remote sensing image fusion using non-separable wavelet frame transform. Pattern Recognition Letters 26, 2006–2014 (2005)

12. Luan, Q., Wen, F., Xu, Y.Q.: Color transfer brush. In: Proceedings of Pacific Graphics, pp. 465–468 (2007)

13. Morovic, J., Sun, P.L.: Accurate 3D image colour histogram transformation. Pattern Recognition Letters 24, 1725–1735 (2003)

14. Neumann, L., Neumann, A.: Color style transfer techniques using hue, lightness and saturation histogram matching. In: Computational Aesthetics in Graphics, Visualization and Imaging, pp. 111–122 (2005)

15. Pitié, F., Kokaram, A., Dahyot, R.: N-dimensional probability density function transfer and its application to colour transfer. In: ICCV 2005: Proceedings of the 2005 IEEE International Conference on Computer Vision, vol. 2, pp. 1434–1439 (2005)

16. Pitié, F., Kokaram, A., Dahyot, R.: Automated colour grading using colour distribution transfer. Computer Vision and Image Understanding 107(2), 1434–1439 (2007)

17. Pouli, T., Reinhard, E.: Progressive histogram reshaping for creative color transfer and tone reproduction. In: NPAR 2010: Proceedings of the 8th International Symposium on Non-Photorealistic Animation and Rendering, pp. 81–90 (2010)

18. Pouli, T., Reinhard, E.: Progressive color transfer for images of arbitrary dynamic range. Computers and Graphics 35(1), 67–80 (2011)

19. Reinhard, E., Ashikhmin, M., Gooch, B., Shirley, P.: Color transfer between images. IEEE Computer Graphics and Applications 21, 34–41 (2001)

20. Reinhard, E., Shirley, P., Ashikhmin, M., Troscianko, T.: Second order image statistics in computer graphics. In: Proceedings of the 1st Symposium on Applied Perception in Graphics and Visualization, pp. 99–106 (2004)

21. Reinhard, E., Akyüz, A.O., Colbert, M., Hughes, C.E., O'Connor, M.: Real-time color blending of rendered and captured video. In: Interservice/Industry Training, Simulation and Education Conference (2004)

22. Reinhard, E., Khan, E.A., Akyüz, A.O., Johnson, G.M.: Color Imaging: Fundamentals and Applications. A K Peters, Wellesley (2008)

23. Ruderman, D., Cronin, T., Chiao, C.: Statistics of cone responses to natural images: implications for visual coding. Journal of the Optical Society of America A 15(8), 2036–2045 (1998)

24. Tai, Y., Jia, J., Tang, C.: Local color transfer via probabilistic segmentation by expectation-maximization. In: IEEE Computer Society Conference on Computer Vision and Pattern Recognition (CVPR 2005), vol. 1, pp. 747–754 (2005)

25. Toet, A.: Natural colour mapping for multiband nightvision imagery. Information Fusion 4, 155–166 (2003)

26. Wang, C.M., Huang, Y.H., Huang, M.L.: An effective algorithm for image sequence color transfer. Mathematical and Computer Modelling 44, 608–627 (2006)

27. Wang, L., Zhao, Y., Jin, W., Shi, S., Wang, S.: Real-time color transfer system for low-light level visible and infrared images in YUV color space. In: Proceedings of the SPIE, vol. 6567, p. 65671G (2007)

28. Wen, C.L., Hsieh, C.H., Chen, B.Y., Ming, O.: Example-based multiple local color transfer by strokes. Computer Graphics Forum 27(7), 1762–1765 (2008)

29. Wyszecki, G., Stiles, W.S.: Color science: Concepts and methods, quantitative data and formulae, 2nd edn. John Wiley and Sons, New York (2000)

30. Xiang, Y., Zou, B., Li, H.: Selective color transfer with multi-source images. Pattern Recognition Letters 30, 682–689 (2009)

31. Xiao, X., Ma, L.: Color transfer in correlated color space. In: VRCIA 2006: Proceedings of the 2006 ACM International Conference on Virtual Reality Continuum and its Applications, pp. 305–309 (2006)

32. Xiao, X., Ma, L.: Gradient-preserving color transfer. Computer Graphics Forum 28, 1879–1886 (2009)

33. Xu, S., Zhang, Y., Zhang, S., Ye, X.: Uniform color transfer. In: IEEE International Conference on Image Processing, pp. III-940–III-943 (2005)

34. Yin, J., Cooperstock, J.R.: Color correction methods with applications to digital projection environments. Journal of the WSCG 12(1-3) (2004)

35. Zhao, Y., Wang, L., Jin, W., Shi, S.: Colorizing biomedical images based on color transfer. In: IEEE/ICME International Conference on Complex Medical Engineering, pp. 820–823 (2007)

Perception Based Representations
for Computational Colour

Maria Vanrell, Naila Murray, Robert Benavente, C. Alejandro Párraga,
Xavier Otazu, and Ramon Baldrich

Computer Vision Center - Universitat Autnoma de Barcelona
Campus UAB, Edifici O, 08193 Bellaterra, Barcelona
{maria.vanrell,naila.murray,robert.benavente,
alejandro.parraga,xavier.otazu,ramon.baldrich}@uab.cat
http://cat.uab.cat

Abstract. The perceived colour of a stimulus is dependent on multiple factors stemming out either from the context of the stimulus or idiosyncrasies of the observer. The complexity involved in combining these multiple effects is the main reason for the gap between classical calibrated colour spaces from colour science and colour representations used in computer vision, where colour is just one more visual cue immersed in a digital image where surfaces, shadows and illuminants interact seemingly out of control.

With the aim to advance a few steps towards bridging this gap we present some results on computational representations of colour for computer vision. They have been developed by introducing perceptual considerations derived from the interaction of the colour of a point with its context. We show some techniques to represent the colour of a point influenced by assimilation and contrast effects due to the image surround and we show some results on how colour saliency can be derived in real images. We outline a model for automatic assignment of colour names to image points directly trained on psychophysical data. We show how colour segments can be perceptually grouped in the image by imposing shading coherence in the colour space.

Keywords: colour perception, psychophysical data, induction, saliency, naming, segmentation.

1 Introduction

Colour science has focused mainly on the study of colour representations, namely colour spaces, that allow to precisely describe the colour of a point. Its usual goal has been to define perceptual spaces where distance correlate with perceived dissimilarities. The dependency of colour with its surroundings has been partially introduced in the procedures to generate these colour spaces albeit in controlled conditions.

This approach is not very useful in computer vision where the inputs are digital images of unknown origin and therefore no information about the real scene

R. Schettini, S. Tominaga, and A. Trémeau (Eds.): CCIW 2011, LNCS 6626, pp. 16–30, 2011.
© Springer-Verlag Berlin Heidelberg 2011

and the acquisition sensor exists. For example, it is usually assumed that the RGB vector component of each image pixel is the integration of three components over the visible wavelengths, that is

$$R = \int R(\lambda), E(\lambda), S_i(\lambda)d\lambda \ \ where \ \ i : R, G, B \tag{1}$$

where $R(\lambda)$ is the reflectance of the surface in the scene, $E(\lambda)$ is the scene illuminant and S_i are the corresponding RGB sensitivities of the camera. This formulation is a simplification of Shafer's dichromatic reflection model [26], after assuming that surfaces in the scene are Lambertian and that there are no reflection components (specularities), two assumptions that in general do not hold resulting in images usually full of shadows, highlights and specularities, unlike the actual appearance of real scenes.

The visual system has a tendency to keep its perceptions invariant to unimportant changes (i.e. illumination changes) and much effort was invested in researching for stable colour representations. Key contributions to this field were concerned with finding colour constancy algorithms capable of placing the image under the effects of a canonical illuminant [6,7], or invariant colour representations where the effects of the illuminant changes were removed from the image [8]. Although some of these approaches have been proven successful in controlled (calibrated) conditions, they are not widely used in common computer vision applications. In the last decade, some of the main advances in the computer vision field were based on the use of powerful machine learning techniques trained on large annotated image datasets. This general approach allowed computer vision scientists to achieve important results in real applications of automatic understanding of visual contents. The main contribution of colour research to this field has been to provide local features to be combined with shape descriptors in recognition tasks [10,9], or features to recover general scene shading [11] or the 3D shape of image objects [12].

2   Perception Based Representations

In this work we present several methods to deal with colour vision problems based on simple bottom-up approaches. The common point of these proposals is that they are not based on any previous learning step on large image-labelled datasets (supervised or unsupervised). Other than using such learning frameworks, we propose to solve a group of vision problems by inserting strong perceptual assumptions. This can be done by training the model (i.e. setting the parameters of the model) based on perceptual data acquired from psychophysical experiments. In this way, the data informs the model about the general behaviour of the underlying visual processes which are involved in performing the corresponding visual task. According to this, our ideas are articulated as follows:

First, we show how the data extracted from psychophysical experiments (based on setting a colour patch immersed in grating backgrounds with different spatial frequency configuration and under different colour combinations) has allowed us to define a mathematical model of colour induction. This model uses the psychophysical data to fit the ECSF function that modulates the perception of colour in its surround and can form the basis of a general colour space that goes further than the colour of a point.

Secondly, we hypothesise that the modulation weights obtained in the induction model could form the basis of a bottom-up attention mechanism. We proved that building a saliency map just recovering the weights obtained by the induction model, we are able to correlate the obtained maps with the fixation data collected over a large image dataset. Sharing the low-level mechanisms trained on psychophysical data with induction effects, we achieve state-of-art results in saliency estimation.

Thridly, we present a general fuzzy set based model for colour naming. Similarly, as we do for induction, we fit specific functions based on a sigmoid basis to model colour naming judgements. The model can be fitted to different sets of naming data that can allow to introduce different perceptual conditions in the naming experiments. Some steps have been done in this direction by fitting the model with different backgrounds conditions [13].

Finally, we present an approach to segment image colour surfaces by modelling the ability of grouping colour on irregular surfaces by estimating the ridges of the colour distribution. In this case we hypothesise that the continuity of the perceived colour space form the basis to recover colour image segments. In this case the model is not based on a parametric function however, the computation of the distribution ridge is shown as a strong visual cue for segments which form the basis for higher level visual processes.

With these examples we try to sustain the view that robust visual cues in colour can be defined based on strong perceptual assumptions. Finding underlying processes of colour perception and inserting them in robust computational approaches may prove to be a valid approach to achieve powerful colour representations. This is the aim of this paper, which has been organised as follows. In section 3 we outline the induction model already developed in [2] and in section 4 we show how the model can be extended to be used for saliency estimation. In section 5 we show how membership functions for eleven basic colour terms have been fitted to a sigmoid based parametric model. Finally, in section 6 we explain how the colour distribution can represent the perceived coherence of the colour shading of a surface.

3   Colour Induction

Colour induction refers to the perceptual change in the colour of a stimulus due to the interactions with its surrounding region. When the perceived colour of a stimulus shifts towards the colour of its surround it is termed "assimilation". Conversely, contrast occurs when the perceived colour of the stimulus diverges from that of its surroundings. These two well-known effects are illustrated in Figure 1, which also shows the dependency of the effects on the local spatial frequency of the stimulus surround.

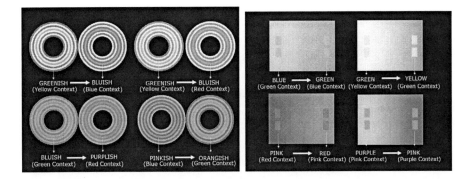

Fig. 1. Examples on induction effects, assimilation (on the left), contrast (on the right)

In a previous work [1,2] we showed that a multi-resolution framework was capable to predict both effects in a unified manner. Our model consisted of four stages in which different image representations were built. The final stage recovers a new image (referred here as the *perceived image*). The pipeline of the model can be summarised as follows:

$$I_c \xrightarrow{WT} \{\omega_{s,o}\} \xrightarrow{CS} \{z_{s,o}\} \xrightarrow{ECSF} \{\alpha_{s,o} \cdot \omega_{s,o}\} \xrightarrow{WT^{-1}} I_c^p \tag{2}$$

where I_c represents a colour channel of the input image, I, in an opponent colour space. The f stages of the model are:

- WT: a multi-resolution wavelet decomposition;
- CS: a center-surround mechanism developed as a divisive normalization [14];
- $ECSF$: a weighting with the extended contrast sensitivity function which was fitted to predict psychophysical data from assimilation and contrast experiments;
- WT^{-1}: an inverse wavelet transform that recovers the corresponding perceived image of the c channel, I_c^p.

In the next paragraphs we give a more detailed explanation of the model stages.

First stage (WT). The input image is convolved with a bank of filters using a multi-resolution wavelet transform. The resulting spatial pyramid contains wavelet planes oriented either horizontally (h), vertically (v) or diagonally (d). The coefficients of the spatial pyramid obtained using the wavelet transform can be considered as an estimation of the local oriented contrast. For an image I, the wavelet transform is denoted as:

$$WT(I_c) = \{w_{s,o}\}_{s=1,2,...,n\,;\,o=h,v,d} \tag{3}$$

where $w_{s,o}$ is the wavelet plane at spatial scale s and orientation o. This wavelet transform contains Gabor-like basis functions and the number of scales used in the decomposition is given by $n = log_2 D$ for an image whose largest dimension is size D.

Second stage (CS). At this level we simulate a center-surround mechanism based on computing a local contrast energy around each wavelet coefficient $w_{x,y}$ centered at position x, y. It is computed by convolving the coefficients with two filters, one for the center energy (small neighbourhood) and another for the surround (larger neighbourhood). By dividing the energy of the center by the energy of the surround window we obtain a measure of the surround contrast (denoted here as $r_{x,y}$). A non-linear scaling of $r_{x,y}$ is performed to produce the final center-surround energy measure $z_{x,y}$:

$$z_{x,y} = r_{x,y}^2/(1 + r_{x,y}^2). \qquad (4)$$

As such, $z_{x,y}$ denotes the output of the second stage of the model or the center-surround energy.

Third stage (ECSF). In this stage the induction effects (assimilation and contrast) are introduced into the model using the *ECSF* function which was defined using psychophysical data. With this function we introduce a blurring effect to simulate assimilation, and a sharpening effect to simulate contrast. Both these effects are achieved simultaneously by using *ECSF* as a weighting function that is parameterized by the z coefficients and the spatial frequency. *ECSF* is defined as

$$ECSF(z, s) = z \cdot g(s) + k(s). \qquad (5)$$

the function $g(s)$ is the combination of two exponential functions

$$g(s) = \begin{cases} \beta e^{-\frac{s^2}{2\sigma_1^2}} & s \leq s_0^g \\ \beta e^{-\frac{s^2}{2\sigma_2^2}} & otherwise \end{cases} \qquad (6)$$

where s represents the spatial scale of the wavelet plane being processed, β is a scaling constant, and σ_1 and σ_2 define the spread of the spatial sensitivity of $g(s)$. The s_0^g parameter defines the peak spatial frequency sensitivity of $g(s)$. In Equation 5, the center-surround activity z of wavelet coefficients are modulated by $g(s)$. This *ECSF* functions is used to weight the center-surround energy $z_{x,y}$ at a location, producing the final response of this stage $\alpha_{x,y}$:

$$\alpha_{x,y} = ECSF(z_{x,y}, s_{x,y}). \qquad (7)$$

Fourth stage (WT^{-1}). This last stage uses the output of the previous stage, $\alpha_{x,y}$, as the weights that modulate the initial wavelet coefficient $w_{x,y}$. The perceived

Table 1. Parameters for $ECSF(z, s)$ obtained using least square regression

Param.	σ_1	σ_2	σ_3	β	s_0^g	s_0^k
Intensity	1.021	1.048	0.212	4.982	4.000	4.531
Colour	1.361	0.796	0.349	3.612	4.724	5.059

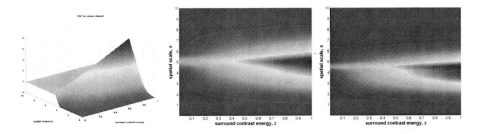

Fig. 2. $ECSF(z, s)$ function profile (left). 2D-plots of $ECSF(z, s)$ for chromaticity channels (center) and for intensity channel (right) (bluer colours represent lower values while redder colours indicate higher values).

image channel $I_c^{perceived}$ is obtained by performing an inverse wavelet transform on the wavelet coefficients $\omega_{x,y}$ at each location, scale and orientation, after the coefficients have been weighted by the $\alpha_{x,y}$ response at that location:

$$I_c^{perceived}(x, y) = \sum_s \sum_o \alpha_{x,y,s,o} \cdot \omega_{x,y,s,o} + C_r. \qquad (8)$$

here o represents the orientation of the wavelet plane of $\omega_{x,y,s,o}$ and C_r represents the residual image plane obtained from WT.

The parameters of the $ECSF$ function (given in table 1) were estimated to predict psychophysical data obtained from two separate experiments. In the first experiment, by Blakeslee *et al* [15], observers performed asymmetric brightness matching tasks in order to match the illusions present in regions of the stimuli to a test patch. The second experiment was performed by Otazu *et al.* [2] in an analogous fashion, but with observers performing asymmetric colour and brightness matching tasks rather than tasks involving only brightness. The experiments were performed on stimuli such as those shown in figure 1. The resulting $ECSF$ functions are plotted in figure 2.

4   Colour Saliency

A great deal of research in computer vision is devoted to modelling attention mechanisms. To this end, models of bottom-up attention in image stimuli which construct saliency maps are popular. Given an image, the corresponding saliency map at each location estimates the probability of attracting the observer's gaze. There have been different approaches to create saliency maps that match the corresponding psychophysically-measured eye-fixation data [18,16,17]. Our contribution has been to extend the induction model defined in the previous section to produce a bottom-up, low-level image representation from which we can build saliency maps.

In the previous section we built a new image channel, I_c^p, that is a modified version of the original channel in which image locations may have been modified

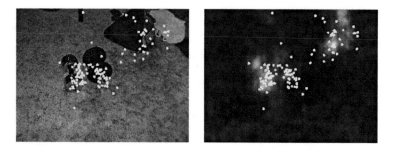

Fig. 3. Original image with fixation points (left). Our recovered saliency map (right).

by the α weight, either by a blurring or an enhancing effect. The colours of modified locations have either been assimilated (averaged) to be more similar to the surrounding colour or contrasted (sharpened) to be less similar to the surround.

To obtain predictions of saliency using this colour representation, we hypothesize that image locations undergoing enhancement are salient, while locations undergoing blurring are non-salient. In this sense we can directly define the saliency map of an specific image channel by the inverse wavelet transform of the α weight. Thus the saliency map, S_c, of the image channel I_c at the location x, y can be easily estimated as

$$I_c \xrightarrow{WT} \{\omega_{s,o}\} \xrightarrow{CS} \{z_{s,o}\} \xrightarrow{ECSF} \{\alpha_{s,o}\} \xrightarrow{WT^{-1}} S_c \qquad (9)$$

where S_c denotes the saliency map of the image I. In figure 3(c) we show an example of one such saliency map. To evaluate the performance of a saliency estimation method, the predictions of the model are compared to eye fixation data. These psychophysical data are provided in large datasets that include image stimuli and eye-fixations, measured using eye-tracking hardware data, for multiple human observers.

We have assessed the accuracy of our model using the well-known receiver operating characteristic (ROC) and Kullback-Leibler (KL) divergence as quantitative metrics. The ROC curve indicates how well the saliency map discriminates between fixated and non-fixated locations for different binary saliency thresholds while the KL divergence indicates how well the method distinguishes between the histograms of saliency values at fixated and non-fixated locations in the image. For both of these metrics, a higher value indicates better performance.

The dataset we used was provided by Bruce and Tsotsos in [16]. This popular dataset is commonly used as the benchmark for comparing eye-fixation predictions between methods. The dataset contains 120 colour images of indoor and outdoor scenes, along with eye-fixation data for 20 different subjects. The mean and the standard error of each metric are reported in Table 2. We performed this evaluation on two state-of-the-art methods as well as our proposed method and as Table 2 shows, our method exceeds the state-of-the-art performance as measured by both metrics.

Table 2. Performance in predicting human eye fixations from the Bruce and Tsotsos dataset (a) KL divergence and ROC Area (SE: Standard Error). (b) ROC curves for Bruce and Tsotsos, Seo and Milanfar, and the proposed method.

(a)   (b)

Model	KL (SE)	AROC (SE)
Bruce & Tsotsos [16]	0.2029 (0.0017)	0.6727 (0.0008)
Seo & Milanfar [17]	0.3432 (0.0029)	0.6769 (0.0008)
Our method	0.4265 (0.0030)	0.7013 (0.0008)

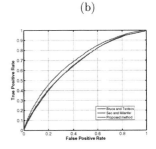

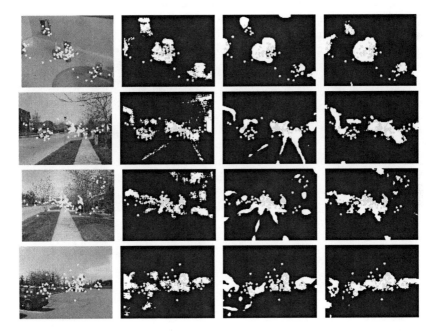

Fig. 4. Qualitative analysis of results for Bruce and Tsotsos dataset: Column A contains original image. Columns B, C, and D contain thresholded saliency maps obtained from Bruce and Tsotsos, Seo and Milanfar and our method, respectively. The saliency maps have each been thresholded to their top 10% most salient locations. Yellow markers indicate eye fixations. Our method is seen to be less sensitive to low-frequency edges such as street curbs and skylights, which is in line with human eye fixations.

5   Colour Naming

Colour naming relies on the assignment of a colour name label either to a point or to an image segment. This visual task has been studied from very different points of view. The anthropological study of Berlin and Kay [19] was a starting point that derived a lot of research about the topic in the subsequent decades. They studied colour naming in different languages and stated the existence of universal colour categories. They also defined the set of 11 basic colour categories that have the most evolved languages. These are white, black, red, green, yellow, blue, brown, purple, pink, orange and grey. Since then, several studies have confirmed and extended their results [20,21].

A computational model of colour naming can be very useful for several tasks such as segmentation, retrieval, tracking, or human-machine interaction. Although some models based on a pure tessellation of a colour space have been proposed [22,23], the most accepted framework has been to consider colour naming as a fuzzy process, that is, any colour stimulus has a membership value between 0 and 1 to each colour category. Kay and McDaniel [24] were the first in proposing a theoretical fuzzy model for colour naming. Later, some approaches from the computer vision field have adopted this point of view.

We proposed in [4] a fuzzy colour-naming model based on a family of membership functions that were fitted to psychophysical naming data. We worked on the CIELab space due to its perceptual properties. Likewise, other spaces could be suitable whenever one of the dimensions correlates with colour lightness and the other two with chromaticity components. Considering the psychophysical data on a chromaticity plane (see figure 5), we proposed to fit colour membership for the eight basic chromatic categories using a triple-Sigmoid function. With this function we are able to fit the configuration of the naming data obtained in a psychophysical experiments such as [25]. Data implied a set of necessary properties that membership functions for the chromatic categories should fulfil: a

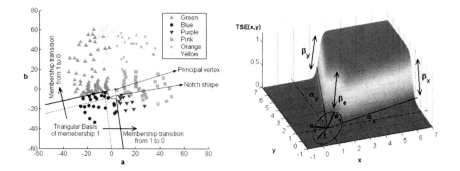

Fig. 5. Psychophysical naming data in CIELab space for a fixed L. Properties of the membership functions of a chromatic category (in this case, blue)(left). TSE function coping with expected properties.

triangular basis, two different slopes on both sides of the category, and a central notch to cope with the transition to the central achromatic category. To achieve these properties we defined the TSE function that for a given colour point $\mathbf{p}$ is defined as

$$TSE(\mathbf{p}, \theta) = DS(\mathbf{p}, \mathbf{t}, \theta_{DS})ES(\mathbf{p}, \mathbf{t}, \theta_{ES}) \tag{10}$$

where $\theta = (\mathbf{t}, \theta_{DS}, \theta_{ES})$ is the set of parameters of the TSE function, which is defined as the product of a Double-Sigmoid function DS and an Elliptical-Sigmoid function ES. The DS function is defined as

$$DS(\mathbf{p}, \mathbf{t}, \theta_{DS}) = S_1(\mathbf{p}, \mathbf{t}, \alpha_y, \beta_y)S_2(\mathbf{p}, \mathbf{t}, \alpha_x, \beta_x) \tag{11}$$

where $\theta_{DS} = (\alpha_x, \alpha_y, \beta_x, \beta_y)$ is the set of parameters of the Double-Sigmoid function and function S_i is a sigmoid function defined as

$$S_i(\mathbf{p}, \mathbf{t}, \alpha, \beta) = \frac{1}{1 + \exp(-\beta \mathbf{u_i} R_\alpha T_t \mathbf{p})}, \qquad i = 1, 2 \tag{12}$$

where T_t and R_α are a translation matrix and a rotation matrix respectively, and u_i is a vector defining the axis on which the function is oriented. This function introduce the triangular basis of the function with two different slopes on both sides.

On the other hand, the ES function introduce the central notch allows to fit the boundary with the achromatic center. It is given by

$$ES(\mathbf{p}, \mathbf{t}, \theta_{ES}) = \frac{1}{1 + \exp\left\{-\beta_e\left[\left(\frac{\mathbf{u_1} R_\phi T_t \mathbf{p}}{e_x}\right)^2 + \left(\frac{\mathbf{u_2} R_\phi T_t \mathbf{p}}{e_y}\right)^2 - 1\right]\right\}} \tag{13}$$

where $\theta_{ES} = (e_x, e_y, \phi, \beta_e)$ is the set of parameters, e_x and e_y are the semiminor and semimajor axis respectively, ϕ is the rotation angle of the ellipse, and β_e is the slope of the Sigmoid curve that forms the ellipse boundary. The function obtained is an elliptic plateau if β_e is negative and an elliptic valley if β_e is positive.

In figure 5(right) we can see how the TSE function adapts to the mentioned properties. By fitting the naming data of each chromatic category with this TSE function we can obtain the memberships of any colour sample in the CIELab space to the basic colour categories.

6   Colour Segmentation

Colour segmentation aims to partition an image into a set of non-overlapped regions corresponding to surfaces of a specific material. A robust and efficient colour segmentation is required as a preprocessing step in several computer vision tasks such as image classification or object detection and recognition. In real images changes due to illumination, shadow, shading and highlights provoke image measurements to vary significantly. These effects, are one of the main difficulties that have to be solved to yield a correct segmentation.

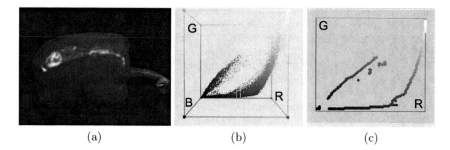

(a)   (b)   (c)

Fig. 6. (a) Original image (b) Colour Distribution. (c) Ridges extracted by RAD.

We proposed in [5] a pure bottom-up approach to recover a model of the material reflectance of the image objects by hypothesizing that our ability to perceive continuity of a coloured surface even the changes due to shading or highlights is a perceptual grouping mechanism that can be modelled by computing the connected ridges of the distribution in the colour space, we refer to it as RAD (Ridge-based Analysis of distributions).

Continuity of the material reflectance (MR) in the colour distribution is supported by the physical model defined by Shafer in [26]. A MR generates many image values due to geometrical and photometric variations that are likely to form a continous set in the histogram space. For this purpose, consider the distribution of a single MR as described by the dichromatic reflection model (DCM)[26] as

$$\mathbf{f}(\mathbf{x}) = m^{b}(\mathbf{x})\,\mathbf{c}^{b} + m^{i}(\mathbf{x})\,\mathbf{c}^{i} \tag{14}$$

where $\mathbf{f} = \{R, G, B\}$, $\mathbf{x}$ is the spatial image coordinate, $\mathbf{c}^{b}$ is the body reflectance, $\mathbf{c}^{i}$ the surface reflectance, m^{b} and m^{i} are geometry dependent scalars representing the magnitude of body and surface reflectance. Bold notation is used to indicate vectors. For one MR we expect both $\mathbf{c}^{b}$ and $\mathbf{c}^{i}$ to be almost constant, whereas $m^{b}(\mathbf{x})$ and $m^{i}(\mathbf{x})$ are expected to vary significantly. Hence, as for this definition, a MR, is formed by a single body reflectance $\mathbf{c}^{b}$ and a surface reflectance $\mathbf{c}^{i}$.

The two parts of the dichromatic reflection model are clearly visible in the histogram of figure 6(b). Firstly, due to the shading variations the distribution of the red pepper traces an elongated shape in histogram-space. Secondly, the surface reflectance forms a branch which points in the direction of the reflected illuminant. In conclusion, the distribution of a single MR forms a ridge-like structure in histogram space.

To extract this perceived MR, we used the multilocal creaseness MLSEC-ST operator introduced by Lopez *et al.* in [27] to enhance ridge points. Afterwards, the structure tensor computes the dominant gradient orientation in a neighbourhood of size proportional to σ_{d}. Basically, this calculus enhances those situations where either a big attraction or repulsion exists in the gradient direction vectors. Thus, it assigns the higher values when a ridge or valley occurs. Given a distribution $\Omega(\mathbf{x})$, (colour histogram in the current context), and a symmetric neighbourhood of size σ_i centered at point $\mathbf{x}$, namely, $N(\mathbf{x}, \sigma_i)$ the structure tensor field S is defined as:

$$S(\mathbf{x}, \sigma) = N(\mathbf{x}, \sigma_i) * (\nabla \Omega(\mathbf{x}, \sigma_d) \cdot \nabla \Omega^t(\mathbf{x}, \sigma_d)) \tag{15}$$

where $\sigma = \{\sigma_i, \sigma_d\}$, and the calculus of the gradient vector field $\nabla \Omega(\mathbf{x}, \sigma_d)$ has been done with a gaussian kernel with standard deviation σ_d.

This operator assigns high values to those point of the distributions more likely to belong to a ridge. This scores comes from the divergence of the main orientation of the gradient in a given neighbourhood against the normal vector in it. The main orientation is extracted using the egeinvectors of the structure tensor $(S(\mathbf{x}, \sigma))$. An example of this resultant distribution is shown in figure 7(b) projected on a chromaticity space.

Once the ridge structure of the distribution has been enhanced with creaseness operator, next step is to extract the exact ridge points that describe the different MRs. As a result only those points necessary to maintain the connectivity of a MR remain. These points form the ridges of Ω^σ. The extraction is essentially based on a zero-crossing detection onto the MLSECT-ST output that maintains the spatial coherence, the whole ridge point detection is given by

$$RP(\Omega^\sigma) = LMP(\Omega^\sigma) \cup TRP(\Omega^\sigma) \cup SP(\Omega^\sigma) \tag{16}$$

that is the union of all different characteristic points found in the ridge of the distribution, these are the local maxima (LMP), the transitional ridge points (TRP) and the saddle points (SP). The final output of this set of point is depicted in figure 7(b) as black dots. The final segmentation is obtained assigning each point in the image to the closest ridge in the colour distribution (figure 7c). The details are explained in [5].

To evaluate quantitatively the performance the method it is compared to four state of art segmentation algorithms using the Berkeley image database (Table 3). Figure 8 shows qualitative results of the method applying different parameters to obtain from fine to coarse segmentation. In all cases the segments behave consistently.

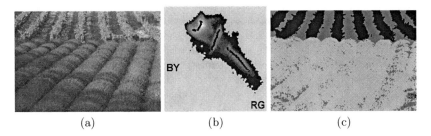

(a)   (b)   (c)

Fig. 7. Example of MR extraction (a) Original image. (b) Result of the creassenes operator on a RG/BY chromaticity space. Extracted ridge points are given in black on top of the distribution. (c) Segmented image.

Fig. 8. Original image. Columns from 2 to 4: RAD-based segmentation on RGB with $(\sigma_d,\sigma_i)=\{(1.5,0.05),(2.5,0.05),(2.5,1.5)\}$.

Table 3. Global Constancy Error: seed [28], fow [30], and mean-shift [31]

	human	RAD	seed	fow	mean-shift
GCE index	0.080	0.2048	0.209	0.214	0.2598

7   Conclusion

As we already mentioned in the introduction this paper reviews a methodological approach to tackle the problem of defining useful computational representations of colour. Our aim is to propose colour representations that go further from the basic three-dimensional spaces by exploring the perceptual processes that underly the role of colour in general visual tasks. To sustain the methodological proposal we have shown some examples of colour representations based on specific perceptual hypothesis.

References

1. Otazu, X., Vanrell, M., Párraga, C.A.: Multiresolution wavelet framework models brightness induction effects. Vision Research 48, 733–751 (2008)
2. Otazu, X., Párraga, C.A., Vanrell, M.: Toward a unified chromatic induction model. Journal of Vision 10(12) (2010)
3. Murray, N., Vanrell, M., Otazu, X., Párraga, C.A.: Non-Parametric Saliency Estimation based on low-level vision mechanism. In: IEEE Computer Society Conference on Computer Vision and Pattern Recognition (2011) (in press)
4. Benavente, R., Vanrell, M., Baldrich, R.: Parametric fuzzy set for automatic color naming. Journal of the Optical Society of America 25(10), 2582–2593 (2008)
5. Vázquez, E., Baldrich, R., van de Weijer, J., Vanrell, M.: Describing Reflectances for Color Segmentation Robust to Shadows, Highlights and Texture. IEEE Trans. on PAMI (2010)
6. Hordley, S.: Scene illuminant estimation: Past, present, and future. Color Research & Application 31, 303–314 (2006)

7. Finlayson, G.D., Hordley, S.D., Hubel, P.: Color by correlation: A simple, unifying framework for color constancy. IEEE Transactions on Pattern Analysis and Machine Intelligence 23, 1209–1221 (2001)
8. Gevers, T., Smeulders, A.: Color based object recognition. Pattern Recognition 32, 453–464 (1997)
9. Khan, F.S., wan de Weijer, J., Vanrell, M.: Top-down color attention for object recognition. In: International Conference on Computer Vision, pp. 979–986 (2009)
10. van de Sande, K.E.A., Gevers, T., Snoek, C.G.M.: Evaluating color descriptors for object and scene recognition. IEEE Transactions on Pattern Analysis and Machine Intelligence 32(9), 1582–1596 (2010)
11. Grosse, R., Johnson, M.K., Adelson, E.H., Freeman, W.T.: Ground-truth dataset and baseline evaluations for intrinsic image algorithms. In: International Conference on Computer Vision, pp. 2335–2342 (2009)
12. Zickler, T., Mallick, S.P., Kriegman, D.J., Belhumeur, P.N.: Color Subspaces as Photometric Invariants. International Journal of Computer Vision 79(1), 13–30 (2008)
13. Benavente, R., Párraga, C.A., Vanrell, M.: European Conference on Visual Perception. Perception Suppl. Series, vol. 38, p. 36 (2009)
14. Heeger, D.H.: Normalization of cell responses in cat striate cortex. Visual Neuroscience 9(2), 181–197 (1992)
15. Blakeslee, B., McCourt, M.E.: Similar mechanisms underlie simultaneous brightness contrast and grating induction. Vision Research 37(20), 2849–2869 (1997)
16. Bruce, N.D., Tsotsos, J.K.: Saliency based on information maximization. In: Advances in Neural Information Processing Systems, vol. 18, pp. 155–162. MIT Press, Cambridge (2006)
17. Seo, H.J., Milanfar, P.: Nonparametric bottom-up saliency detection by self-resemblance. In: IEEE Computer Society Conference on Computer Vision and Pattern Recognition Workshops, CVPR Workshops 2009, pp. 45–52 (2009)
18. Itti, L., Koch, C., Niebur, E.: A Model of Saliency-Based Visual Attention for Rapid Scene Analysis. IEEE Trans. Pattern Anal. Mach. Intell. 20(11), 1254–1259 (1998)
19. Berlin, B., Kay, B.: Basic Color Terms: Their Universality and Evolution. University of California Press, Berkeley (1969)
20. Boynton, R., Olson, C.: Salience of chromatic basic color terms confirmed by three measures. Vision Research 30, 1311–1317 (1990)
21. Sturges, J., Whitfield, T.: Salient features of munsell color space as a function of monolexemic naming and response latencies. Vision Research 37, 307–313 (1997)
22. Tominaga, S.: A color-naming method for computer color vision. In: Proceedings of IEEE International Conference on Cybernetics and Society, pp. 573–577. IEEE, Los Alamitos (1985)
23. Wang, Z., Luo, M., Kang, B., Choh, H., Kim, C.: An algorithm for categorising colours into universal colour names. In: Proceedings of the 3rd European Conference on Colour in Graphics, Imaging, and Vision, Society for Imaging Science and Technology, IS&T, pp. 426–430 (2006)
24. Kay, P., McDaniel, C.: The linguistic significance of the meaning of basic color terms. Language 3, 610–646 (1978)
25. Benavente, R., Vanrell, M., Baldrich, R.: A data set for fuzzy colour naming. Color Research and Applications 31, 48–56 (2006)
26. Shafer, S.: Using color to seperate reflection components. Color Research and Application 10(4), 210–218 (1985)

27. López, A.M., Lumbreras, F., Serrat, J., Villanueva, J.J.: Evaluation of methods for ridge and valley detection. IEEE Transactions on Pattern Analysis and Machine Intelligence 21(4), 327–335 (1999)
28. Micusık, B., Hanbury, A.: Automatic image segmentation by positioning a seed. In: Leonardis, A., Bischof, H., Pinz, A. (eds.) ECCV 2006. LNCS, vol. 3952, pp. 468–480. Springer, Heidelberg (2006)
29. Pantofaru, C., Hebert, M.: A comparison of image segmentation algorithms. Technical Report CMU-RI-TR-05-40, Robotics Institute, Carnegie Mellon University, Pittsburgh, PA (September 2005)
30. Fowlkes, C., Martin, D., Malik, J.: Learning affinity functions for image segmentation combining patch-based and gradient-based approaches. In: IEEE Computer Society Conference on Computer Vision and Pattern Recognition (2003)
31. Comaniciu, D., Meer, P.: Mean shift: A robust approach toward feature space analysis. IEEE Transactions on Pattern Analysis and Machine Intelligence 24(5), 603–619 (2002)

Color Imaging Arithmetic: Physics ∪ Math > Physics + Math

Gaurav Sharma*

University of Rochester, Department of Electrical and Computer Engineering,
Rochester, NY 14627-0126, USA
gaurav.sharma@rochester.edu
http://www.ece.rochester.edu/~gsharma/

Abstract. Color imaging devices for capture, display, and user interaction commonly form the physical interface by which we connect to
the digital cyber-world. Because these devices bridge the physical and
the electronic worlds, elegant and effective solutions to problems in color
imaging can often be found by the synergistic combination of physical
intuition with the mathematical tools of signal and image processing.
In this paper, we support this claim using case studies drawn from our
past research in color imaging. For each of the illustrative examples, we
highlight how the blend of physical insight and mathematical modeling,
offer in the combination, advantages significantly greater than would be
estimated as the sum of the individual parts, thereby justifying the title
for this paper.

1   Introduction

We live in a world governed by the laws of physics. The codification of the physical laws in the form of quantitative mathematical relations, not only aids us in
developing a better understanding of the world, but also provides a potent tool
for solving problems that may sometimes appear insurmountable at the outset.
Newton's laws of motion represent what is, perhaps, the best known example of
this philosophical assertion. The mathematical equations representing Newton's
laws, arm us with the ability to to quantitatively model interactions between
elements in a physical system. This ability allows us to engineer solutions to
a variety of problems, including several problems where the complexity can be
daunting. For instance, using the laws of motion, we can develop propulsion and
control systems for space craft that can undertake inter-planetary travel and
allow us to explore our solar system. Also, equally significantly, the quantitative
modeling using Newton's laws, can also, on occasion, surprise us by enabling solutions to problems that we may intuitively consider infeasible under a less than
thorough first consideration. An example is the inverted pendulum [4] problem,
where the a pole mounted with a pivot on a cart can be balanced in an unstable
upright position by using an appropriate feedback control methodology. For this

---

* Invited paper.

R. Schettini, S. Tominaga, and A. Trémeau (Eds.): CCIW 2011, LNCS 6626, pp. 31–46, 2011.
© Springer-Verlag Berlin Heidelberg 2011

latter category of problems, the physical understanding and the mathematical modeling offer in the combination, advantages significantly greater than would be estimated as the sum of the individual parts. In a mathematical play on the words of the common saying "The whole is greater than the sum of the parts," we denote this synergistic combination by the inequality Physics ∪ Math > Physics + Math. The illustration of this philosophical theme in the context of color imaging systems is the central objective of this paper.

Color imaging systems handle the capture of physical scenes and the reproduction of images on physical devices, commonly serving as the interface between the tangible physical world and the electronic world that operates on mathematical representations. Therefore, the Physics ∪ Math > Physics + Math aphorism rings particularly true for a number of problems in color imaging systems. In this paper, we substantiate this assertion by highlighting specific examples of problems in color imaging for which the combination of physical insight, mathematical tools, and engineering ingenuity leads to particularly elegant and effective solutions.

The rest of this paper is organized as follows. In Section 2, we briefly review colorimetric representations with the dual objectives of introducing relevant notational conventions and to remind our readers that in color imaging the synergistic union of physics and mathematics can be traced back in time to the very the origins of color science. We then bolster the central assertion of the paper by providing, as evidence, two case studies drawn from our research in color imaging, in each case highlighting how the combination of physical modeling/insight with mathematical analysis enables a solutions that each of these tools alone is unable to address adequately. The examples cover two very different applications, the first dealing with numerical metrics for the evaluation of the fidelity of color recording devices and the second addressing the estimation of four separate halftone printing channels from a conventional three channel scan, applied in the specific context of extending phase modulation halftone watermarks to color. We conclude the paper with a summary and a discussion and prognosticate that the harmonious union of Physics and Mathematics will continue to be a happy one in the domain of color imaging.

2   The Union of Physics and Math in Fundamental Color Science

The origins of present day color science can be traced back to the early experiments conducted by the physicists Young, Helmholtz, and Maxwell [9, 14, 15, 29]. These experiments demonstrated that it is possible to produce a color match for a given stimulus by additively combining three light sources and that, in general, fewer than three sources do not suffice for this purpose. The formulation of theories for color perception based on these physical observations *and* the codification of these theories in the form of abstract mathematical relations, exemplified by Grassman's laws of color matching [6], are key ingredients of modern color science. Once mathematical models are available for the physical phenomena, they enable powerful and novel engineering applications that would otherwise be infeasible. In particular, *colorimetry*, i.e. the science of color measurement and representation, arises directly from the incorporation of the insight from (psycho)-physical experiments on color matching within the mathematical framework of linear vector spaces [2, 3, 24, 28]. Specifically, for instance, colorimetry allows us to specify the color of an object using the so-called CIE XYZ tristimulus values [1], given by

$$\mathbf{t} = \mathbf{A}^T \mathrm{diag}(\mathbf{l})\mathbf{r} = \mathbf{A}_\mathbf{L}^T \mathbf{r}, \tag{1}$$

where spectra are represented as $N \times 1$ vectors with a suitably chosen number of samples, N, and in this discrete format, $\mathbf{r}_{N \times 1}$ denotes the spectral reflectance of the object[1], $\mathbf{l}_{N \times 1}$ the spectral power distribution of the illuminant, $\mathbf{A}_{N \times 3}$ the matrix whose 3 columns form the X, Y, and Z, color matching functions, respectively, that characterize the observed psycho-physical color matches, $\mathrm{diag}(\mathbf{x})$ denotes the square diagonal matrix obtained by placing the elements of the vector $\mathbf{x}$ along the diagonal of an otherwise zero square matrix, and $\mathbf{A}_\mathbf{L} \stackrel{\mathrm{def}}{=} \mathrm{diag}(\mathbf{l})\mathbf{A}$ [21, 24].

Once constructed, the framework of colorimetry, suitably augmented, enables a vast array of color imaging applications, spanning the entire gamut from capture, processing, display, and print. For instance, under identical viewing contexts, the color corresponding to a reflectance $\mathbf{r}_1$ can be matched by producing a reflectance $\mathbf{r}_2$, which although spectrally different from $\mathbf{r}_1$, matches in CIE XYZ tristimulus values, i.e.

$$\mathbf{t}_1 \stackrel{\mathrm{def}}{=} \mathbf{A}^T \mathrm{diag}(\mathbf{l})\mathbf{r}_1 = \mathbf{t}_2 \stackrel{\mathrm{def}}{=} \mathbf{A}^T \mathrm{diag}(\mathbf{l})\mathbf{r}_2. \tag{2}$$

The reflectance $\mathbf{r}_2$ is then said to be a *metamer* of the reflectance $\mathbf{r}_1$ (under the illuminant $\mathbf{l}$). The framework can be and is routinely used to obtain reproductions. Under a chosen illumination $\mathbf{l}$, a colorimetrically matched print for a painting, can be obtained, for instance, by selecting for a spatial location in the painting with reflectance $\mathbf{r}_1$, a corresponding reflectance $\mathbf{r}_2$ for the reproduction that satisfies (2). Specifically, if $\mathbf{r}_2 \stackrel{\mathrm{def}}{=} \mathbf{r}_2(\mathbf{v})$ is the output of a color reproduction device with k-dimensional control values $\mathbf{v} = [v_1, v_2, \ldots v_k]^T$, the objective becomes the determination of control values that achieve the match in (2) or the closest approximation thereof under the trade-off imposed by gamut limitations. For our purposes here, the original can also be described, instead of spectra, by a more condensed tristimulus representation, which forms the basis underlying most representations of color images.

The novelty and elegance of colorimetry are sometimes lost on us because its use is now common-place in color imaging. To regain an appreciation, we need to only recognize that without the underlying framework of colorimetry, the metameric matches that one relies on in all of color reproduction would require a cumbersome process of matching by trial and error, analogous to what one may use in the kitchen in order to construct a recipe for matching the taste for a dish obtained from a restaurant!

---

[1] Colorimetry for transmissive and emissive objects can be similarly defined.

3   Figures of Merit for Color Recording Devices

As our first case study, we use our work on developing figures of merit for the evaluation of color recording devices [25]. Scanners and digital cameras are commonly used for recording color images. These devices would, in an ideal setting, report exact colorimetric values corresponding to the spectra that are incident upon their sensors. In practice, however, the accuracy of these devices is limited due to manufacturing limitations and unavoidable noise in the recordings. Consequently, for the purposes of design, a quality factor or figure of merit is desirable that characterizes their color accuracy. For our exposition, we consider the specific case of a scanner based capture, the digital camera scenario can be obtained via a straightforward generalization, albeit with key differences in the formulation that address the fact that the illumination is external to the camera.

Analogous to (1), scanner measurements of the object with reflectance $\mathbf{r}$, with a K channel scanner can be modeled as,

$$\mathbf{t}_s(\mathbf{r}) = \mathbf{M}^T \mathrm{diag}(\mathbf{l}_s)\mathbf{r} + \boldsymbol{\eta} = \mathbf{G}^T\mathbf{r} + \boldsymbol{\eta} , \qquad (3)$$

where $\mathbf{t}_s(\mathbf{r})$ is a $K \times 1$ vector of scanner measurements, $\mathbf{M}$ is the $N \times K$ matrix of scanner filter transmittances (including detector sensitivity and the transmittance of the scanner optical path), $\mathbf{l}_s$ is the $N \times 1$ vector representing the scanning illuminant spectrum, $\boldsymbol{\eta}$ is the $K \times 1$ measurement noise vector, and $\mathbf{G} = \mathrm{diag}(\mathbf{l}_s)\mathbf{M}$.

Colorimetric information must be estimated from the scanner recordings by means of a scanner calibration transform. Since both (3) and (1), represent linear measurement models, a linear calibration transform is mathematically justified, a fact that is also borne out by empirical evaluations [25]. Denoting the scanner calibration transform by a 3×3 matrix $\mathbf{B}$, the estimated tristimulus values from the scanner measurements can be mathematically formulated as

$$\hat{\mathbf{t}}(\mathbf{r}) = \mathbf{B}\mathbf{t}_s(\mathbf{r}), \qquad (4)$$

where the transformation $\mathbf{B}$ is determined so as to minimize the color error, exact details of which we will consider in the sequel.

A useful metric for design purposes is the average magnitude of the perceived color difference between the true color $\mathbf{t}(\mathbf{r})$ and the estimate $\hat{\mathbf{t}}(\mathbf{r})$. We formulate this metric mathematically as

$$\epsilon(\mathbf{A}_L, \mathbf{G}, \mathbf{B}) = E\left\{ \left\| \mathcal{F}(\mathbf{t}(\mathbf{r})) - \mathcal{F}(\hat{\mathbf{t}}(\mathbf{r})) \right\|^2 \right\}, \qquad (5)$$

where $E\{\ \}$ denotes the expectation over the ensemble of scanned objects, $\mathcal{F}()$ is a 3×3 (possibly nonlinear) transformation of the tristimulus values into a perceptually uniform color space such as CIELAB, and $\|\cdot\|$ denotes the Euclidean vector norm [5].

The above error metric quantifies the performance of a scanner "specified by" $\mathbf{G}$ when the transformation $\mathbf{B}$ is used in (4). An error metric for the scanner alone can be obtained by replacing the generic transformation, $\mathbf{B}$, with the optimal transformation that minimizes the error. However, such an error metric is not readily computable since the optimal transformation cannot be determined in closed form for a general non-linear transformation, $\mathcal{F}()$. If the transformation $\mathcal{F}()$ is differentiable, with continuous first partial derivatives, a first order Taylor series provides a fairly accurate locally linear approximation for $\mathcal{F}()$. If $\|\mathbf{t}(\mathbf{r}) - \hat{\mathbf{t}}(\mathbf{r})\|$ is small over the scanned ensemble, as it should be for a well-designed scanner, this first order Taylor series can be used to approximate the error metric in (5) by the expected mean-squared linearized color error,

$$\epsilon(\mathbf{A}_L, \mathbf{G}, \mathbf{B}) \approx \epsilon_l(\mathbf{A}_L, \mathbf{G}, \mathbf{B}) = E\left\{\left\|J_{\mathcal{F}}(\mathbf{t}(\mathbf{r}))\ \left(\mathbf{t}(\mathbf{r}) - \hat{\mathbf{t}}(\mathbf{r})\right)\right\|^2\right\}, \qquad (6)$$

where $J_{\mathcal{F}}(\mathbf{t}(\mathbf{r}))$ denotes the Jacobian matrix [13] of the transformation $\mathcal{F}()$ at $\mathbf{t}(\mathbf{r})$.

The local linearization offers the advantage that the optimal scanner calibration transformation $\mathbf{B}_{opt}(\mathbf{A}_L, \mathbf{G})$ that minimizes the linearized perceptual color error metric in (6) can be computed in closed form(see [25, 27] for details). The minimum mean-squared linearized color error obtained using the optimal transformation can then be written as,

$$\xi(\mathbf{A}_L, \mathbf{G}) = \epsilon\left(\mathbf{A}_L, \mathbf{G}, \mathbf{B}_{opt}(\mathbf{A}_L, \mathbf{G})\right) \qquad (7)$$

which serves as a useful error metric for evaluating the scanner sensitivity $\mathbf{G}$. Through some algebraic manipulation, we can express this error metric in the form

$$\xi(\mathbf{A}_L, \mathbf{G}) = \alpha(\mathbf{A}_L) - \tau(\mathbf{A}_L, \mathbf{G}), \qquad (8)$$

where we refer the reader to [25] for details, only observing here that the terms satisfy $0 \leq \tau(\mathbf{A}_L, \mathbf{G}) \leq \alpha(\mathbf{A}_L)$. As a consequence, we can interpret $\alpha(\mathbf{A}_L)$ as the average "color" energy in a spectrum from the spectral ensemble in perceptually uniform color units and $\tau(\mathbf{A}_L, \mathbf{G})$ as the part of this energy that is recoverable from measurements made with the scanner specified by $\mathbf{G}$ (at the given noise level). Hence, the ratio,

$$q_{\mathcal{F}}(\mathbf{A}_L, \mathbf{G}) = \frac{\tau(\mathbf{A}_L, \mathbf{G})}{\alpha(\mathbf{A}_L)}, \qquad (9)$$

defines a normalized *figure of merit* (FOM) for the color scanner, where the subscript $\mathcal{F}$ has been added to explicitly indicate the dependence on the transformation $\mathcal{F}()$ (which was implicit in the earlier expressions). The normalization ensures that the figure of merit is bounded between 0 and 1 with $q_{\mathcal{F}}(\mathbf{A}_L, \mathbf{G}) = 1$ representing a "perfect" color scanner whose error metric is zero.

The figure of merit of (9) represents, within a common mathematical framework, a number of alternative metrics that can be obtained by a judicious choice of the transformation $\mathcal{F}()$ and assumptions on the ensemble of spectra over which the expectation in (6) is computed and the statistics of the measurement noise [25]. Specifically, a powerful FOM is obtained by using as the color space transformation $\mathcal{F}()$ the transformation from CIE XYZ in to the (approximately) perceptually uniform CIELAB color space [1, 28], which we refer to as the comprehensive FOM. We also consider simpler alternatives that have been used in prior designs: 1) A CIE XYZ *mean-squared error* (MSE) based FOM obtained by using the identity mapping for the color space transformation $\mathcal{F}()$, 2) An orthogonal tristimulus FOM which uses a linear transformation $\mathbf{F}_o$ for the transformation $\mathcal{F}()$, in order to ensure that color errors in (6) are computed within an orthonormal tristimulus color space instead of the highly correlated CIE XYZ space, and 3) A perceptual measure of goodness that ignores the noise (by assuming its amplitude is zero), otherwise utilizes the transformation from CIE XYZ in to the (approximately) perceptually uniform CIELAB color space for the color space transformation $\mathcal{F}()$.

To highlight the utility of the framework, we show in Fig. 1 a subset of the results from [25]. The figure compares the comprehensive FOM against the three other alternative FOMs listed in the preceding paragraph by examining the relationship between the FOM and the average $\triangle E_{ab}^*$ error over a representative ensemble of scanner target reflectances for a number of scanner sensitivities determined by a parametrized set of color filters and varying levels of measurement noise, indicated in the legends by the corresponding signal to noise ration (SNR) (for additional details see [25]). If the FOM is used as a design metric, it is desirable that the relation between the FOM and the perceptual color error as quantified in $\triangle E_{ab}^*$ units follow a smooth monotonic curve so that devices designed to optimize the FOM also result in a small colorimetric error in practical applications. From the plots, in Fig. 1, we see that for the comprehensive FOM, the points in this case are almost ideally distributed, lying along a rather well defined smooth monotonic curve, whereas for the other alternative FOMs this is not so[2]. The agreement is particularly good for values of the comprehensive FOM close to 1, which represents the region of greatest interest in design optimization scenarios.

The advantage of the comprehensive FOM is apparent from the above comparisons, as it was in the original publication on this work [25]. In keeping with the theme of this paper, our objective here is to highlight how the synergistic interplay between physics and mathematics contributes to this advantage. From the vignette we presented of the overall framework, it is apparent that both physics, particularly psycho-physics, and mathematics play a key role in arriving at the powerful comprehensive FOM. The colorimetric representation and the perceptual nonlinearity represented by $\mathcal{F}()$ model the physics and the elegant mathematical tool of local linearization using the Taylor series representation

---

[2] A criticism of the evaluation methodology can be made on the grounds that the comprehensive FOM is designed to infact approximate $\triangle E_{ab}^*$ and therefore the comparison with $\triangle E_{ab}^*$ is unfair. This criticism can be met, however, with the counter that alternative color spaces or color difference metrics that may be shown to offer better agreement with perception in a specific application can also be readily integrated into the framework through an appropriate choice of the transformation $\mathcal{F}()$.

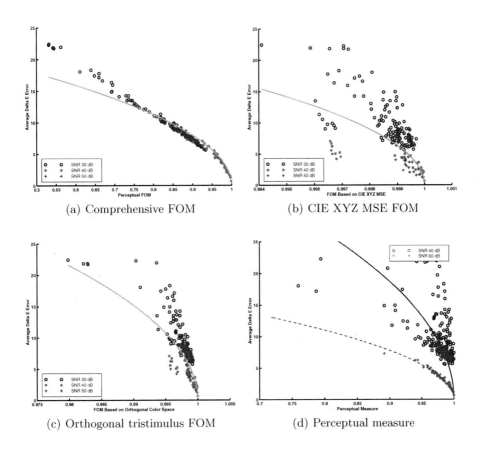

Fig. 1. Correlation between CIELAB $\triangle E_{ab}^{*}$ along the abscissa and (a)Comprehensive FOM, (b) CIE XYZ MSE FOM, (c) Orthogonal tristimulus FOM, and (d) Perceptual measure. A monotone one-to-one relation is desirable for use as a design objective function. The graphs in this figure are adapted from [25].

makes the rest of the analysis feasible, particularly allowing us to compute in closed form the optimal calibration transform and the corresponding color error that forms the basis of our figure of merit framework. The CIE XYZ MSE FOM models only part of the physics of the problem dealing with color representation and adopts the mathematically simplest approach to the problem, allowing a solution without requiring the mathematical sophistication of local linearization. It offers rather poor performance for two reasons. First, the errors in CIE XYZ space do not correlate well with perception. Second, the CIE XYZ MSE FOM also ignores the mathematical correlations between the CIE XYZ coordinate representations for colors. The Orthogonal tristimulus FOM addresses the second of these limitations by orthogonalizing the tristimulus space in order to eliminate the mathematical correlations but continues to ignore the first limitation and therefore offers only modest improvements over the CIE XYZ MSE FOM. The Perceptual measure on the other hand incorporates the (psycho)-physics of perception using the elegant mathematical framework of local linearization but is still divorced from part of physics because it fails to account for inevitable measurement noise. Thus in the mathematically idealized setting of a 60 dB SNR, it offers good agreement with color errors but under even modest degradation at a 40 dB SNR, it correlates rather poorly with perceived color errors. These limitations of the alternate FOMs therefore highlight that the advantage of the comprehensive FOM indeed arises from the combined strengths of the physical modeling and the mathematical analysis supporting our paper's eponymous claim.

4   Separation Estimation from Scanned Color Halftones

As our second case study, we consider an ingredient of our recent work [17]. on extending phase modulation watermarks for monochrome halftones [16] to four color clustered-dot halftone prints. The problem setting for this example is as follows. There exist a number of known methods that allow for embedding of invisible watermark patterns in monochrome clustered-dot halftone images as phase modulation of the halftone dots, where the embedded patterns can then be revealed by overlaying the printed halftone image with a suitably designed physical or simulated transparency mask decoder [10, 16, 26]. These methods, however, do not directly generalize to color prints using the common cyan (C), magenta (M), yellow (Y), and black (K) clustered-dot halftone separations. While the embedding of the watermarks in the individual C, M, Y, and K separations can readily follow the monochrome embedding methodology, the separations are overlaid in the print and cannot be readily separated from conventional red (R), green (G), and blue (B) scans. This problem is highlighted in Fig. 2. The black (K) colorant absorbs uniformly across the spectrum and, thus, the K halftone appears in all three of scanner RGB channels. Also the so-called "unwanted absorptions" of the CMY colorants also cause cross-coupling, i.e., C, M, and Y halftone separations not only appear in the scan R, G, and B channels that complement their spectral absorption bands, respectively, but also in the two other channels as well.

The problem in Fig. 2 seems rather difficult to address from purely a mathematical or physical perspective. Mathematically, the problem of estimating four separations from three scanner channels constitutes an under-determined problem that does not admit a unique solution and therefore offers no guarantees of discovering the correct solution. From a purely physical perspective, the absorptions of the K colorant across the spectrum and the unwanted absorptions indicate that the individual R, G, and B channels cannot directly isolate a single separation. However, as we illustrate in the sequel, and as described in greater detail in [17], the combination of physical insight with mathematical analysis does indeed lead to an effective solution whereby the four color separations can be estimated, which in turn enable per separation phase modulation halftone watermark embedding.

(a) RGB scan of   (b) Scan R channel   (c) Scan G channel   (d) Scan B channel
CMYK halftone

Fig. 2. RGB scan of a printed image that was divided into 4 stripes, where the stripes from left to right contain only C, M, Y, and K colorants, respectively. K colorant can be consistently observed in all scan channels and cross-coupling between C, M, and Y colorant halftone separations can also be clearly seen in the scan R, G, and B channels. Figure reproduced from [17].

For our description, we assume an input contone CMYK image $I_{C,M,Y,K}(x,y)$ that is typically obtained by transforming a device-independent colorimetric representation of the image to the device-dependent CMYK values via a set of color conversions [22, 30], where (x,y) denotes the spatial coordinates. Each separation is then halftoned to obtain a corresponding binary valued halftone separation $I_i^h(x,y)$, where i is one of C, M, Y, or K and rotated clustered-dot halftone screens are utilized for the four separations as is common in lithographic/electrophotographic printing. A spatial watermark pattern w_i is potentially also embedded within $I_i^h(x,y)$ using phase modulation as outlined, for example, in [16]. We adopt the convention that the values 1 and 0 for $I_i^h(x,y)$ correspond, respectively, to whether ink/toner i is, or is not, deposited (or estimated to be deposited) at the pixel position (x,y).

A scan $I_{R,G,B}^s(x,y)$ of the printed image is obtained using a conventional RGB scanner. As previously indicated, coupling between the different colorant halftones is inevitable in the scanned RGB image. Figures 3(a)–(d) show enlarged views of a region from the digital M halftone separation, digital CMYK halftone separation overlay, scanned RGB image, and scan G channel of an image used in our experiments. The M halftone colorant is complementary to the G channel, but the G channel scan clearly displays within it not only the halftone structure of the desired M separation, but also undesired halftone structures for the C, Y, and K separations with varying intensities that arise from the absorption of these colorants in the G scanner channel band.

To develop an effective solution to estimate C, M, Y, and K, halftones from the R, G, and B scans, we begin with the physical insight into the halftone process provided by the mathematical tool of Fourier analysis: the individual colorant halftone images are, phase modulation notwithstanding, narrow-band bandpass images comprised of components located on the fundamental halftone periodicity frequencies and at integer multiples thereof. By employing a suitable rotated halftone configuration, we can ensure that the fundamental halftone frequencies of the separation and their lower order harmonics do not coincide. The individual colorant separation halftones can then be separated by suitable

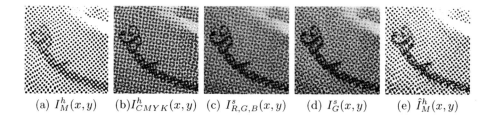

(a) $I_M^h(x,y)$ (b) $I_{CMYK}^h(x,y)$ (c) $I_{R,G,B}^s(x,y)$ (d) $I_G^s(x,y)$ (e) $\hat{I}_M^h(x,y)$

Fig. 3. Subfigure (a) shows enlarged view of a region from the digital M halftone separation of *Hats* halftone image used in our experiments, subfigure (b) shows the same region from the digital CMYK halftone overlay, subfigure (c) shows approximately the same region from the RGB scanned color halftone print, subfigure (d) shows the region from the G channel image of the scanned print showing the couplings between the halftone structures of M and C, Y, and K separations, and subfigure (e) shows the region from the M halftone estimate obtained using the methodology of [17]. Figure reproduced from [17].

filtering in the spatial frequency domain. In order to appreciate this idea, we show in Fig. 4 an enlarged view of the low frequency region for log-magnitude Fourier spectrum of the G channel image from which a section was previously shown in the spatial domain in Fig. 3(d). The fundamental frequencies corresponding to the halftones are labeled in this figure and the inter-color interference that we noted in the spatial domain can also be observed in the frequency domain. The Fourier spectrum exhibits peaks not only about the fundamental frequency vectors (and higher-order harmonics) of the M separation, but also at the fundamental frequency vectors of C, Y, and K separations, and moiré frequencies. However, observing that the primary peaks for rotated clustered-dot screens occur at different (2-D) spatial frequencies, we can also see that these and other unwanted frequency components that do not overlap with the fundamental frequency of a desired halftone can be eliminated by spatial filtering. By suitably designing the rotated halftone configuration so that the fundamental frequencies and the lower-order harmonics for each halftone screen do not coincide with those for any other halftone screen, we can estimate the halftones by employing spatial filtering.

The spatial filtering based methodology encounters some inaccuracies because in the reflectance domain of R, G, B scanner signals, the halftone separations combine multiplicatively causing part of the power in a halftone separation to be transferred to the inter-colorant moiré frequencies via the unwanted colorant interactions. This power transfer and loss of accuracy can be minimized by employing a physically-motivated mathematical model of the print and scan process that leads to an alternate transform domain representation where the combination of halftone separations is better approximated by a linear model. Specifically, if the colorants are modeled as transparent colorants obeying the the Beer-Bouguer law [7, Chap. 7] or the transparent formulation of Kubelka-Munk theory [7, Chap. 7] and the scanner responses are modeled as Dirac delta impulse

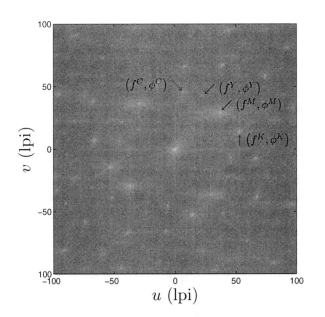

Fig. 4. Enlarged view of the log-magnitude Fourier spectrum of the G channel of the scanned *Hats* halftone print used in our experiments. For illustration purposes, the frequencies of the constituent halftone separations are indicated by arrow and text labels. Figure reproduced from [17].

functions approximating narrow band responsivities, then we can show that [17] the density for the kth channel scan is obtained as

$$d_k(x,y) \stackrel{\text{def}}{=} -\log_{10}\left(\frac{I_k^s(x,y)}{I_k^s(W)}\right) \tag{10}$$

$$= \sum_{i\in\{C,M,Y,K\}} d_k^i I_i^h(x,y), \tag{11}$$

where k denotes one of R, G, or B, $I_k^s(W)$ is the scanned image value corresponding to the paper substrate in the kth color channel and d_k^i is the optical density of the ith colorant layer in the kth scanner channel. Observe that this model is linear in the halftone separations $I_i^h(x,y)$, $i \in \{C,M,Y,K\}$ and therefore avoids avoids inter-separation moiré. Therefore, prior to spatial filtering, the halftone separations are converted into the optical density domain using the mathematical transformation indicated in (10). Even though we recognize that the model used here is an extremely idealized approximation, use of the model provides an improvement over an alternate ad-hoc approach [17].

In actual implementation of the scheme for separation of halftones, additional attention to detail is required to robustly handle all four of the separations. We refer the reader to [17] for details, only mentioning here that we develop a sequential estimation scheme guided by physical intuition; the K colorant is estimated

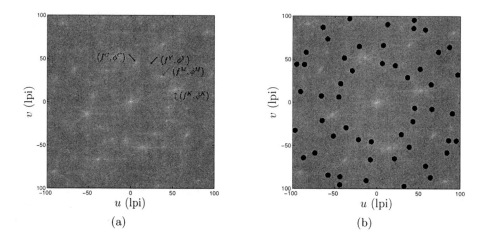

Fig. 5. Spatial filtering for estimation of K halftone $I_K^h(x)$. Subfigure (a) shows enlarged view of the log-magnitude Fourier spectrum of $d_K(x, y)$ for the scanned *Hats* print used in our experiments and subfigure (b) illustrates the elimination of unwanted frequency components of C, M, and Y halftone separations using the narrow-band band-reject filters. Figure reproduced from [17].

first using combined information from the R, G, and B scan channels, followed by an estimation of the C, M, and Y halftones using the complementary R, G, and B, scans and the already obtained estimate for the K colorant halftone. The spatial filtering process for the estimation of the K colorant separation is shown in Fig. 5, where we show the elimination of unwanted frequency components of C, M, and Y halftone separations using the narrow-band band-reject filters.

For purpose of visual assessment, enlarged views of the original CMYK halftone separations and their estimates from a region in one image (also referred to as the *Hats* image in this paper) are shown in Fig. 6. Note that the digital halftone separations undergo a variety of distortions in the printing process and therefore do not exactly correspond to the true printed halftones. Given this inherent variability, the estimates are quite good and enable effective detection of per separation halftone watermarks embedded using phase modulation[3].

The effectiveness of the scheme presented for the estimation of four CMYK halftone separations from three RGB scans is apparent from the results we highlighted above and further substantiated in the original publication on this work [17]. It should be apparent from our presentation of this case study that, just as it was necessary in our last case study example, the synergistic combination of physical intuition with mathematical analysis tools enables a novel solution to a problem that seemed, in our initial analysis, insoluble by purely physical or mathematical means.

---

[3] Because the application is not our focus here, we refer the reader to [17] for results demonstrating watermark detection from the separations obtained.

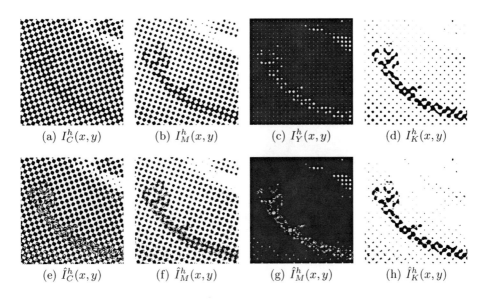

(a) $I_C^h(x,y)$ (b) $I_M^h(x,y)$ (c) $I_Y^h(x,y)$ (d) $I_K^h(x,y)$

(e) $\hat{I}_C^h(x,y)$ (f) $\hat{I}_M^h(x,y)$ (g) $\hat{I}_M^h(x,y)$ (h) $\hat{I}_K^h(x,y)$

Fig. 6. Enlarged view of the digital halftone separations (subfigures (a)–(d)) from a region in the *Hats* image and the corresponding estimates (subfigures (e)–(h)) obtained using the differences in spatial periodicity and colorant spectra.Figure reproduced from [17].

5   Summary and Discussion

Our case studies illustrated how novel and sometimes non-intuitive solutions to problems in color imaging systems can be determined by using suitable physical models and mathematical tools. As we note in the remarks for each of our case studies, in both cases, the synergistic combination of physical insight with the analytical tools of mathematics is what makes the solutions effective and powerful, supporting our assertion that in color imaging, Physics ∪ Math > Physics + Math.

We must also remark here that real-world color imaging systems and color perception rarely adhere strictly to idealized mathematical models. Approximations are therefore often necessary for making mathematical analysis tractable and useful. Both our examples also illustrate this approximation process. For obtaining the comprehensive FOM, we approximate the nonlinear transformation from CIE XYZ to CIE LAB via a local linearization and for the halftone separation case study we approximate the combination of colorant transmittances in print by using a linear in density model that conforms better with the linear Fourier domain filtering framework for separation. Despite the approximations, the models demonstrate their utility when the approximations are also guided by physical insight to align closely with the analysis. Of course, overly simplistic mathematical models that are not physically justified can also result in poor results. This is the situation, for instance, in our first case study, when MSE in CIE XYZ space is utilized as a metric for perceptual color error.

Our presentation in this paper continues the broader "Physics ∪ Math > Physics + Math" philosophical theme that was previously initiated in [23]. The later perspective in time for the current paper allows us to draw our illustrative examples from a larger body of work, including several projects undertaken in the intervening time. The two illustrative case studies that we have chosen for supporting the hypothesis in this paper's title are drawn from our own research because these examples are most familiar to us and because the corresponding published material is readily accessible to us. The research for the individual case studies presented here has previously been published in more detailed individual contributions on figures of merit for color recording devices [25] and on color CMYK halftone separation estimation from RGB scans for color halftone water-marking applications [17]. The exposition in the present paper borrows heavily from these prior publications. Our previous paper on the broader theme [23] included as examples, work on show-through correction [20] and set-theoretic estimation for subtractive color [18, 19]. We encourage readers whose interests may have been stimulated by specific examples, to follow the relevant publications for additional information and details.

Clearly, we cannot and do not claim to monopolize the broader underlying theme of this paper; a far larger set of equally good and perhaps better examples can be found in the works of other researchers. The happy union between Physics and Mathematics underlies not only the origins of color science and numerous pre-existing applications in color imaging, but continues to be a key enabler of future innovations in color imaging systems. Moreover as we indicate in the opening paragraph of the introduction, the theme of the paper is also a subset of the broader idea that pervades a wider arena of applications, where solution methodologies are most successful when they combine the insight offered by the physics underlying the problem with the mathematical framework and tools inherent in digital signal and image processing [8].

Acknowledgments. The examples used in this invited paper are drawn from research on which I have worked over a number of years. The research would not be feasible or complete without my collaborators on these and other research projects. I would like to acknowledge my gratitude to these colleagues, both the direct contributors that are indicated in the associated citations and the indirect contributors who have provided thought-provoking discussions and a lively environment for research. I would also like to thank the various funding agencies and companies that have supported my research at the University of Rochester.

References

1. CIE: Colorimetry. CIE Publication No. 15.2, Central Bureau of the CIE, Vienna (1986), the commonly used data on color matching functions is available at the CIE web site at http://www.cie.co.at/
2. Cohen, J.B., Gibson, W.A.: Vector model for color sensations. J. Opt. Soc. Am. 52(6), 692–697 (1962)

3. Dubois, E.: The structure and properties of color spaces and color image spaces. Synthesis Lectures on Image, Video, and Multimedia Processing 4(1), 1–129 (2009)
4. Franklin, G.F., Powell, J.D., Emami-Naeini, A.: Feedback Control of Dynamic Systems, 6th edn. Prentice Hall, Englewood Cliffs (2009)
5. Golub, G.H., Loan, C.F.V.: Matrix Computations, 2nd edn. The Johns Hopkins University Press, Baltimore (1989)
6. Grassmann, H.G.: Zur theorie der farbenmischung. Poggendorf. Annalen der Physik und Chemie 89, 69–84 (1853); translation titled Theory of compound colors. Philosophic Magazine 4(7), 254–264 (1854), reprinted in [11,12]
7. Grum, F., Bartleson, C.J. (eds.): Optical Radiation Measurements: Color Measurement, vol. 2. Academic Press, New York (1980)
8. Haykin, S.: Signal processing: where physics and mathematics meet. IEEE Sig. Proc. Mag. 18(4), 6–7 (2001)
9. von Helmholtz, H.L.F.: Physiological Optics (1866), extracts reprinted in [11]
10. Knox, K.T., Wang, S.: Digital watermarks using stochastic screens. In: Beretta, G.B., Eschbach, R. (eds.) Proc. SPIE: Color Imaging: Device Independent Color, Color Hardcopy, and Graphic Arts II, vol. 3018, pp. 316–322 (February 1997)
11. MacAdam, D.L. (ed.): Sources of Color Science. MIT Press, Cambridge (1970)
12. MacAdam, D.L. (ed.): Selected Papers on Colorimetry-Fundamentals. SPIE Optical Engineering Press, Bellingham (1993)
13. Magnus, J.R., Neudecker, H.: Matrix Differential Calculus with Applications in Statistics and Econometrics. Wiley, Chichester (1988)
14. Maxwell, J.C.: The diagram of colors. Transactions of the Royal Society of Edinburgh 21, 275–298 (1857), reprinted in [11,12]
15. Maxwell, J.C.: Theory of compound colors and the relations to the colors of the spectrum. Proc. of the Royal Society of London 10, 404–409 (1860), reprinted in [11,12]
16. Oztan, B., Sharma, G.: Continuous phase-modulated halftones. IEEE Trans. Image Proc. 18(12), 2718–2734 (2009), http://www.ece.rochester.edu/~gsharma/papers/OztanSharmaContinPhaseModTIPDec2009.pdf
17. Oztan, B., Sharma, G.: Per-separation clustered-dot color halftone watermarks: Separation estimation based on spatial frequency content. J. Electronic Imaging 19(4), 043007-1–22 (2010), http://www.ece.rochester.edu/~gsharma/papers/OztanPerSepColrHTWMFreqSepJEI043007.pdf
18. Sharma, G.: Set theoretic estimation for problems in subtractive color. Color Res. Appl. 25(4), 333–348 (2000), http://www.ece.rochester.edu/~gsharma/papers/subcolpocsCRNA2000.pdf
19. Sharma, G.: Target-less scanner color calibration. J. Imaging Sci. and Tech. 44(4), 301–307 (2000), http://www.ece.rochester.edu/~gsharma/papers/ntargcaljist00.pdf
20. Sharma, G.: Show-through cancellation in scans of duplex printed documents. IEEE Trans. Image Proc. 10(5), 736–754 (2001), http://www.ece.rochester.edu/~gsharma/papers/showthuip01.pdf
21. Sharma, G.: Color fundamentals for digital imaging. In: Digital Color Imaging Handbook [22], chapter 1
22. Sharma, G. (ed.): Digital Color Imaging Handbook. CRC Press, Boca Raton (2003)
23. Sharma, G.: Imaging Arithmetic: Physics u Math > Physics + Math. In: Eschbach, R., Marcu, G.G. (eds.) Proc. SPIE: Color Imaging X: Processing, Hardcopy, and Applications, vol. 5667, pp. 95–106 (January 2005), http://www.ece.rochester.edu/~gsharma/papers/imagphysmathei05.pdf, invited Paper

24. Sharma, G., Trussell, H.J.: Digital color imaging. IEEE Trans. Image Proc. 6(7), 901–932 (1997), http://www.ece.rochester.edu/~gsharma/papers/dciip97.pdf
25. Sharma, G., Trussell, H.J.: Figures of merit for color scanners. IEEE Trans. Image Proc. 6(7), 990–1001 (1997), http://www.ece.rochester.edu/~gsharma/papers/fomip97.pdf
26. Sharma, G., Wang, S.: Show-through watermarking of duplex printed documents. In: Delp, E.J., Wong, P.W. (eds.) Proc. SPIE: Security, Steganography, and Watermarking of Multimedia Contents VI, vol. 5306, pp. 670–684 (January 2004), http://www.ece.rochester.edu/~gsharma/papers/showthruWMei2004.pdf
27. Sharma, G.: Color scanner characterization, performance evaluation, and design. Ph. D. dissertation, North Carolina State University, Raleigh, NC (August 1996)
28. Wyszecki, G., Stiles, W.S.: Color Science: Concepts and Methods, Quantitative Data and Formulae. John Wiley & Sons, Inc., New York (1982)
29. Young, T.: On the theory of light and colors. Philosophical Transactions of the Royal Society of London 92, 20–71 (1802), extracts reprinted in [11,12]
30. Yule, J.A.C.: Principles of color reproduction, applied to photomechanical reproduction, color photography, and the ink, paper, and other related Industries. Wiley, New York (1967)

Region-Based Annotation of Digital Photographs

Claudio Cusano

DISCo (Dipartimento di Informatica, Sistemistica e Comunicazione),
Università degli Studi di Milano-Bicocca, Viale Sarca 336, 20126 Milano, Italy
cusano@disco.unimib.it

Abstract. We propose a region-based method for the annotation of out-door photographs. First, images are oversegmented using the normalized cut algorithm. Each resulting region is described by color and texture features, and is then classified by a multi-class Support Vector Machine into seven classes: sky, vegetation, snow, water, ground, street, and sand. Finally, a rejection option is applied to discard those regions for which the classifier is not confident enough. For training and evaluation we used more than 12,000 images taken from the LabelMe project.

1 Introduction

In this paper we propose a region-based method for the annotation of outdoor photographs. Our idea is that the provided annotation could be effectively exploited to improve image processing procedures. By following a content-aware processing approach [3] it could be possible to select the most appropriate image enhancement strategy, or the most appropriate region of interest, by taking into account information about the content of the photographs.

In our proposal, homogeneous regions, obtained by a suitable segmentation algorithm, are assigned to seven different classes, or are labeled as "rejected" when they cannot be reliably assigned to one of the classes considered. The classes considered, sky, vegetation, snow, water, ground, street and sand, could be exploited by content-aware processing strategies.

Our method starts with an over-segmentation of the input images. In order to ensure that regions can be assigned to at most one class, we applied a normalized cut algorithm tuned to select regions composed of highly homogeneous pixels. The regions are then described by low-level features: color distribution is represented by statistical moments and by a color histogram; texture is described by a histogram of rotation invariant local binary patterns. Each region is then independently classified by a multi-class (one vs. one) Support Vector Machine (SVM). Finally, a rejection rule is applied to exclude from the annotation those regions which cannot be reliably assigned to one of the seven classes considered.

We based our experimentation on the LabelMe dataset [17]. This dataset is composed of thousands of manually annotated images. We exploited the manual annotation to determine the ground thruth for both the training and the evaluation of the classifier.

R. Schettini, S. Tominaga, and A. Trémeau (Eds.): CCIW 2011, LNCS 6626, pp. 47–59, 2011.
© Springer-Verlag Berlin Heidelberg 2011

2   Related Work

Several approaches have been proposed in the last years for automatic image annotation [20, 11, 6, 7, 12, 16]. Yuan et al. conducted a study which show how spatial context constraints improve automated image region annotation [23]. They classified the regions segmented by the JSEG method into 11 classes: sky, water, mountain, grass, tree, flower, rock, earth, ground, building, and animal. Boutell et al. presented a framework to handle the cases in which a natural scene can be described by multiple class labels [1]. More in detail, they considered combination of classes obtained from six base classes: beach, sunset, foliage, field, mountain, and urban. Millet et al. proposed a method based on the knowledge of how regions should be spatially arranged [14]. In their approach, the regions are classified individually into the classes sky, water, snow, trees, grass, sand, ground, and buildings, using a Support Vector Machine which returns several hypotheses with associated probabilities. For a more complete review of this topic see the survey by Tsai and Hung [19].

A few works in the literature exploited the annotation of regions to drive image enhancement algorithms. Fredembach et al. observed that some regions have specific colors (memory colors) that are perceived consistently by human observers [8]. Therefore their importance, with respect to color correction, is greater than that of other regions in an image. They proposed a method, based on eigenregions, for the detection of regions of blue sky, vegetation, and skin tone. Similarly, Cooper considered memory colors, from skin, sky, and foliage objects, to improve the prediction the scene illuminant [4]. Gasparini and Schettini proposed a method for color cast removal which exploits color and spatial information to identify regions of probable skin, sky, sea, or vegetation [9]. When this regions cover more than 40% of the image, the image is classified as having an intrinsic cast, and the cast remover is not applied.

3   Method

The annotation strategy is composed of four major steps (see Figure 1): i) the input image is segmented into uniform regions; ii) each region is independently described by a set of low-level features; iii) the feature vector is classified by a SVM trained to discriminate between the seven classes considered: sky, vegetation, snow, water, ground, street, and sand; iv) regions corresponding to a low confidence of the classifier are rejected. The following sections provide more details about each step.

3.1   Segmentation

To segment the input images we adopted the Normalized Cut framework proposed by Malik et al. [13]. Our aim is to split regions which probably contain pixels of multiple classes. Therefore, we limited the algorithm to the initial segmentation step. The algorithm treats image segmentation as a graph partitioning problem and uses a global criterion, the normalized cut, for segmenting the

Input Image

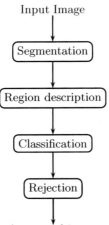

Fig. 1. The main steps which compose the annotation strategy

graph. The normalized cut criterion measures both the total dissimilarity between the different groups as well as the total similarity within the groups.

First, a sparse matrix $\mathbf{W}$ is built to encode the similarity relationships between each pair of pixels in the image. Here, we used a color extension of the weighting scheme proposed by Shi and Malik [18]:

$$W_{ij} = \begin{cases} \exp\left(-\frac{d(I_i,I_j)^2}{\sigma_I^2}\right) \exp\left(-\frac{\|X_i-X_j\|_2^2}{\sigma_X^2}\right) & \text{if } \|X_i - X_j\|_2 < r \\ 0 & \text{otherwise} \end{cases}, \qquad (1)$$

where $d(I_i, I_j)$ is the distance, in the RGB color space, between the values of the i-th and the j-th pixels in the image; $\|X_i - X_j\|_2$ is the Euclidean distance between the locations of the two pixels; σ_I and σ_X are parameters determining the relative importance of color similarity and spatial proximity; r defines a circular neighborhood for each pixel. In practice, high weights are assigned to pairs of pixels with similar color and close positions.

The normalized cut criterion defines a measure of how well a bipartition of the image keeps similar pixels in the same group:

$$ncut(A) = \left(\sum_{i\in A, j\notin A} W_{ij}\right) \left(\frac{1}{\sum_{i\in A, j\in V} W_{ij}} + \frac{1}{\sum_{i\notin A, j\in V} W_{ij}}\right), \qquad (2)$$

where V is the set of all the pixels in the image, which are partitioned into the subsets A and $V \setminus A$.

The problem of minimizing the normalized cut is NP-hard, however an approximate solutions can be found by considering the matrix $\mathbf{W}$ together with the diagonal matrix $\mathbf{D}$ ($D_{ii} = \sum_j W_{ij}$), and by solving the following generalized eigenproblem:

$$(\mathbf{D} - \mathbf{W})\mathbf{y} = \lambda\mathbf{D}\mathbf{y}. \qquad (3)$$

The eigenvectors can be thought of as a transformation of the image into a new feature vector space where the pixels are represented by vectors with the components coming from the corresponding components across the different eigenvectors. The image is segmented by finding the clusters in this eigenvector representation. This is a much simpler problem because the eigenvectors have essentially put regions of coherent descriptors (i.e. connected groups of similar pixels) into tight clusters. We used K-means to find an initial subdivision in 30 clusters which is then refined by aggregating those clusters which do not increase too much the quantization error.

3.2   Regions Description and Classification

To describe the segmented regions we used three different features describing the texture and the color distribution. The first feature is composed of the first two statistical moments of the components in the YCbCr color space (six components).

The second feature is a 37 bin histogram of the hue channel, inspired by the work of Van de Weijer et al. [21]. Since the certainty of the hue is inversely proportional to the saturation, the hue histogram is made more robust by weighting each sample of the hue by its saturation. More in detail, given a region of N pixels, the bins $B_1, \ldots B_{37}$ of the histogram are populated as follow:

$$B_k = \frac{1}{N} \sum_{i=1}^{N} S_i I_{[10(k-1),10k)}(H_i), 1 \le k \le 36, \tag{4}$$

$$B_{37} = \frac{1}{N} \sum_{i=1}^{N} (1 - S_i), \tag{5}$$

where I is the indicator function, and H_i and S_i are the first two components in the HSV color space of the i-th pixel (in the ranges $[0, 360)$ and $[0, 1]$, respectively).

The third feature is based on a histogram of Local Binary Patterns (LBP), which is a highly discriminative texture descriptor [15]. Its robustness comes from the invariance with respect to rotations and contrast. Moreover, the descriptor is very compact, and can be computed very quickly. Briefly, the LBP descriptor is defined as a histogram of the local patterns surrounding each pixel of the region. These patterns are computed by thresholding the intensity of the neighbors of each pixel with the intensity of the pixel itself (see Figure 2). The resulting binary code is then rotated to achieve rotation invariance. More in detail, given the neighbor size P and a radius R, for each pixel the numerical code $LBP_{P,R}$ is computed as follows:

$$LBP_{P,R} = \sum_{p=0}^{P-1} s(g_p - g_c) 2^p, \tag{6}$$

where g_c is the gray level of the current pixel, $g_0, \ldots, g_{P-1}$ are the gray levels of its neighbors, and s is defined as $s(x) = 1$ if $x \ge 0$, $s(x) = 0$ otherwise. The

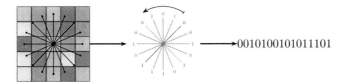

Fig. 2. The first steps of the Local Binary Patter extraction. For each pixel, a circular neighborhood is considered. Each neighbor is thresholded by the intensity of the central pixel determining a binary response. The pattern is formed by concatenating the resulting bits.

P neighbors considered lie on a circular neighbor, of radius R, of the current pixel: the gray value g_p is obtained by interpolating the intensity image at a displacement $(R\cos(2\pi p/P)), R\sin(2\pi p/P))$.

To achieve rotation invariance, the following pattern is defined:

$$LBP^{ri}_{P,R} = \min_{i=0,...,P-1}\{ROR(LBP_{P,R},i)\}, \tag{7}$$

where $ROR(x,i)$ performs i times a circular bit-wise right shift on the P-bits number x. In terms of image pixels this corresponds to rotating the neighbor set clockwise so many times that the longest sequence of zeros is placed in front of the code.

In practice, not all patterns are equally significant and only a selection of all the possible 2^P patterns are individually accounted in the final descriptor. Usually, only patterns describing a somewhat regular neighbor are considered. These patterns are called "uniform" and are defined as those patterns for which there are at most two transitions (bitwise 0/1 changes) between adjacent bits in the code. All non-uniform patterns are considered together in the final descriptor. Since there are $P+1$ uniform patterns $(0\ldots0000_2, 0\ldots0001_2, 0\ldots0011_2, 0\ldots0111_2, \ldots, 1\ldots1111_2)$ the code $LBP^{riu}_{P,R}$ assumes $P+2$ values: one for each uniform pattern, and one for all non-uniform patterns.

As texture descriptor, we used a histogram of 18 bins which counts the occurrences of the $LBP^{riu}_{16,2}$ codes.

The three features are concatenated and fed to a multi-class Support Vector Machine (SVM) [5]. We use the "one-against-one" approach in which $N_c(N_c-1)/2$ (where $N_c = 7$ is the number of classes considered: sky, vegetation, snow, water, ground, street, and sand) binary classifiers are trained to discriminate data from two different classes. Prediction is based on a majority vote among all the trained classifiers (with a random choice in case of tie). Each binary classifier is a SVM with Gaussian RBF kernel. Therefore, before training the kernel scale σ and the penalization coefficient C must be set. To do so, for each binary classifier we uniformly sampled the σC plane and we selected the parameter pair with the highest accuracy estimated by five-fold cross-validation.

The introduction of a rejection option has several advantages: i) regions that are to be classified are not compulsorily assigned to one of the designated classes; ii) ambiguous regions, that is, regions that may be labeled differently by different observers, are likely to be rejected; and iii) classification accuracy for non ambiguous regions is improved. The rejection option is based on estimates of posterior probabilities that the input region belongs to the classes considered, given the value of the features. To estimate the probabilities we used the method proposed by Wu et al. [22]. A region is rejected if the maximum of these probabilities is less than α times larger than the second largest probability (where α is a tunable parameter). Otherwise the region is assigned to the class having the largest posterior probability.

4   Experimental Results

To train and to evaluate our method we used the annotated images provided by the LabelMe project [17]. The dataset is dynamically growing and, as of October 31 2010, includes 62,197 annotated images. Images are annotated online by users who manually segment the images into polygonal regions which are labeled with freely chosen keywords (one keyword per region).

For this work we downloaded all the available annotated images and we looked for keywords matching the seven classes considered. Different keywords may be used to indicate objects matching the classes: Table 1 reports the keyword we selected for each class, together with the resulting number of annotated images containing regions of that class. Note that the images usually contain regions of different classes: a total of 12,755 images has been used during the experiments. These images have been resampled in such a way that the longest side is exactly 1024 pixels long.

To train the classifier, we segmented the images using the approach described in Section 3.1. Each segmented region has been compared with the manual annotation. Only regions with an area exceeding the 10,000 pixels are considered. Moreover, if more than 95% of pixels of a segmented region belong to regions

Table 1. The keywords we selected for each class, the number of annotated regions, and the number of annotated images containing those regions

Class	Keywords	Number of regions	Number of images
Ground	ground, soil, desert ground, rock	2,982	1,510
Sand	sand, sand beach, beach, desert, shore, dune	1,387	523
Sky	sky, cloud, clouds	14,446	7,398
Snow	snow, snow covered ground	399	222
Street	street, asphalt, pavement, highway, road	4,635	4,862
Vegetation	tree, trees, palm tree, pine tree, vegetation, grass, forest, bush, bushes, field	9,870	7,281
Water	water, river, sea, sea water, lake, river water	2,330	1,051

annotated with one of the keywords considered, then that region is further processed as a region of the corresponding class; otherwise the region is discarded. The final number of regions considered is 40,396 as detailed in Table 1. Figure 4 and Figure 5 show a sample of the regions selected for the classes sky and vegetation, respectively. Note that some of the selected regions have been mislabeled. Often this happens when the manual segmentation is too coarse. For instance, sometimes the sky region has been segmented together with trees and buildings, and the automatic segmentation process isolates these objects from the sky. This fact probably causes some degradation in the classification performance. In this work we decided to rely on the annotation provided with the LabelMe dataset. In future works, we plan to manually refine the regions obtained.

The feature vectors extracted from the selected regions has been divided into a training and a test set. For each class 2,000 vectors have been randomly selected for training, with the exception of the sand and snow classes for which all the available feature vectors have been selected (1,387 and 399, respectively). After the model selection and the training procedure, the remaining feature vectors

Table 2. Confusion matrix of classification results obtained on the test set (reported in percentage)

Correct class	Predicted class						
	Ground	Sand	Sky	Snow	Street	Vegetation	Water
Ground	**70.06**	6.92	3.05	1.43	5.80	8.76	3.97
Sky	2.03	1.15	**86.53**	0.76	0.92	5.54	3.06
Street	4.78	3.76	1.18	0.61	**83.98**	0.99	4.71
Vegetation	10.42	1.54	2.95	0.23	0.71	**82.03**	2.12
Water	6.97	2.42	1.52	0.61	4.85	4.24	**79.39**

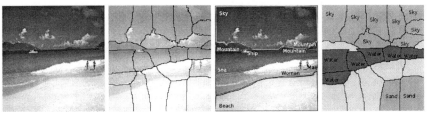

(a) Input image (b) Segmentation (c) LabelMe annotation (d) Final labeling

Fig. 3. Example of the procedure used to determine the ground truth for the experimentation. The input image is segmented using the method described in Section 3.1; the resulting regions are compared with the LabelMe annotation to determine the final labeling. Note that some regions are left unlabeled, for instance, because their keywords are not relevant (mountain, ship, woman, man), or because they are ambiguous (the shoreline).

Fig. 4. A sample of the regions considered for the "sky" class

have been used to evaluate the classifier. The estimated accuracies are reported, as a confusion matrix, in Table 2. Note that, due to the lack of feature vectors, the test set of the sand and snow classes are empty. Therefore, we excluded these classes from the performance evaluation and from any further analysis.

The overall classification accuracy on ground, sky, street, vegetation, and water is 80.4%. Most of the errors concern the ground class which is often misclassified as sand (6.92%) street (5.80%), or vegetation (8.76%). Moreover, vegetation and water classes are often classified as ground (10.42% and 6.97%, respectively). Other common errors are sky regions classified as vegetation (5.54%) and water regions classified as street (4.85%). It should be noted that we completely trusted the LabelMe annotators and that part of the misclassifications could have been caused by annotation errors or inconsistencies.

The rejection option can be used to further improve the accuracy of the classifier. As described before, a region is rejected if the ratio between the two largest estimated posterior probabilities is below a threshold. Figure 6 illustrates that the higher the threshold, the better the classification accuracy is (measured as the mean accuracy of the five classes for which there is a proper test set). That is, rejecting more regions improves classification results on non-rejected regions.

Fig. 5. A sample of the regions considered for the "vegetation" class

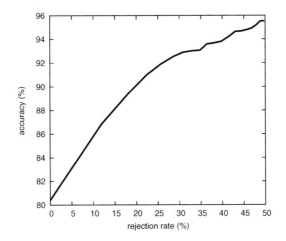

Fig. 6. Trade-off between the amount of rejected regions and the classification accuracy on non-rejected regions

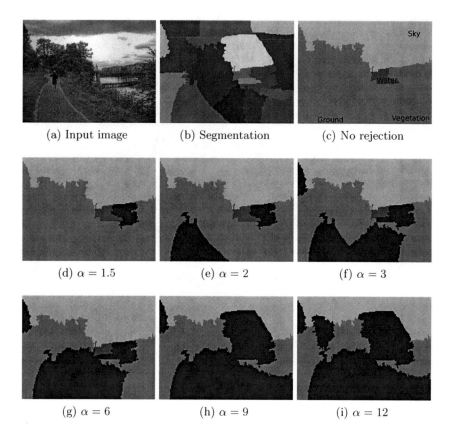

Fig. 7. Examples of the application of the rejection rule: (a) input image; (b) segmentation; (c) annotation without rejection; (d–i) rejection rule applied with different values of the threshold α. Black areas correspond to rejected regions.

For instance, if about 20% of regions are rejection (corresponding to a threshold value of 4) the average accuracy exceeds 91%. The rejection option is also very useful when the method is applied to whole images. In this case, in fact, several regions do not match any of the classes considered. Figure 7 an example of the application of the rejection rule, for different values of the rejection threshold.

Figure 8 reports some examples of application of the annotation strategy, with the rejection threshold α set to the value of 2. As it can be seen, the final annotation is able to capture the most prominent elements composing the pictures. A common source of errors is the segmentation stage which sometimes fails to isolate the objects in the images. Another cause of error is due to the rejection option, which has not been always able to discard those regions corresponding to non relevant concepts. However, this could be fixed by increasing the rejection threshold, at the expenses of a larger number of rejected regions. Classification of water requires a special remark: very often regions of this class present specular reflections which

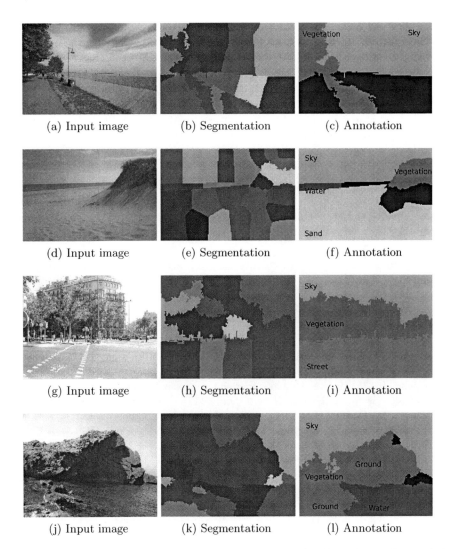

Fig. 8. Examples of annotation. For each input image (a, d, g, j) are shown their segmentation (b, e, h, k), and their final annotation (c, f, i, l). Rejected regions have been painted in black (for these examples we set $\alpha = 2$).

may deceive the classifier since, in these cases, the features represent the reflected objects, not the water itself.

5   Conclusions

We presented a strategy for the automatic annotation of outdoor photographs. Images are over segmented by applying a normalized cut algorithm tuned to select regions composed of highly homogeneous pixels. The regions are then independently classified by a multi-class Support Vector Machine into the classes sky, vegetation, snow, water, ground, street, and sand. The classification accuracy obtained on the LabelMe dataset is higher than 80%. A rejection rule may also be applied to improve the accuracy of the classifier.

We plan to exploit the information provided by the proposed strategy to improve computational color algorithms. For instance, we plan to exploit the automatic annotation for the proble of computational color constancy, as described by Gijsenij and Gevers [10].

We believe that automatic image annotation could also be applied to improve content-based image retrieval systems. In fact, the majority of systems in the state of the art are based on low-level features such as color and texture statistics, or bag-of-features descriptors. The detection of semantically meaningful regions could improve the accuracy of these systems, by reducing the semantic gap between the user's intentions and the representations used to index the images. The information provided by our strategy could also be exploited to further classify the content of the images, for instance, by following the approach proposed by Cheng and Wang [2].

References

1. Boutell, M., Luo, J., Shen, X., Brown, C.: Learning multi-label scene classification. Pattern Recognition 37(9), 1757–1771 (2004)
2. Cheng, H., Wang, R.: Semantic modeling of natural scenes based on contextual Bayesian networks. Pattern Recognition 43(12), 4042–4054 (2010)
3. Ciocca, G., Cusano, C., Gasparini, F., Schettini, R.: Content aware image enhancement. In: Basili, R., Pazienza, M.T. (eds.) AI*IA 2007. LNCS (LNAI), vol. 4733, pp. 686–697. Springer, Heidelberg (2007)
4. Cooper, T.: Color segmentation as an aid to white balancing for digital still cameras, 4300, 164–171 (2000)
5. Cortes, C., Vapnik, V.: Support-vector networks. Machine Learning 20, 273–297 (1995)
6. Cusano, C., Ciocca, G., Schettini, R.: Image annotation using SVM. In: Proc. of Internet Imaging V. SPIE, vol. 5304, pp. 330–338 (2004)
7. Cusano, C., Gasparini, F., Schettini, R.: Image annotation for adaptive enhancement of uncalibrated color images. In: Bres, S., Laurini, R. (eds.) VISUAL 2005. LNCS, vol. 3736, pp. 216–225. Springer, Heidelberg (2006)
8. Fredembach, C., Estrada, F., Süsstrunk, S.: Memory colour segmentation and classification using class-specific eigenregions. Journal of the Society for Information Display 17(11), 921–931 (2009)
9. Gasparini, F., Schettini, R.: Color balancing of digital photos using simple image statistics. Pattern Recognition 37(6), 1201–1217 (2004)
10. Gijsenij, A., Gevers, T.: Color constancy using image regions. In: IEEE International Conference on Image Processing, vol. 3, pp. 501–504 (2007)
11. Guillaumin, M., Mensink, T., Verbeek, J., Schmid, C.: Tagprop: Discriminative metric learning in nearest neighbor models for image auto-annotation. In: IEEE 12th International Conference on Computer Vision, pp. 309–316 (2010)

12. Jeon, J., Lavrenko, V., Manmatha, R.: Automatic image annotation and retrieval using cross-media relevance models. In: Proceedings of the 26th Annual International ACM SIGIR Conference on Research and Development in Informaion Retrieval, pp. 119–126 (2003)
13. Malik, J., Belongie, S., Leung, T., Shi, J.: Contour and texture analysis for image segmentation. International Journal of Computer Vision 43, 7–27 (2001)
14. Millet, C., Bloch, I., Hede, P., Moellic, P.: Using relative spatial relationships to improve individual region recognition. In: European Workshop on the Integration of Knowledge, Semantics and Digital Media Technologies, EWIMT, vol. 5, pp. 119–126 (2005)
15. Ojala, T., Pietikäainen, M., Mäaenpää, T.: Multiresolution gray-scale and rotation invariant texture classification with local binary patterns. IEEE Transactions on Pattern Analysis and Machine Intelligence 24(7), 971–987 (2002)
16. Rui, X., Li, M., Li, Z., Ma, W., Yu, N.: Bipartite graph reinforcement model for web image annotation. In: Proceedings of the 15th International Conference on Multimedia, pp. 585–594 (2007)
17. Russell, B., Torralba, A., Murphy, K., Freeman, W.: LabelMe: a database and web-based tool for image annotation. International Journal of Computer Vision 77(1), 157–173 (2008)
18. Shi, J., Malik, J.: Normalized cuts and image segmentation. IEEE Transactions on Pattern Analysis and Machine Intelligence 22(8), 888–905 (2000)
19. Tsai, C., Hung, C.: Automatically annotating images with keywords: A review of image annotation systems. Recent Patents on Computer Science 1(1), 55–68 (2008)
20. Wang, C., Jing, F., Zhang, L., Zhang, H.: Content-based image annotation refinement. In: IEEE Conference on Computer Vision and Pattern Recognition, pp. 1–8 (2007)
21. Van de Weijer, J., Gevers, T., Bagdanov, A.: Boosting color saliency in image feature detection. IEEE Transactions on Pattern Analysis and Machine Intelligence 28(1), 150–156 (2006)
22. Wu, T., Lin, C., Weng, R.: Probability estimates for multi-class classification by pairwise coupling. The Journal of Machine Learning Research 5, 975–1005 (2004)
23. Yuan, J., Li, J., Zhang, B.: Exploiting spatial context constraints for automatic image region annotation. In: Proceedings of the 15th International Conference on Multimedia, pp. 595–604 (2007)

Adaptive Edge Enhancing Technique of Impulsive Noise Removal in Color Digital Images

Bogdan Smolka

Silesian University of Technology, Department of Automatic Control,
Akademicka 16, 44-100 Gliwice, Poland
smolka@ieee.org

Abstract. In this paper a novel class of noise attenuating and edge enhancing filters for color image processing is introduced and analyzed. The proposed adaptive filter design is minimizing the cumulative dissimilarity measure of a cluster of pixels belonging to a sliding filtering window and outputs the most centrally located pixel. The proposed filter is computationally efficient, easy to implement and very effective in suppressing impulsive noise, while preserving image details and enhancing its edges. Therefore it can be used in any application in which simultaneous denoising and edge enhancement is a prerequisite for further steps of the color image processing pipeline.

Keywords: color image enhancement, impulsive noise reduction.

1 Introduction

During image formation, acquisition, storage and transmission many types of distortions limit the quality of digital images [1, 2, 3]. Quite often, images are corrupted by the *impulsive noise* caused mainly either by faulty image sensors or due to transmission errors. Common sources of impulse noise include also lightenings, industrial machines, car starters, faulty or dusty insulation of high voltage powerlines and various unprotected electric switches. These noise sources generate short time duration, high energy pulses which block the regular signal, resulting for example in bothering spots on the TV screen and sharp click sounds in the audio [4].

The Vector Median Filter (VMF) is the most popular filter intended for smoothing out spikes injected into the color image by the impulse noise process, [5, 6, 7]. This filter is very efficient at reducing the impulses, preserves sharp edges and linear trends, however it does not retain fine image structures, which are treated as noise and therefore generally the VMF tends to produce blurry images. This unwanted feature of the VMF is quite important as much of the image information is contained in its edges and sharp edges are pleasing to humans and are desirable for machine processing [8, 9, 10]. As a result much research has been devoted to the construction of filters which can cope with image noise while simultaneously preserving image details and enhancing image edges.

R. Schettini, S. Tominaga, and A. Trémeau (Eds.): CCIW 2011, LNCS 6626, pp. 60–74, 2011.
© Springer-Verlag Berlin Heidelberg 2011

In this paper a solution to the problem of image noise filtering with edge enhancing abilities is presented. Extending the VMF concept using the *peer groups* introduced in [11, 12], it is possible to efficiently remove impulse noise while sharpening the color image edges. The proposed filtering design excels over the VMF, preserves much better image details and produces images with sharp object boundaries. Additionally, the proposed design ia able to adapt to the noise intensity level so that no tuning parameters are required.

2   Vector Median Filter

In this paper the color image is defined as a two-dimensional matrix of size $N_1 \times N_2$ consisting of pixels $\boldsymbol{x}_i = (x_{i1}, x_{i2}, x_{i3})$, indexed by i, which gives the pixel position on the image domain. Components x_{ik}, for $i = 1, 2, \ldots, N$, $N = N_1 \cdot N_2$ and $k = 1, 2, 3$ represent the color channel values quantified into the integer domain.

As color images are highly non-stationary, the filtering operators work on the assumption that the local image features can be extracted from a small image region centered at pixel $\boldsymbol{x}_i$ called a *sliding filtering window*, W. Thus, the output of the filtering operation will depend only on the samples from the filtering window. Of course, the size and shape of the window influence the properties and efficiency of the image processing operations and are therefore application dependent. However, in order to preserve image details, mostly a 3×3 window is used to process the central pixel surrounded by its neighbors.

To remove the impulse noise various filtering approaches based on the order statistics theory have been devised. The most popular filtering class operating on a sliding window is based on the *reduced* or *aggregated ordering* which assigns an aggregated dissimilarity measure to each color pixel from the filtering window [1, 13]. The aggregated dissimilarity measure assigned to pixel $\boldsymbol{x}_i$ is defined as

$$R_i = \sum_{j=1}^{n} \rho(\boldsymbol{x}_i, \boldsymbol{x}_j), \quad \boldsymbol{x}_i, \boldsymbol{x}_j \in W, \tag{1}$$

where $\rho(\cdot)$ is the chosen dissimilarity measure. The scalar accumulated dissimilarity measures are then sorted and the vectors are correspondingly ordered

$$R_{(1)} \leq \ldots \leq R_{(n)} \Rightarrow \boldsymbol{x}_{(1)} \leq \ldots \leq \boldsymbol{x}_{(n)}. \tag{2}$$

The dissimilarity measure depends on the kind of relationship between the sample vectors used to measure their difference. Usually the distance between vectors and the angle between them is utilized. The combination of the magnitude and directional processing can also be used, [14, 15].

In this paper we will focus on the *vector median filter* defined using the accumulated sum of distances between vectors, which serves as a dissimilarity measure. The vector median of a set of vectors belonging to a filtering mask W is defined as the vector $\boldsymbol{x}_{(1)}$ for which the sum of distances to all other vectors from W is minimized, [5, 16, 17, 18]

$$\boldsymbol{x}_{(1)} = \arg\min_{\boldsymbol{x} \in W} \sum_{j=1}^{n} \|\boldsymbol{x} - \boldsymbol{x}_j\|, \tag{3}$$

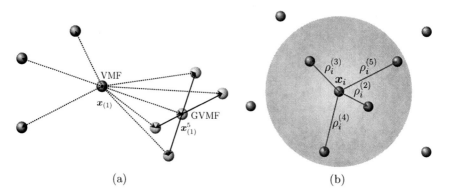

Fig. 1. Illustration of the peer group concept: (a) output of the VMF, $(n = 9)$ and GVMF for $\alpha = 5$ and (b) the peer group associated with $\boldsymbol{x}_i$, $\alpha = 5$

where $\|\cdot\|$ denotes the Euclidean distance. The construction of the VMF is illustrated in Fig. 1a, where the Euclidean distance is used. As can be seen, the vector median of the set of pixels is centrally located within the samples from the filtering window, meaning that the sum of distances to all other samples from W is minimized.

3   Generalized Vector Median Filter

As in the definition of the VMF the sum of distances is used (Eqs. 1, 3), we can say that the vector median is the vector $\boldsymbol{x}_{(1)}$ whose average distance to the n vectors from W is minimized. So we see that the vector median and also the scalar median is utilizing the concept of averaging, which is a little bit surprising, taking into account its properties, which are clearly opposed to the averaging based filters.

In this paper we propose to generalize the definition of the vector median. In the new approach the vector median will be the vector $\boldsymbol{x}_{(1)}^{\alpha}$ for which the sum of α smallest distances to other vectors from W is minimized. For $\alpha = n$ the output of the Generalized VMF (GVMF) is identical with the standard VMF and for $\alpha = 1$ the identity filter is obtained, as the smallest distance is always zero, because it is the distance of the reference pixel to itself.

If the distance between the vector $\boldsymbol{x}_i$ and $\boldsymbol{x}_j$ is denoted as $\rho_{i,j}$, then we can order the set of distances $\rho_{i,j}$, for $j = 1, \ldots, n$ and obtain the following sequence: $\rho_i^{(1)} \leq \ldots \leq \rho_i^{(\alpha)} \leq \ldots \leq \rho_i^{(n)}$, where $\rho_i^{(k)}$ is the k-th smallest distance from $\boldsymbol{x}_i$ and $\rho_i^{(1)} = \|\boldsymbol{x}_i - \boldsymbol{x}_i\| = 0$. For each pixel in the filtering window the cumulated sum R_i^{α} is calculated

$$R_i^{\alpha} = \sum_{k=1}^{\alpha} \rho_i^{(k)} , \tag{4}$$

and the output of the generalized VMF is the pixel for which the trimmed sum of distances R^{α} is minimized.

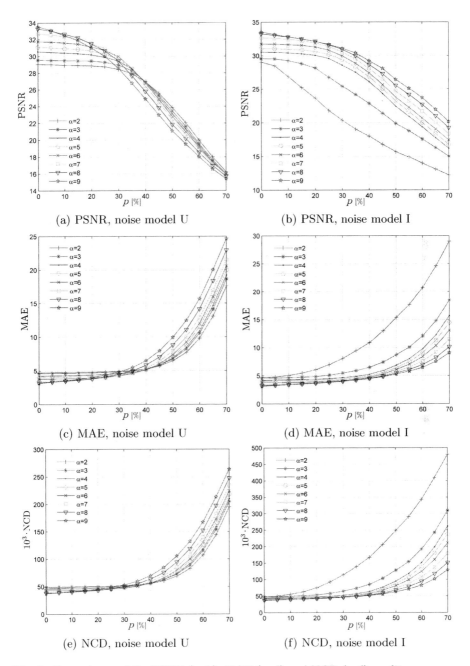

Fig. 2. Dependence of the PSNR (a, b), MAE (c, d) and NCD (e, f) quality measures on the contamination intensities for the used noise models U and I applied to the *LENA* test image filtered with the GVMF for various values of the α parameter

In [11] a concept of the so called *peer group* filtering was introduced. This concept can be used to describe the construction of the proposed filtering approach. The *peer group* $\mathcal{P}(\boldsymbol{x}, \alpha)$, denotes the set of α pixels consisting of $\boldsymbol{x}$ and $(\alpha - 1)$ nearest pixels belonging to W. Using the *peer group concept* we can define the generalized vector median filter output as the sample $\boldsymbol{x}$ whose peer group of size α has the smallest accumulated sum of distances R^α, (see Fig. 1b). In other words the output of the GVMF is the pixel centrally located within a peer group of pixels with minimal dispersion, expressed as the sum of distances.

It is worth noticing the similarity of the new filter design with the α-*trimmed vector median filter*. The trimming operation in the α-trimmed filter is however being performed on the ordered set of vectors, whereas in the construction of the new filter, the trimming is applied to the ordered set of distances associated with a pixel from the filtering window.

So, the new filtering design is utilizing the concept of a peer group which has been already successfully utilized for impulse noise removal [19, 20, 21] and can be regarded as a generalization of the vector median filter, which is obtained as a special case of the new filtering technique.

4   Adaptive Design

As can be observed in Fig. 2, the quality measures, which will be defined later together with the used noise models, depend significantly on the α parameter of the GVMF, which evokes the need for an adaptive scheme of adjusting this parameter to the local image structures.

In [22] the following criterion for choosing the α parameter was proposed

$$\alpha = \max \alpha' \quad \text{subject to} \quad \left(\sum_{l=1}^{\alpha'} \rho_j^{(l)} \right) \leq \rho_j^{(n)}, \ j = 1, \ldots, n, \tag{5}$$

where $\rho_j^{(n)}$ is the largest distance between the central pixel $\boldsymbol{x}_j$ and its neighbors from W. This rule for the setting of the α values works well for pixels corrupted by impulsive noise, however for uncorrupted pixels in homogeneous image areas, usually the number of the pixels α in the peer-group is very small, as the distances between pixels are comparable. Therefore a new scheme for the adaptive determination of the choosing the α value has been elaborated.

The adaptive algorithm which will be denoted as Adaptive Generalized VMF (AGVMF) requires to calculate for each pixel $\boldsymbol{x}_k$, the distances $\rho_{k,l}$, $l = 1, \ldots, n$, $l \neq k$ to other pixels belonging to the filtering window. The largest distance $\rho_k^{(n)}$ is used for building the peer-groups $\mathcal{P}(\boldsymbol{x}_k, \alpha_k)$ which consist of α_k pixels contained in a sphere centered at $\boldsymbol{x}_k$ with diameter $\rho_k^{(n)}$. In this way the peer group consists of α_k pixels $\boldsymbol{x}_l$ satisfying: $\rho_{k,l} \leq \rho_k^{(n)}/2$. The highest value of the α_k for $k = 1, \ldots, n$, denoted as α serves as an self-adaptive parameter of the proposed filter. Thus, the filter output is the pixel $\boldsymbol{x}_k$ for which the aggregated, trimmed distance R_k^α defined in (4) is minimized

$$k = \arg \min_j \sum_{l=1}^{\alpha} \rho_j^{(l)}, \quad j = 1, \ldots, n, \quad \text{where} \tag{6}$$

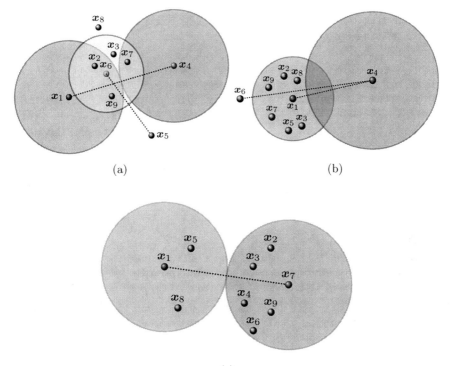

(a)   (b)

(c)

Fig. 3. Illustration of the adaptive determination of the maximum size cluster

$$\alpha = \arg\max_{l} \ \rho_j^{(l)} \leq \frac{1}{2}\rho_j^{(n)}, \quad j = 1, \ldots, n. \tag{7}$$

Figure 3a shows an exemplary configuration of pixels. For the pixel x_1 the most distant neighbor is the outlying pixel x_4 and in the sphere centered at x_1 with the diameter equal to the distance $\rho_{1,4}$ four pixels are contained. The peer group of pixel x_4, whose most distant neighbor is x_1 contains 2 pixels and the largest peer group consisting of 5 pixels is assigned to pixel x_6 whose most distant pixel is x_5. In this way the proposed filter is searching for a cluster of $\alpha = 5$ pixels with the lowest trimmed sum of distances.

As can be observed in Fig. 3b the proposed design is able to cope with the outliers introduced by the noise process as their peer groups do not contain any other pixels or like in a situation depicted in Fig. 3c the peer group size is quite low.

As often a few clusters with the same maximum number of pixels is found, then the pixel centrally located in the most compact cluster is chosen as the filter output. In other words, the output is the center of the peer-group whose aggregated distances to its members attains a minimum value.

Additionally, in order to preserve image details a switching mechanism has been incorporated into the adaptive filter design. As can be observed, the adaptive filter removes efficiently the impulses and enhances the image edges. The changes introduced into the image are significant at pixels corrupted by impulse noise and at edges. If the differences between the channel components of the original and filtered image pixels are small, then most probably these pixels are not corrupted and do not belong to an edge.

If $x_i = \{x_{i1}, x_{i2}, x_{i3}\}$ denotes a pixel at a position indexed by i and $y_i = \{y_{i1}, y_{i2}, y_{i3}\}$ is the output of the Adaptive Generalized VMF (AGVMF), then the final output will be x_i if $|x_{ik} - y_{ik}| < \delta$ for $k = 1, 2, 3$ and y_i otherwise. In other words, if the changes in the RGB components are less than a threshold δ then the color image pixels are not changed, otherwise they are replaced by the AGVMF. Extensive experiments indicate that the value of δ equal to 30 provides a good compromise between detail preservation and noise reduction.

5   Experiments

For the evaluation of the efficiency of the proposed adaptive denoising design a set of standard color images has been contaminated with two noise types. In the first model, which will be called impulsive *salt* and *pepper* noise model denoted as I, the noisy signal is modeled as $x_i = \{x_{i1}, x_{i2}, x_{i3}\}$, where

$$x_{ik} = \begin{cases} \rho_{ik} & \text{with probability } \pi, \\ o_{ik} & \text{with probability } 1 - \pi, \end{cases} \tag{8}$$

where o_i is the original, uncorrupted image pixel and the contamination component ρ_{ik} is a random variable, which takes the value 0 or 255 with the same probability. In this noise model the contamination of the color image components is uncorrelated and the overall contamination rate is $p = 1 - (1 - \pi)^3$.

The second type of noise, called *random-valued* or *uniform* noise denoted as U is modeled as

$$x_i = \begin{cases} \rho_i & \text{with probability } p, \\ o_i & \text{with probability } 1 - p, \end{cases} \tag{9}$$

where ρ_i is a noisy pixel with all channels corrupted by noise of uniform distribution in the range $[0, 255]$. In the first model the noise can corrupt one, two or all three channels. In the second all channels are contaminated by random values within the range $[0, 255]$.

For the measurement of the restoration quality the commonly used *Root Mean Squared Error* (RMSE) expressed through the *Peak Signal to Noise Ratio* (PSNR) was used as the RMSE is a good measure of the efficiency of impulsive noise suppression. For the evaluation of the detail preservation capabilities of the proposed filtering design the *Mean Absolute Error* (MAE) has been used.

The PSNR, which measures the impulsive noise removal efficiency of a filter, is defined as

$$\text{PSNR} = 20 \log_{10} \left(\frac{255}{\sqrt{MSE}} \right), \quad \text{MSE} = \frac{1}{N} \sum_{i=1}^{N} \|x_i - o_i\|_2^2, \tag{10}$$

where N is the total number of image pixels, and x_{ik}, o_{ik} denote the k-th component of the noisy image pixel channel and its original, undisturbed value at a pixel position i, respectively. The MAE defined as

$$\text{MAE} = \frac{1}{N} \sum_{i=1}^{N} \|x_i - o_i\|_1, \tag{11}$$

where $\| \cdot \|_\gamma$ denotes the L_γ Minkowski norm, is a good measure of detail preservation.

Since RGB is not a perceptually uniform space, in the sense that differences between colors in this color space do not correspond to color differences perceived by humans, the restoration errors were also analyzed using the *Normalized Color Difference* (NCD) based on the CIE Lab color space, [1].

$$\Delta E = \frac{1}{N} \sum_{i=1}^{N} \sqrt{\left(L^*_{o_i} - L^*_{x_i}\right)^2 + \left(a^*_{o_i} - a^*_{x_i}\right)^2 + \left(b^*_{o_i} - b^*_{x_i}\right)^2}, \tag{12}$$

$$NCD = \frac{N \, \Delta E_1}{\sum\limits_{i=1}^{N} \sqrt{\left(L^*_{o_i}\right)^2 + \left(a^*_{o_i}\right)^2 + \left(b^*_{o_i}\right)^2}}, \tag{13}$$

where L^* represents lightness values and (a^*, b^*) chrominance values corresponding to original o_i and noisy (filtered) x_i samples expressed in CIE LAB color space.

In order to evaluate the edge enhancing and noise canceling properties of the proposed filter a synthetic color test image has been prepared, (Fig. 4a). This image has been blurred by rotating it clockwise about 3 degrees, applying moving average smoothing and rotating back about 3 degrees. The rotation operation has been performed in order to avoid the generation of totally symmetric ramp edges which would be produced by direct linear smoothing. Then the blurry image has been contaminated by 10% impulsive noise (I) as shown Fig. 4d.

Figures 4b and 4e depict the output of the VMF when applied to the blurred and noisy test image. As can be noticed the VMF removes the impulse noise and preserves the blurred edges. This behavior is not present when inspecting the output of the GVMF filter, which is able to enhance image edges, (Fig. 4c) while suppressing the impulsive noise, (Fig. 4f). It is worth noticing that the ramp edges tend to be converted into ideal step edges which separate piecewise constant image regions.

The ability of the GVMG to remove impulses while sharpening the color image edges by reducing their width is also depicted in Fig. 5 which exhibits the row 60 of the blue channel of color test image shown in Fig. 4d. As seen in the magnified part of the main plot the spikes originating from the noise are removed and the ramp edges tend to be converted into step edges.

This filter behavior is also clearly seen in Fig. 6 which presents three dimensional representation of the blue channel of the artificial test images. The comparison of the GVMF technique with the standard VMF shows that the latter removes efficiently the impulse noise but preserves the blurred edges. The proposed filtering design replaces the impulses as efficiently as the VMF does but generates an

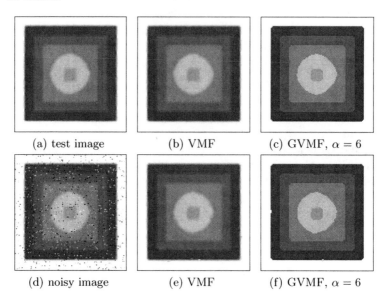

Fig. 4. Edge enhancing and noise attenuating properties of the GVMF as compared with VMF: (a) blurry test image, (b) its VMF output, (c) GVMF with $\alpha = 6$, (d) test image distorted by impulsive noise (noise model I, $p = 0.1$), (d) VMF and (e) GVMF output with $\alpha = 6$

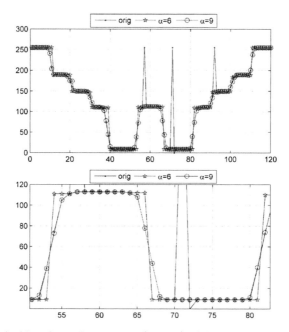

Fig. 5. Plot of the blue channel intensities (row 60) of the corrupted and enhanced synthetic test image depicted in Fig. 4c and below a zoomed part of the graph

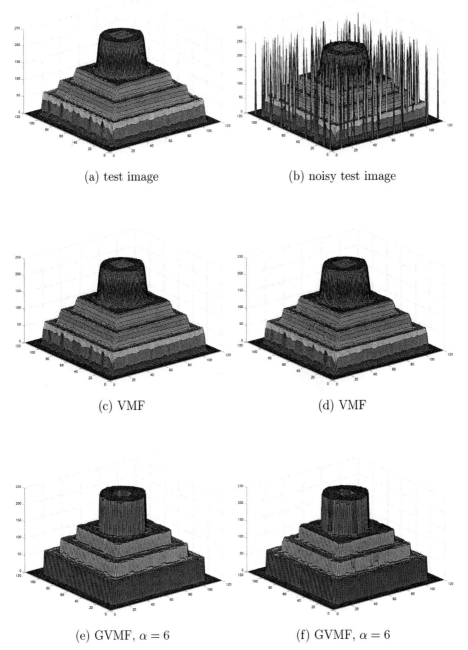

(a) test image   (b) noisy test image

(c) VMF   (d) VMF

(e) GVMF, $\alpha = 6$ (f) GVMF, $\alpha = 6$

Fig. 6. Visualization of the edge enhancing and noise reduction capabilities of the generalized VMF (GVMF) with fixed $\alpha = 6$: (a) 3D representation of the inverted blue channel of the test image depicted in Fig. 4a, (b) visualization of the inverted blue channel of the noisy test image shown in Fig. 4d, (c) and (d) the result of the VMF, (e) and (f) output of the GVMF

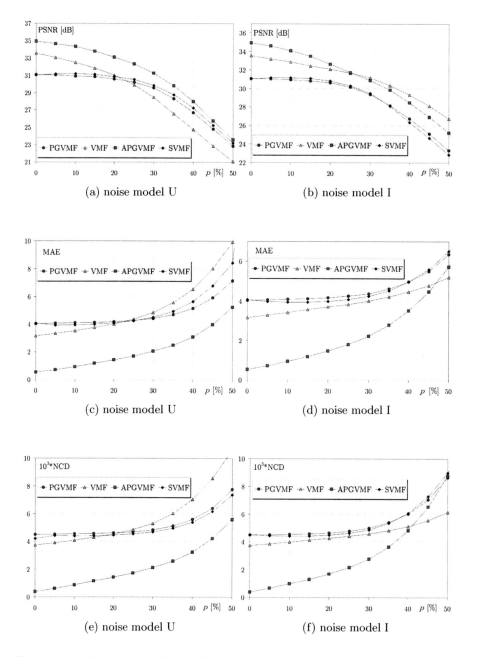

Fig. 7. Dependence of the PSNR (a, b), and MAE (c, d) and NCD (e, f) quality measures on the contamination intensities for the noise model U and I applied to the *LENA* test image filtered with AGVMF with $\delta = 30$ as compared with other denoising techniques

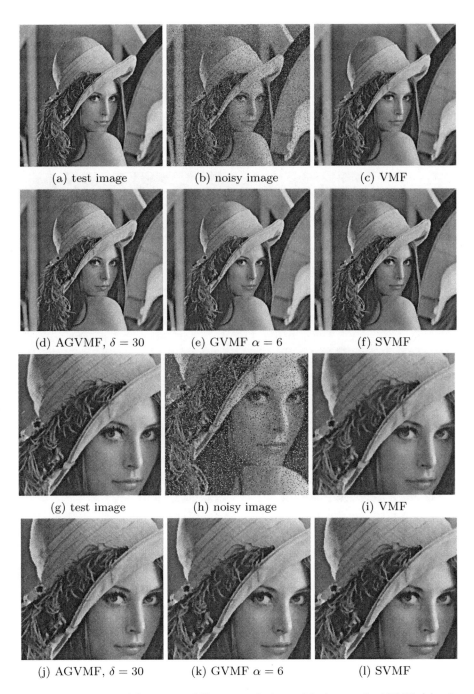

Fig. 8. Comparison of the proposed filtering technique with the standard VMF: (a) color test image, (b) test image distorted by 20% noise U, (c) VMF output, (d) AGVMF output with $\delta = 30$, (e) GVMF with $\alpha = 6$, (f) SVMF output

(a) test image FRUITS   (b) noisy image, noise model U, $p = 0.4$

(c) VMF output, 2 iterations   (d) DDF output, 2 iterations

(e) GVMF output, 2 iterations, $\alpha = 6$ (f) AGVMF, 2 iterations, $\delta = 30$

(g) VMF   (h) GVMF   (i) AGVMF

Fig. 9. Efficiency of the proposed Adaptive Generalized VMF - AGVMF (f) as compared with the VMF (c), DDF [14, 15] (d) and GVMF (e) using a color test image (a) contaminated with 40% noise U (b). Below cropped and zoomed parts of the outputs of VMF (g), GVMF (h) and AGVMG with $\delta = 30$ (i).

image with sharp, almost ideal edges. Extensive experiments revealed that very similar results were obtained for images distorted by the uniform noise model.

The overall good noise reduction abilities of the proposed adaptive filtering design, are presented in Fig. 7, which show the dependance of the PSNR and MAE on the uniform noise (U) intensity p when restoring the *LENA* noisy image. As can be observed the efficiency of the proposed adaptive GVMF (AGVMF) is superior to that of the Sharpening VMF (SVMF) proposed in [22] and the Generalized VMF (GVM F) with fixed parameter $\alpha = 5$. As can be observed the efficiency of the proposed adaptive filter in terms of the used quality measures is lower for the impulsive noise I. This behavior is caused by the creation of clusters of similar pixels which are injected by the impulsive noise. For contamination intensity exceeding 30%, the number of such clusters of noisy pixels is rapidly increasing and as a result the noisy pixels are preserved by the proposed filter.

Apart from the good denoising efficiency, the proposed adaptive filtering scheme has the unique ability to sharpen the edges present in the color images. This feature is visible in Fig. 8 which depicts the filtering results delivered by the new filter as compared with the VMF, GVMF and SVMF. As can be observed the new filtering design not only removes efficiently the impulses but also preserves image details due to the incorporated switching mechanism.

The detail preservation can be also observed when evaluating the output of the novel filter operating on a very noisy image depicted in Fig. 9. As can be seen the proposed filter removes the noise component while preserving fine image structures and significantly outperforms the basic filters like VMF, Directional Distance filter (DDF) [14, 15] and the GVMF with a fixed α parameter.

6   Conclusions

In the paper an adaptive filtering design for impulsive noise removal has been presented. The proposed adaptive scheme of choosing the optimal value of the peer group size used in the construction of the filter exhibits very good denoising properties outperforming the vector median based solutions. Extensive simulations revealed very good noise attenuation properties of the proposed filtering scheme combined with its unique ability to sharpen image edges while preserving image details. As a result, the novel class of filters exhibits very good noise reduction efficiency which combined with its edge enhancing properties makes the new filtering design an attractive tool for low level color image processing. The simplicity of the new algorithm and its computational speed, which is comparable to that of the VMF makes the new noise removal method very useful in the preprocessing of color images corrupted by impulse noise.

Acknowledgments. This work has been supported by the Polish Ministry of Science and Higher Education Development Grant OR 00002111.

References

1. Plataniotis, K.N., Venetsanopoulos, A.N.: Color Image Processing and Applications. Springer, Heidelberg (2000)
2. Boncelet, C.G.: Image Noise Models. In: Bovik, A. (ed.) Handbook of Image and Video Processing, pp. 325–335. Academic Press, London (2000)
3. Zheng, J., Valavanis, K.P., Gauch, J.M.: Noise Removal from Color Images. Journal of Intelligent and Robotic Systems 7, 257–285 (1993)
4. Lukac, R., Smolka, B., Martin, K., Plataniotis, K.N., Venetsanopoulos, A.N.: Vector Filtering for Color Imaging. IEEE Signal Processing Magazine 22, 74–86 (2005)
5. Astola, J., Haavisto, P., Neuvo, Y.: Vector Median Filters. Proc. of the IEEE 78, 678–689 (1990)
6. Tang, K., Astola, J., Neuvo, Y.: Multichannel Edge Enhancement in Color Image Processing. IEEE Transactions on Circuits and Systems for Video Technology 4, 468–479 (1994)
7. Tang, K., Astola, J., Neuvo, Y.: Nonlinear Multivariate Image Filtering Techniques. IEEE Transactions on Image Processing 4, 788–798 (1995)
8. Leu, J.G.: Edge Sharpening Through Ramp Width Reduction. Image and Vision Computing 18, 501–514 (2000)
9. Schavemaker, J.G.M., Reinders, M.J.T., Gerbrands, J.J., Backer, E.: Image Sharpening by Morphological Filtering. Pattern Recognition 33, 997–1012 (2000)
10. Lin, W.S., Gai, Y.L., Kassim, A.A.: Perceptual Impact of Edge Sharpness in Images. IEE Proceedings - Vision, Image and Signal Processing 153, 215–223 (2006)
11. Kenney, C., Deng, Y., Manjunath, B.S., Hewer, G.: Peer Group Image Enhancement. IEEE Transactions on Image Processing 10, 326–334 (2001)
12. Deng, Y., Kenney, S., Moore, M.S., Manjunath, B.S.: Peer Group Filtering and Perceptual Color Image Quantization. Proc. of ISCAS 4, 21–24 (1999)
13. Pitas, I., Venetsanopoulos, A.N.: Nonlinear Digital Filters, Principles and Applications. Kluwer Academic Publishers, Boston (1990)
14. Karakos, D., Trahanias, P.E.: Generalized Multichannel Image Filtering Structures. IEEE Trans. on Image Processing 6, 1038–1045 (1997)
15. Trahanias, P.E., Karakos, D.G., Venetsanopoulos, A.N.: Directional Processing of Color Images: Theory and Experimental Results. IEEE Trans. on Image Processing 5, 868–881 (1996)
16. Astola, J., Kuosmanen, P.: Fundamentals of Nonlinear Digital Filtering. CRC Press, Boca Raton (1997)
17. Lukac, R.: Color Image Filtering by Vector Directional Order-Statistics. Pattern Recognition and Image Analysis 12, 279–285 (2002)
18. Lukac, R.: Adaptive Vector Median Filtering. Pattern Recognition Letters 24, 1889–1899 (2003)
19. Smolka, B., Plataniotis, K.N., Chydzinski, A., Szczepanski, M., Venetsanopulos, A.N., Wojciechowski, K.: Self-adaptive Algorithm of Impulsive Noise Reduction in Color Images. Pattern Recognition 35, 1771–1784 (2002)
20. Smolka, B., Lukac, R., Chydzinski, A., Plataniotis, K.N., Wojciechowski, K.: Fast Adaptive Similarity Based Impulsive Noise Reduction Filter. Real Time Imaging 9, 261–276 (2003)
21. Smolka, B., Chydzinski, A.: Fast Detection and Impulsive Noise Removal in Color Images. Real-Time Imaging 11, 389–402 (2005)
22. Lukac, R., Smolka, B., Plataniotis, K.N.: Sharpening Vector Median Filters. Signal Processing 87, 2085–2099 (2007)

Human Skin Color Simulator Using Active Illumination

Motonori Doi[1], Akira Kimachi[1], Shogo Nishi[1], and Shoji Tominaga[2]

[1] Osaka Electro-Communication University, 18-8 Hatsu-cho, Neyagawa,
Osaka 572-8530, Japan
[2] Chiba University, 1-33, Yayoi-cho, Inage-ku, Chiba 263-8522, Japan
{doi,kima,s-nishi}@isc.osakac.ac.jp, shoji@faculty.chiba-u.jp

Abstract. Skin color simulation is one of the most important topics. We propose a novel method to reproduce realistic skin color under different conditions by projecting active illumination to a real human skin surface. The active illumination is generated by a programmable light source, which can emit illuminant in high speed with any spectral distribution. The spectral reflectances of human skin with different concentrations of pigments in the skin are estimated based on the Kubelka-Munk theory. Then, the appearance of the skin surface under arbitrary illuminant is displayed by projecting the programmed light onto a real human skin surface. The experimental results show the feasibility of the proposed method.

Keywords: color simulation, skin color, programmable light source, spectral radiance.

1 Introduction

Color simulation of human skin is one of the most important topics. Skin color appearance is changed by illumination and the concentration of pigments in the skin. The surface layer of human skin is composed of two turbid layers of the epidermis and dermis. Each layer includes pigments of melanin and hemoglobin respectively. The surface spectral reflectance then depends on the concentration of the pigments. Production of realistic appearance of human skin under a variety of conditions is useful for many research fields including medical imaging, cosmetic development and computer graphics.

In the previous work [1] we described an algorithm for estimating surface-spectral reflectance of human skin using the Kubelka-Munk theory [2,3]. The skin color was then reproduced using the estimated spectral reflectance on a calibrated RGB color display. However, it was difficult to calibrate the color on the monitor correctly. The color matching between spectral data and RGB values on monitor is not simple problem. In this paper, we propose a direct approach to spectral reproduction of human skin under different conditions by using an active illumination system and a real human skin. Tominaga, et al. constructed a visual evaluation system for objects in a scene under arbitrary illuminants [4,5]. The system was a high-speed spectral imaging system using an active spectral illumination, where 3D object surfaces in a real scene can be observed by synthesizing illuminant with arbitrary spectral-power distribution. In this paper we produce realistic appearance of skin by projecting illuminant

R. Schettini, S. Tominaga, and A. Trémeau (Eds.): CCIW 2011, LNCS 6626, pp. 75–84, 2011.

with a specific spectral-power distribution onto real skin surface. The surface appearance of human skin with curved texture can be produced directly under different pigment conditions, without using tristimulus calculation and RGB color conversion.

2 Color Simulation by Active Illumination

2.1 Principles of Color Simulation

We assume a simple model for the surface reflection. The observed object surface color is determined from the spectral distributions of light and the spectral reflectance of the surface. Fig. 1 shows the model of color simulation by active illumination. In this model, the observed spectral radiance $V_o(\lambda)$ of the object with spectral reflectance $R_o(\lambda)$ under the illumination with the spectral power distribution $E(\lambda)$ is described as the following equation,

$$V_o(\lambda) = R_o(\lambda)E(\lambda) \tag{1}$$

where λ is the parameter of wavelength. The reproduction of the simulated color on the object is done by the illumination with the spectral power distribution $E'(\lambda)$ to the object,

$$E'(\lambda) = E(\lambda)\frac{R_s(\lambda)}{R_o(\lambda)} \tag{2}$$

where $R_s(\lambda)$ is the simulated spectral reflectance of object. The observed spectral radiance $V_s(\lambda)$ of the object with reflectance $R_s(\lambda)$ under the illumination with the spectral power distribution $E(\lambda)$ is equal to the observed color of object with reflectance $R_o(\lambda)$ under the illumination with the spectral power distribution $E'(\lambda)$.

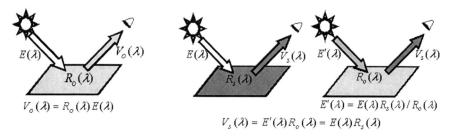

$$V_o(\lambda) = R_o(\lambda)E(\lambda)$$
$$V_s(\lambda) = E'(\lambda)R_o(\lambda) = E(\lambda)R_s(\lambda)$$
$$E'(\lambda) = E(\lambda)R_s(\lambda)/R_o(\lambda)$$

Fig. 1. Principles of color simulation by active illumination

2.2 Programmable Light Source

It is difficult to control the spectral power distribution of illumination by using conventional light source. We use a programmable light source (Optronic Laboratories, Inc. OL490) to control the illumination spectra. Fig. 2 shows the programmable light source. The light source can emit light with arbitrary spectral-power distribution.

Fig. 2. Programmable light source

The programmable light source is composed of a xenon lamp source, a grating, a digital micro mirror device (DMD) chip, and a liquid light guide. The light beam of xenon is separated by the grating into its constituent wavelength. The intensity of the light on each wavelength is controlled by the DMD chip.

3   Skin Color Estimation

The skin color depends on some histological variables such as the concentration of pigments of melanin and hemoglobin. Our previous work [1] showed that the skin surface reflectance was controllable by the density parameters of melanin and hemoglobin. In our method, the human skin was modeled in the two turbid layers of the epidermis including melanin and dermis including hemoglobin as shown in Fig.3. In this model, the incident light penetrating the skin surface is absorbed and scattered in these two layers. The spectral reflectance and spectral transmittance of each layer was determined from density parameters by the Kubelka-Munk theory [2,3].

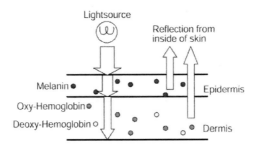

Fig. 3. Skin optics model

The body reflectance function of the skin surface $R_b(\lambda)$ is described as a function of wavelength as

$$R_b(\lambda) = R_e(\lambda) + \frac{T_e(\lambda)^2 R_{dt}(\lambda)}{1 - R_e(\lambda) R_{dt}(\lambda)},$$ (3)

where $R_e(\lambda)$ and $T_e(\lambda)$ are, respectively, the spectral reflectance and transmittance of epidermis. The spectral reflectance $R_{dt}(\lambda)$ represents the reflectance of dermis and the equation for $R_{dt}(\lambda)$ is described as

$$R_{dt}(\lambda) = R_d(\lambda) + \frac{T_d(\lambda)^2}{1 - R_d(\lambda)} , \qquad (4)$$

where $R_d(\lambda)$ and $T_d(\lambda)$ are the spectral reflectance and transmittance of the dermis, respectively. We assume that the reflectance of tissues under dermis is 1.

The spectral reflectances and transmittances of the respective layers are given as follows:

Epidermis:

$$R_e(\lambda) = \frac{1}{a_e(\lambda) + b_e(\lambda)\coth b_e(\lambda)S_e(\lambda)D_e}$$

$$T_e(\lambda) = \frac{b_e(\lambda)}{a_e(\lambda)\sinh b_e(\lambda)S_e(\lambda)D_e + b_e(\lambda)\coth b_e(\lambda)S_e(\lambda)D_e} \qquad (5)$$

$$a_e(\lambda) = \frac{S_e(\lambda) + K_e(\lambda)}{S_e(\lambda)}, b_e(\lambda) = \sqrt{a_e(\lambda)^2 - 1}$$

Dermis:

$$R_d(\lambda) = \frac{1}{a_d(\lambda) + b_d(\lambda)\coth b_d(\lambda)S_d(\lambda)D_d}$$

$$T_d(\lambda) = \frac{b_d(\lambda)}{a_d(\lambda)\sinh b_d(\lambda)S_d(\lambda)D_d + b_d(\lambda)\coth b_d(\lambda)S_d(\lambda)D_d} \qquad (6)$$

$$a_d(\lambda) = \frac{S_d(\lambda) + K_d(\lambda)}{S_d(\lambda)}, b_d(\lambda) = \sqrt{a_d(\lambda)^2 - 1}$$

where $S_e(\lambda)$ and $S_d(\lambda)$ are spectral scattering coefficients in epidermis and dermis, respectively. The spectral absorption coefficients $K_e(\lambda)$ and $K_d(\lambda)$ in the two layers are determined by the pigments in the following forms:

$$K_e(\lambda) = w_m K_m(\lambda)$$
$$K_d(\lambda) = w_h K_h(\lambda) + w_{dh} K_{dh}(\lambda) \qquad (7)$$

where $K_m(\lambda)$, $K_h(\lambda)$, and $K_{dh}(\lambda)$ represent the spectral-absorption coefficients of melanin, oxy-hemoglobin, and deoxy-hemoglobin, respectively. The constant coefficients w_m, w_h, and w_{dh} represent the weights of the pigment absorption coefficients.

For applying the estimation algorithm to real measurements, we need the optical and histological data of skin tissue. The spectral absorption data, the spectral scattering data, and the layer thickness values published in Refs [6,7] are used in this paper.

4 Procedure of Skin Color Simulation on Skin Surface

The simulation is done by the estimation of spectral reflectance of skin surface with the change of pigment concentration and the display of the estimated color by the projection of the active illumination on the real skin surface. Fig. 4 shows the scheme of the skin color simulation. Spectral reflectances of skin surface with different concentrations of pigments are simulated. Then, the simulated colors are displayed on real skin surface by the projection of active illumination.

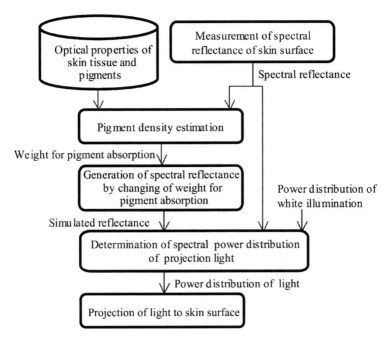

Fig. 4. Scheme of simulation procedure

4.1 Simulation of Spectral Reflectance of Skin Surface with Condition Change

The estimation of spectral reflectance of skin surface and the generation of new spectral reflectance of skin is done by the following procedures. First, the spectral reflectance of skin surface is measured. The measured skin surface area is the same area that is used for the display by the projection of the active illumination. Then, the fitting of the estimation data to the measured data is done by the control of the variables of pigment density in equation (7).

Next, new spectral reflectance data are generated by the changing of pigment density variables. When the weight for melanin is increased, the generated skin color shows the suntanned skin. The increase of hemoglobin generates reddish skin color by inflammation.

4.2 Display of Simulated Color on Real Skin Surface by Projection of Active Illumination

The spectral power distributions of illuminations for simulated colors are calculated from the measured original spectral reflectance, the estimated spectral reflectances and the spectral power distribution of white illumination by equation (2). The spectral power distributions are converted to inputs of the programmable light source. The output of the programmable light source is calibrated in advance.

Then, the synthesized illumination is projected to the measured skin surface area in a room without other light sources. Simulated color appears on real skin surface under the synthesized illumination.

5 Experiments

We simulated melanin-increased skin color and hemoglobin-increased skin color on a back of hand. The programmable light source was adjusted beforehand. First, the spectral reflectance of skin was measured by a spectrometer. Fig.5 shows the image of target skin and the spectral reflectance measured from the skin. The wavelengths of

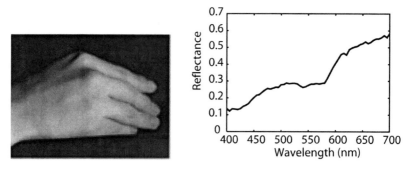

(a)   Measurement target: back of hand   (b) Spectral reflectance of target

Fig. 5. Measurement of spectral skin reflectance

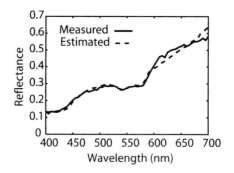

Fig. 6. Measured reflectance and fitted estimated reflectance

Table 1. Weights for pigment absorption coefficients

Pigment	Density coefficient
Melanin (w_m)	470
Oxy-hemoglobin (w_h)	152
Deoxy-hemoglobin (w_{dh})	200

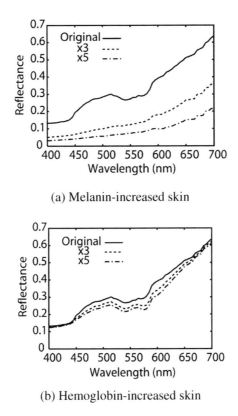

(a) Melanin-increased skin

(b) Hemoglobin-increased skin

Fig. 7. Simulated spectral reflectance

the measured spectral reflectance were from 400nm to 700nm with the interval of 5nm. The weights of the pigment absorption coefficients were estimated from the measured spectral reflectance by the fitting of estimation data to the measured data. Figure 6 shows the measured data and the fitted estimation data. Table 1 shows the estimated weight parameters. Second, the spectral reflectances of skin with pigment density changes were simulated. In this experiment, the weights of pigment absorption coefficients were increased by a factor of three and five. Fig. 7 shows the spectral reflectances of original skin, simulated melanin-increased skin and simulated hemoglobin-increased skin.

Next, the spectral power distributions of illuminations for the simulated colors were calculated from the measured original spectral reflectance, the estimated spectral reflectances and the spectral power distribution of white illumination by equation (2). Fig. 8 (a) shows the spectral power distribution of white illumination as $E(\lambda)$. One of the calculated spectral power distributions of illuminations for a simulated color, $E'(\lambda)$, is shown in Fig. 8 (b).

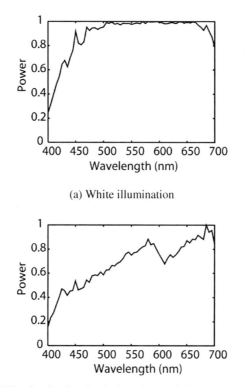

(a) White illumination

(b) Illumination for simulation of melanin-increased skin

Fig. 8. Spectral power distributions of illuminations of white and simulated color

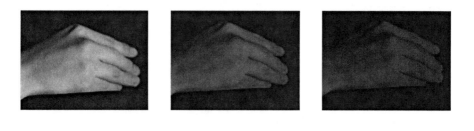

(a) Original   (b) Melanin x3   (c) Melanin x5

Fig. 9. Results of simulation for melanin-increased skin color

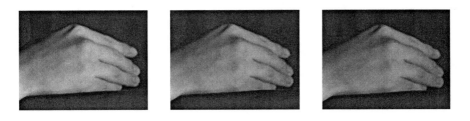

(a) Original   (b) Hemoglobin x3   (c) Hemoglobin x5

Fig. 10. Results of simulation for hemoglobin-increased skin color

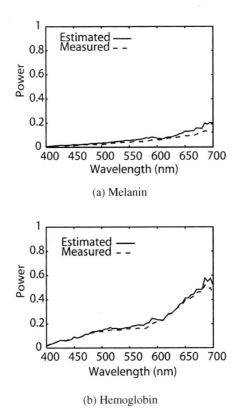

(a) Melanin

(b) Hemoglobin

Fig. 11. Comparison between estimated and measured spectral power distribution of light reflected on skin surface

Then, the colors of hand under these illuminations were observed. Fig. 9 shows pictures of hand with (a) original color, (b) simulated melanin-increased color by a factor of three and (c) simulated melanin-increased color by a factor of five. Fig. 10 shows pictures of hand with (a) original color, (b) simulated hemoglobin-increased color by a factor of three and (c) simulated hemoglobin-increased color by a factor of five. These pictures were taken by a digital camera with fixed camera parameters. These pictures show the feasibility of the proposed method.

Fig. 11 shows the comparison between the estimated spectral power distribution of reflected light on skin surface and measured spectral power distribution. Fig. 11 (a) shows the case of melanin-increased skin and Fig. 11 (b) shows the case of hemoglobin-increased skin. Average of absolute differences between the estimated data and measured data was 0.02 for each case.

6 Conclusions

This paper described the skin color simulation that displays simulated colors as spectral power distribution on real skin surface. The reproduction of the simulated color on skin is done by the illumination with the spectral power distribution calculated from the measured original spectral reflectance, the simulated spectral reflectances and the spectral power distribution of white illumination. We use a programmable light source to synthesize illuminant with arbitrary spectral-power distribution. We simulated skin color change by the concentration of pigments in skin. We estimated the spectral reflectances of melanin-increased skin and hemoglobin-increased skin by the method based on the Kubelka-Munk theory. Then, the estimated colors are displayed by the projection of the synthesized light on the real skin surface. The experimental results showed the feasibility of the proposed method.

References

1. Doi, M., Tanaka, N., Tominaga, S.: Spectral Reflectance Estimation of Human Skin and its Application to Image Rendering. J. Image Science and Technology 49(6), 574–582 (2005)
2. Kubelka, P.: New Contributions to the Optics of Intensely Light-Scattering Materials. Part I. J. Optical Society of America 38(5), 448–457 (1948)
3. Kubelka, P.: New Contributions to the Optics of Intensely Light-Scattering Materials. Part II. J. Optical Society of America 44(4), 330–335 (1954)
4. Tominaga, S., Horiuchi, T., Kakinuma, H., Kimachi, A.: Spectral Imaging with a Programmable Light Source. In: IS&T/SID's 17th Color Imaging Conference, pp. 133—138 (2009)
5. Horiuchi, T., Kakinuma, H., Tominaga, S.: Effective Illumination Control for an Active Spectral Imaging System. In: 12th International Symposium on Multispectral Color Science (2010)
6. Anderson, R.R., Parrish, J.A.: The Optics of Human Skin. J. Investigative Dermatology 77(1), 13–19 (1981)
7. Gemert, M.J.C.V., Jacques, S.L., Sterenborg, H.J.C.M., Star, W.M.: Skin Optics. IEEE Transactions on Biomedical Engineering 36(12), 1146–1154 (1989)

Estimation of Multiple Illuminants Based on Specular Highlight Detection

Yoshie Imai[1,2], Yu Kato[1], Hideki Kadoi[1], Takahiko Horiuchi[1],
and Shoji Tominaga[1]

[1] Graduate School of Advanced Integration Science, Chiba University, Japan
[2] Toshiba Corporation
{yoshie.imai,yu_kato,kadoi}@graduate.chiba-u.jp,
{horiuchi,shoji}@faculty.chiba-u.jp

Abstract. This paper proposes a method for estimating the scene illuminant spectral power distributions of multiple light sources under a complex illumination environment. The spectral power distributions including natural and artificial illuminants are estimated based on the image data from a high-dimensional spectral imaging system. We note that specular highlights on inhomogeneous dielectric object surfaces includes much information about scene illumination according to the dichromatic reflection model. First, we describe several methods for detecting specular highlight areas. We assume a curved object surface illuminated by multiple light sources from different directions. Then we estimate the illuminant spectrum of each light source from the image data of that highlight area. Based on this principle, we present an algorithm to estimate multiple illuminants. The feasibility of the proposed method is shown in experiments.

Keywords: Multiple light sources, dichromatic reflection model, specular highlight area, illuminant estimation.

1 Introduction

Estimation of scene illumination from image data has important imaging applications, including illumination design, color constancy, image processing, image rendering, and image retrieval. The scene illuminant estimation problem has a long history. In the past, many algorithms were proposed for scene illuminant estimation; however most algorithms assumed uniform illumination from a single light source [1-10]. It should be noted that our illumination environment is not necessarily a single light source such as daylight or a light bulb, but often consists of multiple light sources from different directions.

Recently, artificial light sources such as various fluorescent lights and light emitting diode (LED) are now in use in daily life. A complex illumination environment is constructed by the multiple illuminants including these artificial light sources and natural daylight.

This paper proposes a method for estimating the scene illuminant spectral power distributions of multiple light sources under a complex illumination environment. A high-dimensional spectral imaging system is first realized using a liquid-crystal tunable filter,

R. Schettini, S. Tominaga, and A. Trémeau (Eds.): CCIW 2011, LNCS 6626, pp. 85–98, 2011.

a monochrome CCD scientific camera with a cooling system, and a personal computer. We assume that objects captured by the imaging system in a scene are composed of inhomogeneous dielectric material like plastic or paint. In this case, the dichromatic reflection model suggests that light reflected from the object is decomposed into two additive components: the specular and the diffuse reflection components. The spectral power distribution of the specular component is coincident with the illuminant spectrum [2]; therefore the illuminant estimation can be reduced to detect the specular reflection component.

Moreover we note that, when a curved object surface is illuminated by multiple light sources from different directions, the illuminant spectrum estimated from each highlight area corresponds to each of the light sources. So the multiple illuminants can be estimated from different specular highlight areas on the curved object.

The first step of illuminant estimation is to detect highlight areas from the observed object image. Though many algorithms have been developed to detect highlights [11-14], in this paper we describe several detection methods: (1) use of variable thresholding of luminance, (2) use of luminance and hue components, and (3) use of a polarization filter.

The second step is to develop an algorithm for estimating the illuminant spectrum from the extracted highlight area. As mentioned above, the two-dimensionality of the object surface, the high-dimensional image data of the highlight area are projected onto a two-dimensional space spanned by the first two principal-components. Then the pixel distribution (histogram) in this space is divided into two straight clusters, corresponding to the specular and diffuse reflections. The directional vector of the specular highlight cluster is coincident to the vector of the light source. Therefore, the illuminant spectrum can be estimated by extracting the principal-component vector of the highlight cluster.

The feasibility of the proposed method is shown in experiments using plastic objects in a real scene. First, the performance of the highlight detection methods is compared in detail. Second, the accuracy of illuminant estimation is investigated in a complex environment using multiple light sources of LED, fluorescence, and daylight.

2 Imaging System

Figure 1 shows the camera system for spectral imaging system. A high-dimensional spectral imaging system is realized using a liquid-crystal tunable filter, a monochrome CCD scientific camera (Retiga 1300 - with a cooling system using a Peltier device), and a personal computer. We represent illuminant spectra with 69-dimensional vectors, where the visible wavelength range [400-700nm] is sampled at equal intervals of 5nm and also sampled at eight wavelengths (404, 436, 488, 544, 584, 588, 612, 656nm) that correspond to peaks of general fluorescent spectra.

The total sensitivity function $R_k(\lambda)$ of the spectral camera system at k-th channel is computed by multiplying the transmittance $t_k(\lambda)$ of liquid-crystal tunable filter, the sensitivity function $r(\lambda)$ monochrome CCD scientific camera, and exposure time e_k as shown below

$$R_k(\lambda) = e_k \cdot t_k(\lambda) r(\lambda), \quad (k=1, 2,\ldots, 69). \tag{1}$$

Figure 2 shows the total sensitivity function. The original CCD camera was modified so that the shutter speed could easily be changed from the outside computer. We justify exposure time e_k so that the imaging system has constant sensitivity at each channel.

The spectral radiance of the reflected light (color signal) $Y(\lambda)$ from an object surface is described as

$$Y(\lambda) = E(\lambda) S(\lambda), \tag{2}$$

where $E(\lambda)$ is the spectral power distribution of the incident light to the object, and $S(\lambda)$ is the spectral reflectance of the surface. The sensor output ρ_k of k-th channel is written as

$$\rho_k = \int_{400}^{700} Y(\lambda) R_k(\lambda) d\lambda. \tag{3}$$

If the band of the total sensitivity $R_k(\lambda)$ is narrow, the color signal can be obtained approximately as

$$Y(\lambda_k) = \rho_k \left/ \int_{400}^{700} R_k(\lambda) d\lambda \right., \tag{4}$$

where λ_k is the wavelength for k-th channel. So we interpolate $Y(\lambda_k)$ $(k=1, 2,\ldots, 69)$ to obtain the color signal $Y(\lambda)$ at arbitrary wavelength in the visible range. Thus, the color signal observed from each pixel point of an object surface can be estimated from the outputs of the imaging system by knowing the total spectral sensitivity functions $R_k(\lambda)$.

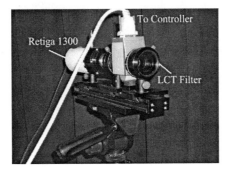

Fig. 1. Spectral imaging system

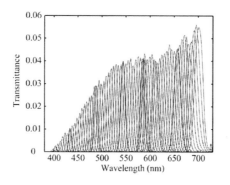

Fig. 2. Total sensitivity properties

3 Detection of Highlight Area

We consider three methods for detecting highlight areas on object surfaces.

3.1 Detection Using Variable Luminance Thresholds

The luminance value Y for the color signal is computed as

$$Y = \int_{400}^{700} Y(\lambda)\bar{y}(\lambda)d\lambda , \tag{5}$$

where $\bar{y}(\lambda)$ is the luminance function which is one of the CIE color matching functions for the standard observers. A simple way for detecting highlight areas is to use a luminance threshold for the whole image area. It should be noted however, that the intensity of highlight on an object surface depends on the object color. Therefore the detection of multiple highlight areas is not always performed by simple thresholding if various object colors are contained in a scene.

In such a case, a method is proposed for repeatedly detecting multiple highlight areas by adaptively changing the luminance threshold. Figure 3 shows the procedure of this method. First, we calculate luminance value at every pixel and make the luminance histogram for the entire image. Second, the highlight candidates are extracted using a single threshold value, that corresponds to the luminance at a clear valley in the distribution shape of the luminance histogram. Third, the detected areas are labeled based on connectivity of pixels, so if the connected pixel count is small, the area is neglected. Then the connected regions with enough pixel counts are reserved as the target regions. Fourth, each target area is narrowed by increasing the threshold value, in order to determine precisely the highlight area. The above process is repeated for the respective target regions.

For instance, in Figure 3 (also see the color image in Figure 8), highlight areas on the blue cup is first detected with a low luminance threshold. Highlight areas on green and yellow objects are detected with higher luminance thresholds after four iterations of the above process. We can implement a semi-automatic thresholding technique. Thus, multiple highlight areas on different color objects are detected.

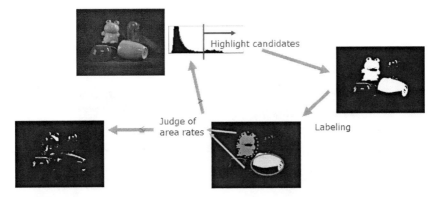

Highlight candidates

Judge of
area rates

Labeling

Fig. 3. Procedure of highlight area detection using variable luminance thresholds

3.2 Detection Using Luminance and Hue Components

The second method proposed for detecting highlight areas uses the luminance and hue components (Figure 4 illustrates an example of this method). We calculate the tristimulus values XYZ of the color signal by the color matching functions, and the chromaticity coordinates (x, y) as

$$x = \frac{X}{X+Y+Z}, \quad y = \frac{Y}{X+Y+Z}. \tag{6}$$

In this study, we define the hue H as

$$H = \arctan((y - y_0)/(x - x_0)), \tag{7}$$

where (x_0, y_0) are standard white coordinates.

Normally the chromaticity coordinates of most scene illuminants are located closely to the chromaticity locus of the black-body radiator. Therefore the standard white coordinates (x_0, y_0) should be placed at the black-body radiator locus on the xy diagram. Since the color temperature however, of scene illuminant is unknown, we select the suitable coordinates of (x_0, y_0) in three ways, such as (1) $(x_0, y_0) = (1/3, 1/3)$, (2) the average (x, y) of all pixels by the Gray-World assumption [15], and (3) (x, y) of brightest pixel by the White-Patch assumption.

We think that the hue of specular reflection part is different from surroundings as long as the light-source color is not the same hue as the object color when the specular reflection happens to the object usually. Therefore, high luminance area surrounded by different hue must be detected as a highlight area. The second method detects such area by setting a luminance threshold and hue thresholds. First, the candidates of highlight areas are detected by luminance thresholding. Second, the hue threshold of object color is determined by boundary color of the surface detected by the first luminance thresholding. By considering only high luminance area, the influence of the noise in the low luminance area can be eliminated.

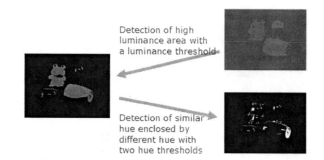

Detection of high
luminance area with
a luminance threshold

Detection of similar
hue enclosed by
different hue with
two hue thresholds

Fig. 4. Highlight area detection using luminance and hue components

3.3   Detection Using a Polarization Filter

The polarization property of light reflected from an object surface is available for highlight detection. When a polarization filter is attached to the front of the camera system, the linear polarization of the arbitrary direction can be observed by rotating the polarization filter. The proportion of the linear polarization element in the reflected light is represented by a polarization degree ρ

$$\rho = \left(I_{max} - I_{min}\right) \Big/ \left\{ I_{max} + \left(\frac{T_p(\lambda)}{T_N(\lambda)} - 1\right) I_{min} \right\}, \qquad (8)$$

where $T_p(\lambda)$ and $T_N(\lambda)$ are the spectral transmittances for linearly polarized light and unpolarized light respectively and I_{max} and I_{min} are the maximum and minimum intensities of reflected light, respectively [16]. Light reflected from an inhomogeneous dielectric is decomposed into two linear components: the diffuse reflection component and the specular reflection component. The diffuse component is not polarized and so invariant with polarization orientations, while the specular component is significantly polarized and varies greatly with polarization orientations. The polarization degree varies between 0 and 1. One extreme $\rho = 1$ represents the unpolarized state, such as reflection consisting of only the diffuse component and the other extreme $\rho = 0$ represents the completely polarized state, such as pure specular reflection without the diffuse component.

Figure 5 depicts the transmitted radiance of light reflected from dielectric as a function of polarizer orientation. The transmitted light intensity oscillates sinusoidally between a minimum I_{min} and a maximum I_{max}. For dielectrics this magnitude of oscillation is quite large in the specular highlight area, and then becomes smaller in the off-specular highlight area. Therefore, because the polarization degree ρ is large for specular highlight area, we can detect the highlight area by thresholding of ρ computed from all pixels.

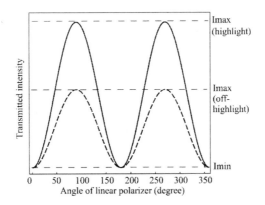

Fig. 5. Transmitted radiance of reflected light as a function of polarizer orientation

4 Illuminant Estimation Algorithm

The observed color signal from an inhomogeneous dielectric object is described by the dichromatic reflection model as follows:

$$Y(\lambda) = Y_S(\lambda) + Y_D(\lambda),$$ (9)

where the suffix S and D indicate the specular reflection component and the diffuse reflection component, respectively. To express the model in terms of the surface-reflectance function, let $S_S(\lambda)$ be the surface-spectral reflectance for the diffuse component, and let $E(\lambda)$ be the spectral power distribution of the incident light. Then the color signal is described as

$$Y(\lambda) = S_S(\lambda)E(\lambda) + CE(\lambda),$$ (10)

where C is constant over the visible wavelength. Therefore the specular reflection component can be used for illuminant estimation.

Let **Y** be an n-dimensional vector of the camera output. As mentioned before, the surface with the specular reflection is two-dimensional. So for each highlight area the image data are projected onto a two-dimensional space spanned by two principal components. These components $\mathbf{p}_1$ and $\mathbf{p}_2$ are computed from the set of the n-dimensional image data. Then we can derive the mapping equation:

$$\begin{bmatrix} C_1 \\ C_2 \end{bmatrix} = \begin{bmatrix} \mathbf{p}_1^t \\ \mathbf{p}_2^t \end{bmatrix} \mathbf{Y},$$ (11)

Figure 6 shows an example of pixel distribution (histogram) on the two-dimensional space (C_1, C_2), projected from the image data of a highlight area. The pixel distribution in this space is divided into two straight clusters. One cluster corresponds to highlight pixels by specular reflection, and the other cluster corresponds to matte pixels by diffuse reflection. Therefore we note that the directional vector of the highlight cluster represents the illuminant vector.

Estimation of the illuminant vector is reduced to finding the gradient of straight lines in the pixel cluster. Such a line component can be extracted by applying the principal component analysis or the Hough transform to the pixel distribution. We found that the line detection by the principal-component analysis is better in computational cost than the Hough transform.

Then, the illuminant vector $\mathbf{E}$ can be estimated by extracting the directional vector (C_1', C_2') of the highlight cluster and transforming it inversely into the high-dimensional spectral space as follows:

$$\mathbf{E} = \begin{bmatrix} \mathbf{p}_1' \\ \mathbf{p}_2' \end{bmatrix}^{+} \begin{bmatrix} C_1' \\ C_2' \end{bmatrix}, \tag{12}$$

where + indicates a generalized inverse.

We note that, when an object with convex surface is illuminated by several light sources from different directions, the illuminant spectrum estimated from each highlight area corresponds to each of the light sources. That is, we assume that each highlight area is illuminated by only one source and not a combination of spectra power distributions of several light sources. Moreover, reflections generated by highlight areas do not interfere with other objects, i.e., that are not secondary sources.

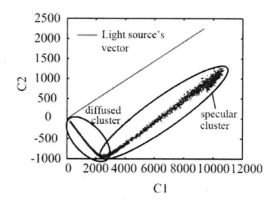

Fig. 6. Pixel distribution of image data on the two-dimensional space (C_1, C_2)

5   Experimental Results

We have examined the proposed method for estimating illuminant spectral power distribution under multiple light sources, based on the image data of the multiband imaging system. The feasibility of the method was examined in two steps: the highlight detection and the illuminant estimation.

5.1   Experimental Conditions

Figure 7 shows our experimental setup. Plastic objects placed on a table are illuminated with three different lightings: (1) daylight outside through the window, (2) fluorescent light source with D65 color temperature and (3) light emitting diode (LED) source. The multiband camera system aims from the front at the target object placed on the table. We also measure the illuminant spectra by using a reference white plate and a spectro-radiometer (Photo Research, PR655). These measurements are used as the ground truth.

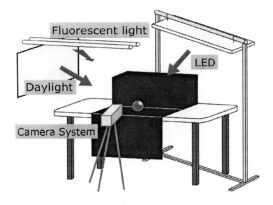

Fig. 7. Experimental setup

5.2 Detection of Highlight Areas

The scene in Figure 8 with different colored objects was used in experiments. Figure 9 shows bright areas detected by threshold of a low luminance value. We note that highlight areas are not properly detected by this simple thresholding.

Figure 10 shows the experimental results by the method (1) using the variable thresholding of luminance. The threshold of area counts (area rate) in Figure 10 (a) was set to 5 % of all pixels. A highlight in the upper part of the yellow object cannot be appropriately detected. However, when we decrease the threshold in the recursive process, the detection accuracy improves as shown in Figure 10 (b) with the result by the threshold 0.3 %.

Figure 11 shows the results of the method (2) using luminance and hue compo-nents, where (a) is the result by the standard white coordinates (1/3, 1/3), (b) is the result by the Gray-World Assumption, (c) is the result by the White-Patch Assump-tion. The detection of highlight areas is influenced by object color. Three binary images in Figure 11 (a)-(c) are combined into Figure 11 (d). Look at the white bot-tom of the yellow cup. The entire white area is detected wrong as a highlight area.

Figure 12 shows the results by the method (3) using a polarization filter. Highlight areas on yellow and green objects are not properly detected. The image of polariza-tion degree is depicted in Figure 12 (a), where image intensity indicates the value of polarization degree. Therefore, the highlight or glossy areas with specular reflection correspond to brighter areas in the image. It should be noted that the polarization degree depends greatly on the angle of incidence to object surface. As the angle is distant from the Brewster angle, the polarization degree decreases. No highlight area is detected on the yellow cup and green frog.

Table 1 summarizes the detection characteristics of the three methods (1)-(3). Most highlight areas are extracted by (1). However, highlight on white object surface can not be detected sometimes by the method. In addition, it is necessary to examine application to the object with the pattern. The advantage of (3) using polarization is independence of object color. Therefore this method is applicable to colored texture

Fig. 8. Scene with different colored objects used in experiments

Fig. 9. Areas detected by threshold of a low luminance value

(a) Area rate threshold 5 %   (b) Area rate threshold 0.3 %

Fig. 10. Detected highlight areas by using the variable thresholding of luminance

surface. However the polarization degree depends on the angle of light incidence. That is, the method is unstable, depending on illumination geometry. Moreover rotation of the filter takes time, and the images captured with different rotation angles require much memory storage.

Thus it is suggested that the method (1) is the most suitable for detecting highlight areas by a normal imaging system.

(a) White coordinates (1/3, 1/3)

(b) Gray-World Assumption

(c) White-Patch Assumption

(d) Combined image of (a)-(c)

Fig. 11. Detected highlight areas by using luminance and hue components

(a) Image of polarization degree

(b) Thresholding of polarization degree

Fig. 12. Detected highlight areas by using a polarization filter

Table 1. Comparison of detection characteristics among three methods

Detection method	White object surface	Colored texture surface	Measurement time	Memory capacity	Computation time	Illumination geometry
(1) variable thresholding	✓		✓✓	✓✓	✓	✓✓
(2) luminance& hue			✓✓	✓✓	✓✓	✓✓
(3) polarization	✓✓	✓✓				

5.3 Estimation of Illuminant Spectra

Figure 13 (a) shows a part of the scene in Figure 3. Figures 13 (b)-(d) are the illuminant estimation results by the proposed algorithm. The blue curve in each figure is the estimated spectral power distribution, and the red curve is the direct measurement by a spectro-radiometer.

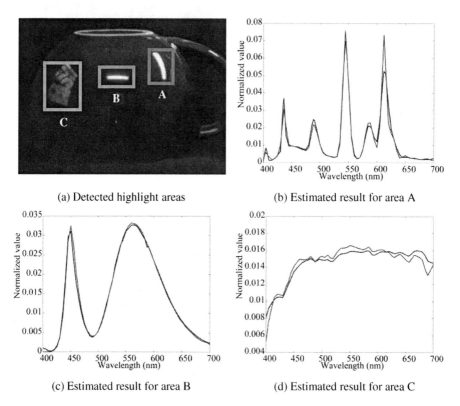

(a) Detected highlight areas

(b) Estimated result for area A

(c) Estimated result for area B

(d) Estimated result for area C

Fig. 13. Experimental results of illuminant estimation of multiple light sources

Three light sources illuminate the surface of a blue cup from different directions. In this case, three highlight areas correspond to the three light sources. The ability of estimating multiple illuminants is based on this fact.

The area A consists of fluorescent light with strong spikes. We can identify the fluorescent light source by knowing the wavelengths of the spike peaks. The area B provides us a LED light source. Moreover, notice that the area C reflects the outside scene through a window. We can estimate the daylight spectrum of natural light source from this highlight area.

We see that the estimated spectral curves of the respective light sources are very close to the direct measurements. These results suggest the feasibility of the proposed illuminant estimation method.

Moreover, we examined illuminant estimation from an object with color texture. In this case, when the highlight area on the object surface included the color texture, the estimation accuracy of illuminant spectrum decreased, compared with an object surface with uniform color.

6 Conclusion

We have proposed a method for estimating the scene illuminant spectral power distributions of multiple light sources under a complex illumination environment. The spectral power distributions were estimated based on the image data from a high-dimensional spectral imaging system. Since specular highlights on inhomogeneous dielectric object surfaces included much information about scene illumination according to the dichromatic reflection model, we proposed three methods of highlight detection: (1) use of variable thresholding of luminance, (2) use of luminance and hue components, and (3) use of a polarization filter. Then we estimated the illuminant spectrum of each light source from the image data of that highlight area based on assumption that a curved object surface illuminated by multiple light sources from different directions. The feasibility of the proposed method was shown in experiments using plastic objects in a real scene. The experimental results suggested that the method of highlight detection using the variable thresholding of luminance was the most suitable for detecting highlight areas by a normal imaging system. These results also showed the accuracy of the estimated illuminant spectral power distributions of the respective light sources. Further examination of highlight detection of objects with texture remains as a future work.

References

1. Tominaga, S.: Multichannel vision system for estimating surface and illumination functions. J. Optical Society of America A 13(11), 2163–2173 (1996)
2. Tominaga, S., Wandell, B.A.: Standard surface-reflectance model and illuminant estimation. J. Optical Society of America A 6(4), 576–584 (1986)
3. Maloney, L.T.: Evaluation of linear models of surface spectral reflectance with small numbers of parameters. J. of the Optical Society of America A 3(10), 1673–1683 (1986)
4. Maloney, L.T., Wandell, B.A.: Color constancy: a method for recovering surface spectral reflectance. J. Optical Society of America A 3(1), 29–33 (1986)

5. Tominaga, S., Haraguchi, H.: Estimation of fluorescent scene illuminant by a spectral camera system. In: Color Imaging X: Processing, Hardcopy, and Applications, San Jose, Calif, USA. Proceedings of SPIE, vol. 5667, pp. 128–135 (2005)
6. Tominaga, S.N., Tanaka, N.: Feature article: omnidirectional scene illuminant estimation using a mirrored ball. Journal of Imaging Science and Technology 50(3), 217–227 (2006)
7. Schultz, S., Doerschner, K., Maloney, L.T.: Color constancy and hue scaling. Journal of Vision 6(10), 1102–1116 (2006)
8. Tominaga, S.: Estimation of composite daylight-fluorescent light components based on multi-spectral scene images, In: Proceedings of the 14th IS&T/SID Color Imaging Conference, Scottsdale, Ariz, USA, pp.125–130 (2006)
9. van de Weijer, J., Gevers, T., Gijsenij, A.: Edge-based color constancy. IEEE Transactions on Image Processing 16(9), 2207–2214 (2007)
10. Zhou, W., Kambhamettu, C.: A unified framework for scene illuminant estimation. Image and Vision Computing 26(3), 415–429 (2008)
11. Klinker, G.J., Shafer, S.A., Kanade, T.: The Measurement of Highlights in Color Images. International Journal of Computer Vision 2(1), 7–26 (1992)
12. Tan, R.T., Nishino, K., Ikeuchi, K.: Separating Reflection Components Based on Chromaticity and Noise Analysis. IEEE Transaction on Pattern Analysis and Machine Intelligence 26(10), 1373–1379 (2004)
13. Xu, S.C., Ye, X., Wu, Y., Zhang, S.: Highlight detection and removal based on chromaticity. In: Kamel, M.S., Campilho, A.C. (eds.) ICIAR 2005. LNCS, vol. 3656, pp. 199–206. Springer, Heidelberg (2005)
14. Angelopoulou, E.: Specular Highlight Detection Based on the Fresnel Reflection Coefficient. In: IEEE 11th International Conference on Computer Vision, pp. 1–8 (2007)
15. Buchsbaum, G.: A spatial processor model for object colour perception. J. Franklin Institute 310(1), 1–26 (1980)
16. Tominaga, S., Kimachi, A.: Polarization imaging for material classification. Optical Engineering 47(12), 123201 (2008)

Subjective Evaluation of Specular Appearance for Multiple Observations Using Projector-Based Appearance Reproduction

Mayu Yokoya[1], Shoji Yamamoto[2], Yasuki Yamauchi[3], Satoshi Yamamoto[4], Osama Ouda[5], Toshiya Nakaguchi[6], and Norimichi Tsumura[1,5]

[1] Department of Information & Image Science, Chiba University, Japan
z7t0732@students.chiba-u.jp
[2] Tokyo Metropolitan College of Industrial Technology, Japan
[3] Graduate School of Yamagata University, Japan
[4] Graduate School of Medicine, Chiba University, Japan
[5] Graduate School of Advanced Integration Science, Chiba University, Japan
[6] Graduate School of Engineering, Chiba University, Japan

Abstract. This paper presents the subjective evaluations of multiple observers as part of an investigation into the relationship between CG parameters of digital mockups and visual sensibility. In our experiments, the specular appearance of CG imagery is reproduced on an actual mockup using a projector-camera system. The specular intensity and position are evaluated in terms of magnitude and inauthenticity. For the specular intensity evaluation, it was found that changes to specular intensity in the CG parameters were equal to the changes in the brightness sensibility of the object viewed. Furthermore, the results of inauthenticity evaluations clarified the limitations of the viewpoint range. The specular appearance from the 60° viewpoint gave observers the impression that the form and position of the specular reflection were inauthentic. Therefore, it was determined that the control of appearance in our digital mockup was only suitable for observations within the range from -45° to 45°.

Keywords: Specular appearance, subjective evaluation, projector-camera system, digital mockup.

1 Introduction

Research in the field of computer science is advancing steadily towards the realization of seamless integration of the real and virtual worlds [1]. For example, as a result of remarkable progress in the field of computer graphics (CG), it has become possible to accurately reproduce various visual scenes by exploiting the physical properties of the ways in which light interacts with the real world, such as reflection, absorption, and interference [2]. Furthermore, the combination of CG and computer vision (CV) has paved a way toward developing advanced three dimensional (3D) vision systems that are further erasing borders between actual and virtual reality.

R. Schettini, S. Tominaga, and A. Trémeau (Eds.): CCIW 2011, LNCS 6626, pp. 99–112, 2011.
© Springer-Verlag Berlin Heidelberg 2011

Because the appearance of computer-generated 3D objects can be controlled easily, 3D reproduction has become increasingly common in various research and industrial applications. In particular, accurate 3D reproduction is very important in a wide range of industrial processes such as design assessment, reverse engineering, and quality inspection. For instance, the visual appearance of physical or virtual objects (such as digital mockups [3]) can be changed easily by controlling specular and diffuse light reflections. Thus, the ability to change the appearance of digital mockups using 3D reproduction techniques can enrich our imaginations.

In general, there are two types of digital mockup: full digital mockups and composite-type digital mockups. Full digital mockups reproduce both the shape and appearance of an object in virtual reality. There are several 3D reproduction methods that use full digital mockups such as holograms, integral photography displays, and light field displays. Unfortunately, employing such methods introduces significant practical challenges [4,5]. In fact, while head-mounted displays or active stereographic 3D shutter glasses might be the simplest ways to reproduce the 3D appearance of a full digital mockup, wearing such glasses can sometimes cause uncomfortable sensations that hinder their practical use [6].

In contrast, composite-type digital mockups address the issues inherent with full digital mockups by reproducing 3D appearance using projection displays and unfinished actual mockups. One advantage of composite-type digital mockups is that they eliminate the need for special glasses, while a disadvantage is that an actual 3D form of the object must be fabricated. Fortunately, recent developments in the field of 3D printing have enabled us to create mockups of almost any shape [7]. The images projected onto such mockups are generated by calculating the desired appearance using well-developed CG techniques. The use of projection images can allow reproduction of various composite-type digital mockup views, which allow multiple observers to make observations from different positions and thus produce a thorough evaluation of the image design. However, there are some difficulties related to finding correct settings for CG images, such as reflectance and position, so that they match seamlessly with human visual sensibilities on composite-type digital mockups. In order to achieve an authentic visual appearance, it is important clarify how CG parameter changes correlate with visual sensibility through projection image changes.

Accordingly, this paper presents subjective evaluations made by multiple observers when investigating the relationships between changes in CG parameters and the perceived specular appearance of a composite-type digital mockup. Specular appearance is considered to be the most important appearance attribute, and, during design validation, plays a crucial role in the final decision making process for a variety of products. In specular appearance reproduction, both the intensity and position of the specular reflectance must be set. Specular intensity is controlled by the reflectance coefficient defined by the reflection model used. According to the Weber–Fechner's law, the relationship between the intensity of reflected light and its perceived magnitude is logarithmic [8]. Therefore, it was

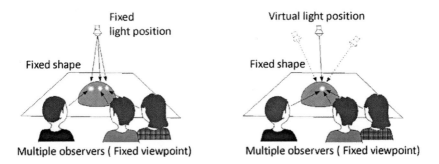

Fig. 1. Illustrated explanation of virtual light positioning for multiple observers (a):Freedom at specular reflection position, (b):Freedom at light position

necessary to determine whether this law is applicable for the CG setting and observer perceptions.

In contrast, in CG settings, the position of a specular reproduction is specified by three parameters, the position of the light source, the shape of the object, and the viewpoint of the observer. Here, a contradiction appears in that each viewpoint is unique, even if the shape and position of the light source are fixed. Two or more specular reflections corresponding to multiple observations may be reproduced on digital mockups, as shown in Fig. 1(a). Note that, during our observations, no negative sensations were experienced, even when a single specular reflection was observed from various viewpoints, as shown in Fig. 1(b). This result infers that single specular reproduction with shape fixation can cause two or more observers to perceive the existence of a virtual light at an arbitrary position. Therefore, for a design assessment system, we determined that it was necessary to examine the viewpoint range of multiple observers.

This paper focuses on the construction of a projector-based reproduction system and subjective evaluations of the relationship between CG parameters and visual sensibility. A brief review of related works is presented in Section 2. Section 3 presents our experimental system, while our rendering method is discussed in Section 4. The results of subjective evaluations of sensibility magnitude and viewpoint range of specular appearance are described in Section 5 and 6 respectively. Finally, in the conclusion, we discuss the evaluation results and the limitations of our system.

2   Related Works

The virtual reality production technology that integrates projected images and digital mockups arose simultaneously with development in computers and projectors. The initial form of this technology was simple image transcription, where virtual information was projected onto walls and screens without using actual mockups [9,10]. The fusion with CV made it possible to precisely measure the position and the shape of an actual 3D object, which then made possible the development of 3D projector-camera systems. Projector-camera systems can produce various image combinations with authentic appearing visual textures [11,12]. Other recent research has resulted in improvements to the projection image quality, by taking into consideration the object's surface reflectance and surrounding ambient light [13,14].

Still other research efforts have worked to reproduce projection images that include not only texture, but appearance elements such as specular reflectance or shading [15,16]. Rasker *et al.* developed a realistic projection system, as shown in Fig. 2. This work succeeded in producing visual texture and appearance of complex shapes using 3D measurement technology and a control method utilizing multiple projectors [17]. Kamimigaki *et al.* have also developed a reproduction system that was able to project specular appearance onto a cylinder mockup, as shown in Fig. 3. This system utilizes high speed rendering to reproduce the desired specular appearance based on the observer's viewpoint [18]. Figure 4 shows a flexible system consisting of a multiple projector-camera setup suitable for multiple observers [19].

As mentioned previously, it is already possible to create actual 3D appearance textures on an object by projecting imagery information that conforms to the shape of mockup. Furthermore, with the integration of CV and CG techniques, it now appears possible to design digital mockups incorporating arbitrary color

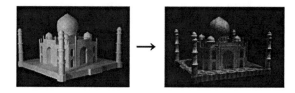

Fig. 2. Realistic visual texture and appearance can be produced using shader lamps to project light information on a 3D object, as seen in this example

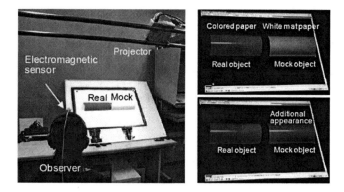

Fig. 3. Experimental system using a projector and head tracking system
(a): Experimental arrangement (b): Result of specular appearance reproduction

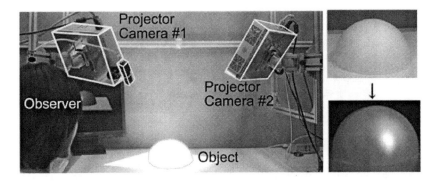

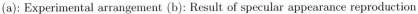

Fig. 4. Prototype system for reproducing actual visual appearance information on a mock 3D object
(a): Experimental arrangement (b): Result of specular appearance reproduction

and specular reflection. The practical simulation of various appearances is performed by controlling the CG parameters. Unfortunately, no amount of control guarantees that the image produced will satisfy visual sensibility requirements. To create an accurate matching between the virtual and real worlds, it is necessary to clarify the gain and control range necessary to satisfy visual sensibility requirements.

Therefore, in this research, we subjectively evaluated the relationship between reproduction results and visual sensibility using an appearance reproduction system that can be controlled by the projected image. We focused on the visual sensibility as difference is verified about the magnitude and the position of the specular reflectance. Significant attention has been paid to the specular appearance of an image recently, because of its important role in evaluating the quality of materials.

3   Projector-Camera System

To project an exact desired appearance on a 3D object, it is first necessary to know the shape of the object and its precise location relative to the projector. For increased system versatility, it is preferable to be able to reproduce such an appearance even the object is moved to another position. Therefore, our projector-camera system enabled to perform an auto geometric calibration.

In the first step, the projector-camera system should correct for any geometrical lens distortion. Next, it is necessary to accurately acquire the positions of both the camera and projector. Lens distortion and focal length are calculated as internal parameters [20]. Position and orientation of the projector and camera are calculated as external parameters. Note that the projector and camera optics are assumed using a pinhole camera model. Each parameter could be obtained using the capture method and calculations developed by S. Zhang et al. [21]. In our system, the camera first captures an image of a checkerboard projected via

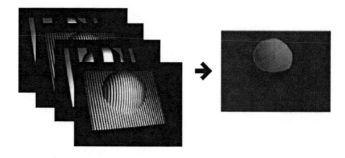

Fig. 5. Shape measurement illustration images
(a): Some structured light on the object (b): Calibrating shape and position of the 3D object

structured light. The calculation then determines the relationship of the corresponding pixels and coordinates using the captured image. Using these obtained parameters, the lens is calibrated and the transformation matrix between the devices is clarified.

After the system is calibrated, the coded structured light method is utilized to measure the position and shape of the mockup. Figure 5(a) shows examples of the images used for shape measurements with the coded structured light method. The images of multiple coded patterns are necessary to construct an accurate model of the shape. Then, based on these images, the 3D position and shape of the mockup is calculated via triangulation, as shown in Fig. 5(b). Calculated 3D data are used as vertex information in CG software. Here, it should be noted that the 3D data includes the relative position of the mockup at the projected plane. Therefore, accurate image projection onto the mockup becomes possible without misalignment.

4   Rendering Equation for Specular Appearance

In this section, we describe the rendering process used to reproduce the desired appearance based on the mockup vertex data. To reproduce a colored mockup with specular reflectance characteristics, a dichromatic reflection model was adopted in our rendering process. Figure 6 shows dichromatic reflection model. In the dichromatic model, incident light is reflected at the surface, while the rest enters the object and is absorbed. In the specular model, when light is reflected at the object's surface, the angle of incidence equals the angle of reflection. Diffuse light is generated by multiple reflections and scattering in the object. There are various dichromatic reflection models including Phong [22], Torrance–Sparrow [23], and Ward [24]. In our system, Phong's model was adopted due to its low computational costs and few adjustable parameters. Here, reflected light I_r without ambient is modeled as follows:

$$I_r = I_i(k_d \cos \alpha + k_s \cos^n \beta), \tag{1}$$

Fig. 6. Reflected light distribution in Phong's Model
(a): Dichromatic reflectance (b): Specular reflectance (c): Diffuse reflectance

where I_i denotes incident radiance from the light source, k_d is the coefficient of the diffuse reflectance, k_s is the coefficient of the specular reflectance, α is the angle between the surface normal of the object and the light source direction, β is the angle between the viewpoint and the specular reflection, and n is the specular reflection characteristics. The intensity distribution of reflected light in Phong's model is shown in Fig. 6(a). Specular reflection refers to light that is reflected symmetrically to the normal, as shown in Fig. 6(b). Diffuse reflected light is independent of the incident light direction and viewpoint location because it scatters evenly in all directions, as shown in Fig. 6(c).

Projection image pixels are calculated by Phong's model according to the viewpoint and light source positions. Observers perceive the reflected light from the surface of the digital mockup, which is generated by the projection image. In this experiment, the coefficient of the diffuse reflectance, k_d is fixed because the digital mockup color is constant. In contrast, the coefficient of the specular reflectance, k_s is a variable parameter used to evaluate the relationship between visual sensitivity and specular intensity, where n is fixed. Furthermore, the position of the light source and viewpoint are also fixed in Phong's model in order to facilitate appearance evaluations from various positions by multiple observers.

5   Experiment

Using our projector-camera system, we were able to produce reflected specular light appearance on a mockup and could subjectively evaluate the relationship between the results and visual sensibility. In our experiments, the specular intensity and position generated by each viewpoint were evaluated as the magnitude and authenticity of visual sensibility. Ideally, these evaluations should be performed as separate experiments. However, it was believed that the excessively long evaluation periods required would introduce instability, and thus produce uncertain results. Therefore, we developed a method of conducting these evaluations simultaneously, as described in Chapter 5.1. For the intensity evaluation, observers described their sensibility appraisals based on the magnitude estimation method according to the changes to the specular coefficient k_s [25]. At the same time, they were asked to complete a questionnaire about the authenticity of the specular reproduction at each intensity and viewpoint.

5.1   Experimental Layout

Figure 7 shows our experimental layout. In this system, a 3LCD type projector with 1024×768 resolution (Panasonic, PT0LB51NT), and a monochrome CCD camera with 1280×960 resolution (IMI Tech, IMC-17FT) were used. The mockup was a styrene foam hemisphere placed in the center of the projection area. Furthermore, in this system, the projector-camera system was covered with a blackout curtain because it was considered important that the observer perceive only the appearance projected onto the mockup during the evaluation period. Viewpoints, defined as the observer sitting positions, were set at 0°, 15°, 30°, 45°, and 60°, respectively. Here, the 0° position is defined as the location where specular reflection directly faced the observer, as shown in Fig. 8. The distance from the hemisphere to the observer was set at 2.5 meters, at which point the patterned indented surface of the styrene foam was not visible. At each viewpoint, we recorded the observer's answers regarding magnitude and any comments about the specular image superimposed on the mockup.

It is understood that, for a digital mockup, limitations in projector brightness will lead to specular intensity limitations. As a result of a preliminary experiment in our system, we found that the practical intensity of the digital mockup saturated at $k_s = 0.4$. Therefore, the specular coefficient k_s was set at 0.1, 0.2, 0.3, and 0.4, respectively, as shown in Fig. 9. The intensity of the perceived specular reflection was evaluated using the magnitude estimation method. This method

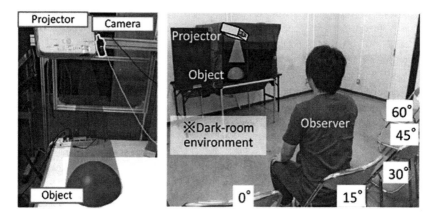

Fig. 7. Experimental layout
(a): Projector-camera system (b): Viewpoints for subjective evaluation

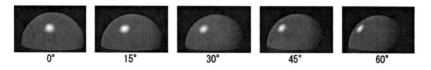

Fig. 8. Specular appearance at each viewing position

ks=0. 1   ks=0. 2   ks=0. 3   ks=0. 4

Fig. 9. Specular appearance for each coefficient k_s

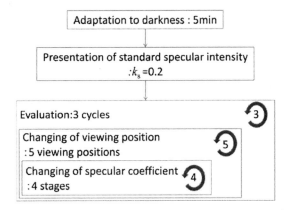

Fig. 10. Flow of experimental process

makes it possible to determine the sensitivity of an observer as a numerical value. Based on our arbitrary definition that a standard specular intensity at $k_s = 0.2$ would receive a score of 100, observers were asked to evaluate and record scores for various specular reflection intensities displayed at random. Some other limitations were set as experimental conditions. For example, observers were asked to make their evaluations while moving their heads as little as possible and to answer intuitively. However, we did not limit observation time. Under these conditions, 10 men and women in their twenties participated in the experiment.

The experimental process flow is shown in Fig. 10. After five minutes of dark adaptation, observers were asked to observe and evaluate the specular intensity of the standard appearance at 0° viewpoint. Then, they experienced intensity changes in four stages and were moved among five positions, while providing their evaluations at each change. A total of three experiment cycles were performed for each observer.

6   Subjective Evaluation

6.1   Intensity of Specular Appearance Using Magnitude Estimation Method

Typical subjective evaluation results are shown in Fig. 11. The x-axis indicates the luminance at the center of the specular reflection appearance, while the y-axis

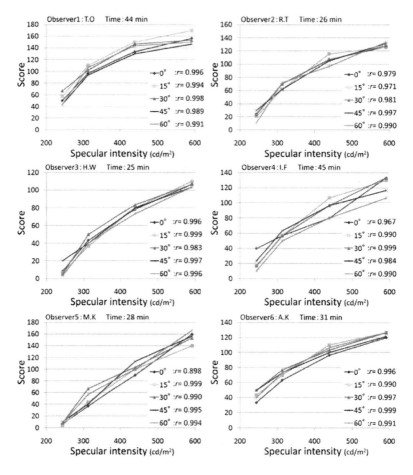

Fig. 11. Magnitude estimation results
The x-axis is the luminance at the center of specular appearance while the y-axis is the subjective evaluation score for specular intensity.

indicates the subjective evaluation score for specular intensity recorded using the magnitude estimation method. The values of r in Fig. 11 indicate correlation coefficient with a logarithm at each viewpoint. The luminance correspond to each specular reflectance coefficients of $k_s = 0.1, 0.2, 0.3, 0.4$, as shown in Table 1.

The subjective evaluation results showed good correlation with a logarithm, and it was clear that the specular reflection intensity of our system followed Weber–Fechner's law. Additionally, it was determined that the evaluation score for the specular appearance intensity did not differ at each viewpoint. Thus, with the projector-camera system, we could conclude that visual sensitivity reported for specular intensity changes were similar to actual brightness variations that occur when coefficient k_s was changed.

6.2 Verification of Inauthenticity Due to Changes in Viewing Position

Figure 12 shows the number of observers that reported ginauthenticity" at each viewpoint. The x-axis indicates the specular intensity k_s, while the y-axis indicates the viewpoint, the z-axis indicates the numbers of observers that reported inauthenticity two or more times during their three experiment cycles.

Numerous inauthenticity reports were received in the case of $k_s = 0.1$ and $k_s = 0.4$, and inauthenticity was also reported for all cases of the k_s at 60° viewpoint. The reason given by most observers at the $k_s = 0.1$ scenes, was that the specular reflection looked artificial because its specular intensity was too weak. When explaining their inauthenticity report at $k_s = 0.4$, most observers commented that the specular intensity was quite different from reality because the specular intensity was too strong.

In contrast, the specular appearance from the 60° viewpoint gave observers a different impression of inauthenticity, with many comments that the form and position of the specular reflection were strange. Such observers said that the

Table 1. Luminance at the specular reflection center

k_s	Luminance:$Y(cd/m^2)$
0.1	224
0.2	313
0.3	439
0.4	591

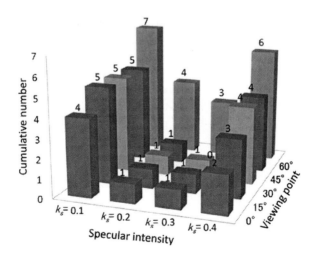

Fig. 12. Evaluation results for inauthenticity
The x-axis is the specular intensity k_s, the y-axis is the viewpoint, and the z-axis is the number of observers that reported inauthenticity two or more times during their three experiment cycles.

specular shape was strangely circular and that the specular position was too low. Based on the above-mentioned comments, we concluded that in our system, specular reproduction can only provide authentic sensibility within the range of $0°$ to $45°$.

7   Conclusion

This paper presented subjective evaluations of multiple observers in order to investigate the relationship between changes in CG parameters and visual sensibility. Using a composite-type digital mockup system, the specular appearance of a CG generated image was reproduced on a mockup using a projector-camera system. The pixels of the projection image were calculated using Phong's model based on the viewpoint position and light source. In our experiment, the specular coefficients k_s in Phong's model were set at 0.1, 0.2, 0.3, and 0.4, and the specular reflection position was fixed. Observer viewpoints were sitting positions set at $0°$, $15°$, $30°$, $45°$, and $60°$. The specular intensity and position generated at each viewpoint were evaluated using the magnitude estimation method and authenticity of visual sensibility was determined. Evaluation results of specular intensity clarified that the specular reflection intensity of our system followed Weber–Fechner's law. Additionally, it was found that the intensity evaluation score for specular appearance did not differ by viewpoint. Therefore, for the specular intensity evaluation, it was determined that the change in specular intensity in the CG parameter was equal to the change in the sense of brightness, regardless of the viewpoint. An evaluation of the sense of inauthenticity experienced clarified limitations within the viewpoint range. In particular, many observers reported feelings of inauthenticity at the $60°$ viewpoint. Therefore, in our system, we concluded that CG image settings such as reflectance and position only corresponded accurately to visual sensibility from $-45°$ to $45°$.

In the future, it is believed that using projector-camera systems, 3D reproduction will become an increasingly common tool in various research and industrial applications because it allows the appearance attributes of computer-generated 3D objects to be controlled easily.

8   Limitation and Future Work

Our experiments focused on a simple hemispherical shape, which simplified evaluations into the relationship between CG parameters and visual sensibility. However, practical digital mockups will require reproducing the appearance of complex shapes. Therefore, it will be necessary to verify the clarification results for each different mockup shape. Furthermore, reports of inauthentic specular appearances were obtained via a questionnaire, even though specular intensity was evaluated on a numerical scale. Therefore, it is not clarified of the magnitude of inauthenticity. The quantitative evaluation will be examined to the inauthenticity observation in the future.

As part of our future developments, we intend to improve the practical application and expansion of digital mockups so that rendering techniques and device settings can be revised to reproduce various appearances other than specular reflections. Furthermore, to improve the practical utility of the system, will be necessary to enable it to be used for close-up observations, which will require higher levels of reproduction accuracy in terms of image detail, grain, etc. Accordingly, we expect to focus on the development of advance reproduction techniques that can render high resolution images and bump mapping.

Acknowledgements

Norimichi Tsumura is partly supported by JSPS Grants-in-Aid for Scientific Research (19360026). Shoji Yamamoto and Norimichi Tsumura are also partly supported by JSPS Grants-in-Aid for Scientific Research (20500198).

References

1. Weiser, M.: The computer for the 21st century. Scientific American 272(3), 78–89 (1995)
2. Foley, J.: Computer graphics: principles and practice. Addison-Wesley Professional, Reading (1995)
3. Beyer, H., Holtzblatt, K.: Contextual design. Interactions 6(1), 32–42 (1999)
4. Pastoor, S., Wöpking, M.: 3-D displays: A review of current technologies. Displays 17(2), 100–110 (1997)
5. Jones, A., McDowall, I., Yamada, H., Bolas, M., Debevec, P.: Rendering for an interactive 360 light field display. In: ACM SIGGRAPH 2007 Emerging Technologies, p. 13. ACM, New York (2007)
6. Lantz, E.: The future of virtual reality: head mounted displays versus spatially immersive displays (panel). In: Proceedings of the 23rd Annual Conference on Computer Graphics and Interactive Techniques, pp. 485–486. ACM, New York (1996)
7. Hiller, J., Lipson, H.: Tunable digital material properties for 3D voxel printers. Rapid Prototyping Journal 16(4), 241–247 (2010)
8. Fechner, G., Adler, H., Howes, D., Boring, E.: Elements of psychophysics (1966)
9. Raskar, R., Welch, G., Cutts, M., Lake, A., Stesin, L., Fuchs, H.: The office of the future: A unified approach to image-based modeling and spatially immersive displays. In: Proceedings of the 25th Annual Conference on Computer Graphics and Interactive Techniques, pp. 179–188. ACM, New York (1998)
10. Kruger, W., Bohn, C., Frohlich, B., Schuth, H., Strauss, W., Wesche, G.: The responsive workbench: A virtual work environment. Computer 28(7), 42–48 (2002)
11. Pinhanez, C., Kjeldsen, R., Levas, A., Pingali, G., Podlaseck, M., Sukaviriya, N.: Applications of steerable projector-camera systems. In: Proceedings of the IEEE International Workshop on Projector-Camera Systems at ICCV 2003 (2003), Citeseer
12. Yoshida, T., Horii, C., Sato, K.: A virtual color reconstruction system for real heritage with light projection. In: Proceedings of VSMM, pp. 161–168 (2003)

13. Grossberg, M., Peri, H., Nayar, S., Belhumeur, P.: Making one object look like another: Controlling appearance using a projector-camera system. In: Proceedings of the IEEE Computer Society Conference on Computer Vision and Pattern Recognition, CVPR 2004, vol. 1, IEEE, Los Alamitos (2004)

14. Amano, T., Kato, H.: Appearance control by projector camera feedback for visually impaired. In: 2010 IEEE Computer Society Conference on Computer Vision and Pattern Recognition Workshops (CVPRW), pp. 57–63. IEEE, Los Alamitos (2010)

15. Mukaigawa, Y., Nishiyama, M., Shakunaga, T.: Realization of virtual photometric environment by photometric pattern projection. In: Proceedings of the IEEE International Symposium on Computational Intelligence in Robotics and Automation, 2003, vol. 1, pp. 435–440. IEEE, Los Alamitos (2003)

16. Konieczny, J., Meyer, G.: Material and color design using projectors. In: CGIV 2006: Third European Conference on Colour in Graphics, Imaging, and Vision, pp. 438–442. Citeseer (2006)

17. Raskar, R., Welch, G., Low, K., Bandyopadhyay, D.: Shader lamps: Animating real objects with image-based illumination. In: Rendering Techniques 2001: Proceedings of the Eurographics Workshop, London, United Kingdom, June 25-27, p. 89. Springer, Wien (2001)

18. Yamamoto, S., Tsuruse, M., Takase, K., Tsumura, N., Nakaguchi, T., Miyake, Y.: Real-Time Control of Appearance on the Object by using High Luminance PC Projector and Graphics Hardware. In: The 13th Color Imaging Conference, Scottsdale, USA (2005)

19. Kamimigaki, S., Yamamoto, S., Tsumura, N., Nakaguchi, T., Miyake, Y.: Real reproducing of 3D appearance with multi-projectors and cameras. In: The 17th Color Imaging Conference (2009)

20. Zhang, Z.: Flexible camera calibration by viewing a plane from unknown orientations. In: ICCV, p. 666. IEEE Computer Society, Los Alamitos (1999)

21. Zhang, S., Huang, P.: Novel method for structured light system calibration. Optical Engineering 45, 083601 (2006)

22. Phong, B.: Illumination for computer generated pictures. Communications of the ACM 18(6), 311–317 (1975)

23. Torrance, K., Sparrow, E.: Theory for off-specular reflection from roughened surfaces. Journal of the Optical Society of America 57(9), 1105–1114 (1967)

24. Ward, G.: Measuring and modeling anisotropic reflection. In: Proceedings of the 19th Annual Conference on Computer Graphics and Interactive Techniques, pp. 265–272. ACM, New York (1992)

25. Torgerson, W., Social Science Research Council (US). Committee on Scaling Theory and Methods: Theory and methods of scaling, vol. 1967. Wiley, New York (1958)

Spatial Colour Gamut Mapping by Means of Anisotropic Diffusion

Ali Alsam[1] and Ivar Farup[2]

[1] Sør-Trøndelag University College, Trondheim, Norway
[2] Gjøvik University College, Gjøvik, Norway

Abstract. We present a computationally efficient, artifact-free, spatial colour gamut mapping algorithm. The proposed algorithm offers a compromise between the colorimetrically optimal gamut clipping and an ideal spatial gamut mapping. It exploits anisotropic diffusion to reduce the introduction of halos often appearing in spatially gamut mapped images. It is implemented as an iterative method. At iteration level zero, the result is identical to gamut clipping. The more we iterate the more we approach an optimal, spatial gamut mapping result. Our results show that a low number of iterations, 10–20, is sufficient to produce an output that is as good or better than that achieved in previous, computationally more expensive, methods. The computational complexity for one iteration is $O(N)$, N being the number of pixels. Results based on a challenging small destination gamut supports our claims that it is indeed efficient.

Keywords: spatial gamut mapping, colour reproduction, anisotropic diffusion.

1 Introduction

To accurately define a colour, three independent variables need to be fixed. In a given three dimensional colour space, the colour gamut is the volume enclosing all the colour values that can be reproduced by the reproduction device or present in the image. Colour gamut mapping is the problem of representing the colour values of an image within the gamut of a reproduction device, typically a printer or a monitor. Furthermore, in the general case, when an image gamut is larger than the destination gamut some visual image information will be lost. We therefore redefine gamut mapping as the problem of representing the colour values of an image within the gamut of a reproduction device with minimum loss of visual information, i.e., as visually close as possible.

Unlike single colours, images are represented in a higher dimensional space than three, i.e. knowledge of the exact colour values is not, on its own, sufficient to reproduce an unknown image. In order to fully define an image, the spatial context of each colour pixel needs to be fixed. Based on this, we define two categories of gamut mapping algorithms. In the first, colours are mapped independent of their spatial context [1]. In the second, the mapping is influenced by the local context of each colour value [2,3,4,5]. The latter category is referred to as spatial colour gamut mapping.

R. Schettini, S. Tominaga, and A. Trémeau (Eds.): CCIW 2011, LNCS 6626, pp. 113–124, 2011.

Eschbach [6] stated that although the accuracy of mapping of a single colour is well defined, the reproduction accuracy of images isn't. To elucidate this claim, with which we agree, we consider a single colour that is defined by its hue, saturation and lightness. Assuming that such a colour is outside the target gamut, we can modify its components independently. That is to say, if the colour is lighter or more saturated than what can be achieved inside the reproduction gamut, we shift its lightness and saturation to the nearest feasible values. Further, in most cases it is possible to reproduce colours without shifting their hue.

Taking the spatial context of colours into account presents us with the challenge of defining the spatial components of a colour pixel and incorporating this information into the gamut mapping algorithm. Generally speaking, we need to define rules that would result in mapping two colours with identical hue, saturation and lightness to two different magnitudes depending on their context in the image. The main challenge is, thus, defining the spatial context of an image pixel in a manner that results in an improved gamut mapping. By improved we mean that the appearance of the resultant in-gamut image is closer to the original as judged by a human observer. Further, from a practical point of view, the new definition needs to result in an algorithm that is fast and does not result in image artifacts.

It is well understood that the human visual system is more sensitive to spatial ratios than to absolute luminance values [7]. This knowledge is at the heart of all spatial gamut mapping algorithms. A rephrasing of spatial gamut mapping is then the problem of representing the colour values of an image within the gamut of a reproduction device while preserving the spatial ratios between different colour pixels. In an image, spatial ratios are the difference, given some metric, between a pixel and its surround. This can be the difference between one pixel and its adjacent neighbors or pixels far away from it. Thus, we face the problem that spatial ratios are defined in different scales and dependent on the chosen difference metric.

McCann suggested to preserve the spatial gradients at all scales while applying gamut mapping [8]. Meyer and Barth [9] suggested to compress the lightness of the image using a low-pass filter in the Fourier domain. As a second step the high-pass image information is added back to the gamut compressed image. Many spatial gamut mapping algorithms have been based upon this basic idea [2,4,10,11,12].

A completely different approach was taken by Nakauchi et al. [13]. They defined gamut mapping as an optimization problem of finding the image that is perceptually closest to the original and has all pixels inside the gamut. The perceptual difference was calculated by applying band-pass filters to Fourier-transformed CIELAB images and then weighing them according to the human contrast sensitivity function. Thus, the best gamut mapped image is the image having contrast (according to their definition) as close as possible to the original. Kimmel et al. [3] presented a variational approach to spatial gamut mapping where it was shown that the gamut mapping problem leads to a quadratic programming formulation, which is guaranteed to have a unique solution if the gamut of the target device is convex. However, they did not apply their method to colour images.

Finding an adequate description of the surface of the gamut, commonly denoted a gamut boundary descriptors (GBDs) is an important step in any colour gamut mapping algorithm. One of the main challenges is the fact that gamut surfaces are most often concave. Many methods for finding the GBD have been proposed over the years. Recently, Bakke et al. [14] presented a survey and evaluation of the most common method, showing that the modified convex hull algorithm by Balasubramanian and Dalal [15] is generally the most reliable one.

The algorithm presented in this paper adheres to our previously stated definition of spatial gamut mapping in that we aim to preserve the spatial ratios between pixels in the image. We start by calculating the gradients of the original image in the CIELAB colour space. The image is then gamut mapped by projecting the colour values to the nearest, in gamut, point along hue-constant lines. The difference between the gradient of the gamut mapped image and that of the original is then iteratively minimized with the constraint that the resultant colour is inside the destination gamut and has the same hue as the original. The scale at which the gradient is preserved is related to the number of iterations and the extent to which we can fit the original gradients into the destination gamut.

The main contributions of this work are as follows. We first present a mathematical formulation of the gamut mapping problem in colour space. Our formulation can be extended to a higher dimensional space than three. Secondly, to avoid halos which are a main drawback in previous spatial gamut mappings techniques we introduce a modification of the algorithm presented by Alsam and Farup [16]. In [16] we observe that halos are visible in the resultant gamut mapped images at strong lightness or chromatic edges. Furthermore, those edges are generally visible in the gamut clipped image. That is to say that halos are the result of over enhancing visible edges. In this article we avoid this problem by using anisotropic diffusion [17] where the gradients of the gamut mapped image are improved based on their strength. This methods is known to improve the classic strategy for a number of applications such as zooming [18] and image compression [19]. With anisotropic diffusion, the diffusion is encouraged within regions and prohibited across strong edges thus avoiding the introduction of halos. Finally, our results show that as few as ten iterations are sufficient to produce an output that is similar or better than previous methods. Being able to improve upon previous results using such low number of iterations allows us to state that the proposed algorithm is fast.

2   Spatial Gamut Mapping: A Mathematical Definition

Let's say we have an original image with pixel values $\mathbf{p}(x, y)$ (bold face to indicate vector) in CIELAB or any similarly structured colour space. A gamut clipped image can be obtained by leaving in-gamut colours untouched, and projecting the out-of-gamut colours onto the gamut surface along straight lines defined by

g, the center of the gamut on the L axis and the nearest in-gamut colour. Let's denote the gamut clipped image, which is the outcome of such a conventional gamut clipping algorithm as $\mathbf{p}_c(x, y)$. Clearly, the gamut clipped image is a convex linear combination of the original image and the grey point,

$$\mathbf{p}_c(x, y) = \alpha_c(x, y)\mathbf{p}(x, y) + (1 - \alpha_c(x, y))\mathbf{g} \tag{1}$$

which can be solved for α_c:

$$\alpha_c(x, y) = \frac{||\mathbf{p}_c(x, y) - \mathbf{g}||}{||\mathbf{p}(x, y) - \mathbf{g}||} . \tag{2}$$

A spatial gamut mapped image is obtained by further compressing the pixel value towards the grey by some hitherto unknown amount $\alpha_s(x, y)$, i.e.,

$$\begin{aligned} \mathbf{p}_s(x, y) &= \alpha_s(x, y)\mathbf{p}_c(x, y) + (1 - \alpha_s(x, y))\mathbf{g} \\ &= \alpha_s(x, y)\alpha_c(x, y)\mathbf{p}(x, y) + (1 - \alpha_s(x, y)\alpha_c(x, y))\mathbf{g} \\ &= \alpha(x, y)\mathbf{p}(x, y) + (1 - \alpha(x, y))\mathbf{g}, \end{aligned} \tag{3}$$

where $\alpha(x, y) = \alpha_s(x, y)\alpha_c(x, y)$ has been introduced. A visual illustraion of the parameters involved is shown in Figure 1.

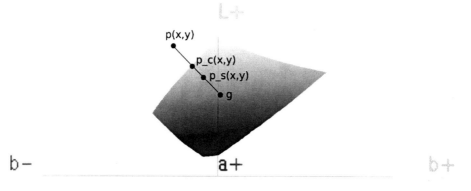

Fig. 1. A representation of the spatial gamut mapping problem. $p(x, y)$ is the original colour at image pixel (x, y), this value is clipped to the gamut boundary resulting in a new colour $p_c(x, y)$ which is compressed based on the gradient information to a new value $p_s(x, y)$.

In a previous paper [16], we demonstrated that a reasonable spatial gamut mapping algorithm can be achieved by minimising

$$\min \int ||\nabla \mathbf{p}_s(x, y) - \nabla \mathbf{p}(x, y)||^2 \, dA \quad \text{subject to} \quad \alpha_s(x, y) \in [0, 1]. \tag{4}$$

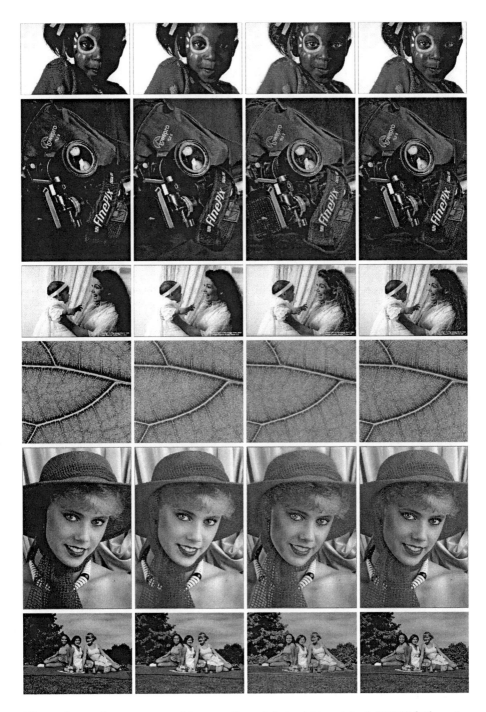

Fig. 2. A set of gamut mapped images. From left to right: original, SGCK [21], variational GMA [16], and proposed solution with $\kappa = 2$, $\alpha_{min} = 0.8$ and $N_{it} = 100$.

A numerical solution to this problem was found by solving the corresponding Euler–Lagrange equation,

$$\nabla^2(\mathbf{p}_s(x,y) - \mathbf{p}(x,y)) = 0 \tag{5}$$

subject to the same constraint using a finite difference method with Jacobi iteration with homogeneous Neumann boundary conditions to ensure zero derivative at the image boundary. The problem was reduced from three to one dimension using the constraint (3) and least squares optimisation.

One of the problems with this approach – a common problem with diffusion based image processing – was the creation of halos near strong edges. In this paper we overcome this problem by employing a non-linear diffusion algorithm. Specifically, we propose to exchange the simple diffusion equation with an anisotropic diffusion equation inspired by Perona and Malik [17]:

$$\nabla \cdot (D(x,y)\nabla(\mathbf{p}_s(x,y) - \mathbf{p}(x,y))) = 0, \tag{6}$$

where the diffusion coefficient is a function of the image properties, $D(x,y) = D(\mathbf{p}(x,y), \nabla\mathbf{p}(x,y))$. In reference [16], we transformed the vectorial diffusion equation to a scalar equation for α_s using the constraint (3) and least squares optimisation. With the more advanced diffusion coefficient of Perona and Malik, this is not a straight forward procedure. Thus, in order to simplify the problem further, we solve this equation for the grayscale versions of the original, p, and gamut mapped images, p_s, where the greyscale image is obtained by taking the second norm of the colour vectors. The final colour gamut mapped image can be obtained based on the assumption that it is a convex linear combination of the original image and the neutral gray color at any pixel position, Equation (3).

The diffusion coefficient is chosen in accordance with Perona and Malik:

$$D(x,y) = \frac{1}{1 + (|\nabla p(x,y)|/\kappa)^2}, \tag{7}$$

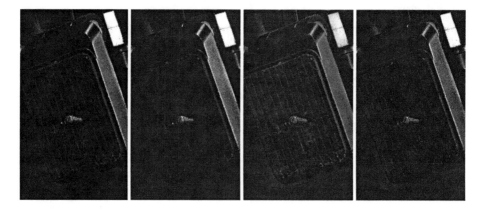

Fig. 3. A close-up of one of the rows in Figure 2: original, SGCK [21], variational GMA [16], and proposed solution with $\kappa = 2$, $\alpha_{min} = 0.8$ and $N_{it} = 100$.

Fig. 4. Effect of changing the κ value in the algorithm. The κ values are, from left to right, 0.5, 1, 2, and 5. For all of them, $N_{it} = 100$ and $\alpha_{min} = 0.8$.

where the constant is chosen such that $\max_{x,y}((|\nabla p(x,y)|/\kappa)^2) \gg 1$ in order to stop the diffusion over sharp egdes. This results in the following scalar equation:

$$\nabla \cdot \left(\frac{\nabla(p_s(x,y) - p(x,y))}{1 + (|\nabla p(x,y)|/\kappa)^2} \right) = 0. \tag{8}$$

This equation is discretised using the finite difference method with homogeneous boundary conditions, and iterated using the steepest decent method with N_{it} iterations, in analogy with [16]. This gives a solution for $\alpha_s(x,y)$ which can be inserted in Equation (3). However, like in Reference [16], the resulting images tend to preserve details at the cost of losing saturation, since no fidelity term is in used (see, e.g., [20]). Therefore, in analogy with conventional gamut mapping algorithms [1], we set a limitation to how small α_s can be. That is, the constraint in Equation (4) is replaced with $\alpha_s(x, y) \in [\alpha_{min}, 1]$ for a suitable choice of α_{min}.

3   Results and Discussion

Figure 2 shows the result of gamut mapping some images with the algorithm proposed in the previous section. For comparison, the images were also mapped using pure clipping, the SCGK algorithm [21], and the previously proposed variational scheme [16]. We see that the proposed algorithm preserves more of the details present in the original image than the SCGK algorithm without introducing the artificial looking edges and haloes produced by the previously proposed method [16]. It should be noted, though, that the number of iterations for the previously proposed algorithm was set too high ($N_{it} = 100$) in order to be directly comparable to the current proposal. This is much higher than suggested in [16], and exaggerates the problems of that algorithm. A close-up of one of the images is shown in Figure 3.

3.1   The κ Parameter

Figure 4 illustrates the behaviour of the algorithm for various choices of κ. The κ parameter controls the anisotropy of the diffusion. The smaller the value of κ, the more sensitive the diffusion coefficient (7) is to the local variations in the image. Intuitively, this should mean that the κ parameter should be set as small as possible. However, the resulting images become unnaturally sharp for too small κ values. Further, for very low κ values, the algorithm becomes too sensitive to noise in the image. Finally, smaller κ increases the risk of numerical instabilities. A close-up is shown in Figure 5.

On the other side, if κ is set to a large value, the diffusion coefficient will be insensitive to edges. This results in diffusion across the edges in the image, with

Fig. 5. A close-up of one of the rows in Figure 4. The κ values are, from left to right, 0.5, 1, 2, and 5. For all of them, $N_{it} = 100$ and $\alpha_{min} = 0.8$.

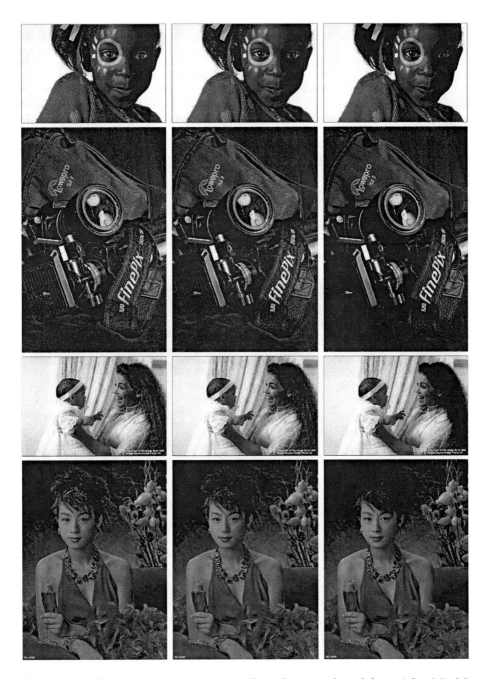

Fig. 6. The effect of the α_{min} parameter. The values are, from left to right: 0.7, 0.8 and 0.9. For all of them, $N_{it} = 100$ and $\kappa = 2$.

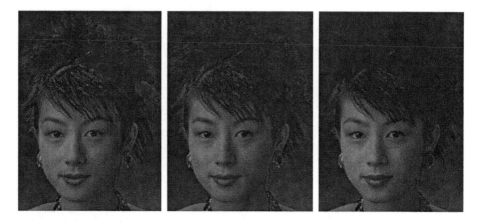

Fig. 7. Close-ups of one row in Figure 6. The α_{min} parameter values are, from left to right: 0.7, 0.8 and 0.9. For all of them, $N_{it} = 100$ and $\kappa = 2$.

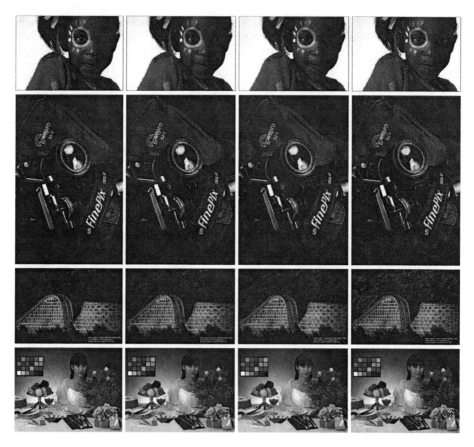

Fig. 8. The effect of the N_{it} parameter. The values are, from left to right: 0, 10, 20, and 100. For all of them, $\alpha_{min} = 0.8$ and $\kappa = 2$.

halo artefacts as the consequence. If $\alpha_{min} = 0$, the algorithm reduces to that proposed in Reference [16] in the limit $\kappa \rightarrow \infty$. In our experiments, the best performance is found for values in the range $\kappa \in [1, 2]$.

3.2 The α_{min} Parameter

The α_{min} parameter limits the amount of compression. Thus, similar to the SGCK algorithm [21], the parameter is a tradeoff between preservation of details and preservation of saturation. An $\alpha_{min} = 0$, represents no preservation of saturation while for an, $\alpha_{min} = 1$, the algorithm reduces to clipping. The most convincing results are obtained by choosing values around 0.8, cf. Figure 6 with close-ups in Figure 7.

3.3 The Number of Iterations

Figure 8 shows how the result of our algorithm develops with the number of iterations. Due to the anisotropic diffusion, the algorithm converges slower than the one proposed in Reference [16]. After 100 iterations, the result is quite stable for most images. The most noticeable changes are, however, observed in the first iterations. Thus, for practical implementations, when speed is called for, 10–20 iterations should be sufficient. Already after 10 iterations, the result resemble that presented in [4], which is, according to Dugay et al. [22] a state-of-the-art algorithm. Thus, the algorithm is very fast, the complexity of each iteration being $O(N)$ for an image with N pixels.

4 Conclusion

The efficient variational spatial colour gamut mapping algorithm suggested in Reference [16] has been refined by the introduction of anisotropic diffusion. As a consequence, the problem of halo creation is strongly reduced, or even totally removed. The problem of too strong desaturation has been solved by introducing a limit to how much the colours can be compressed as an additional constraint in the equations.

To reduce the complexity of the algorithm, we performed the calculations of the gradient and the resulting compression map on the luminance image only. This simplification holds for all colour regions apart from those known as isoluminance, i.e. neighboring colours that have the same luminance values. Thus the algorithm will not recover details that are lost in the conversion between the colour gamut mapped image and its greyscale version.

The resulting algorithm shows promising results for a broad range of images for the same choice of parameters, $\alpha_s = 0.8$ and $\kappa = 2$.

References

1. Morovič, J., Ronnier Luo, M.: The fundamentals of gamut mapping: A survey. Journal of Imaging Science and Technology 45(3), 283–290 (2001)
2. Bala, R., de Queiroz, R., Eschbach, R., Wu, W.: Gamut mapping to preserve spatial luminance variations. Journal of Imaging Science and Technology 45(5), 436–443 (2001)

3. Kimmel, R., Shaked, D., Elad, M., Sobel, I.: Space-dependent color gamut mapping: A variational approach. IEEE Trans. Image Proc. 14(6), 796–803 (2005)

4. Farup, I., Gatta, C., Rizzi, A.: A multiscale framework for spatial gamut mapping. IEEE Trans. Image Process. 16(10) (2007), doi:10.1109/TIP.2007.904946.

5. Giesen, J., Schubert, E., Simon, K., Zolliker, P.: Image-dependent gamut mapping as optimization problem. IEEE Trans. Image Process. 16(10), 2401–2410 (2007)

6. Eschbach, R.: Image reproduction: An oxymoron? Colour: Design & Creativity 3(3), 1–6 (2008)

7. Land, E.H., McCann, J.J.: Lightness and retinex theory. Journal of the Optical Society of America 61(1), 1–11 (1971)

8. McCann, J.J.: A spatial colour gamut calculation to optimise colour appearance. In: MacDonald, L.W., Luo, M.R. (eds.) Colour Image Science, pp. 213–233. John Wiley & Sons Ltd., Chichester (2002)

9. Meyer, J., Barth, B.: Color gamut matching for hard copy. SID Digest, 86–89 (1989)

10. Morovič, J., Wang, Y.: A multi-resolution, full-colour spatial gamut mapping algorithm. In: Proceedings of IS&T and SID's 11th Color Imaging Conference: Color Science and Engineering: Systems, Technologies, Applications, Scottsdale, Arizona, pp. 282–287 (2003)

11. Eschbach, R., Bala, R., de Queiroz, R.: Simple spatial processing for color mappings. Journal of Electronic Imaging 13(1), 120–125 (2004)

12. Zolliker, P., Simon, K.: Retaining local image information in gamut mapping algorithms. IEEE Trans. Image Proc. 16(3), 664–672 (2007)

13. Nakauchi, S., Hatanaka, S., Usui, S.: Color gamut mapping based on a perceptual image difference measure. Color Research and Application 24(4), 280–291 (1999)

14. Bakke, A.M., Farup, I., Hardeberg, J.Y.: Evaluation of algorithms for the determination of color gamut boundaries. Journal of Imaging Science and Technology 54(5), 050502–050511 (2010)

15. Balasubramanian, R., Dalal, E.: A method for quantifying the color gamut of an output device. In: Color Imaging: Device-Independent Color, Color Hard Copy, and Graphic Arts II, San Jose, CA. Proc. SPIE, vol. 3018 (January 1997)

16. Alsam, A., Farup, I.: Colour gamut mapping as a constrained variational problem. In: Salberg, A.-B., Hardeberg, J.Y., Jenssen, R. (eds.) SCIA 2009. LNCS, vol. 5575, pp. 109–118. Springer, Heidelberg (2009)

17. Perona, P., Malik, J.: Scale-space and edge detecion using anisotropic diffusion. IEEE Trans. Image Proc. 12(7), 629–639 (1990)

18. Battiato, S., Gallo, G., Stanco, F.: Smart interpolation by anisotropic diffusion. In: International Conference on Image Analysis and Processing, vol. 0, p. 572 (2003)

19. Gali, I., Weickert, J., Welk, M., Bruhn, A., Belyaev, A., Seide, H.-P.: Image compression with anisotropic diffusion. Journal of Mathematical Imaging and Vision 31(255-269) (2008)

20. Lin, Z., Islam, S.: An adaptive edge-preserving variational framework for color image regularization. In: IEEE International Conference on Image Processing, ICIP 2005, pp. 101–104 (2005)

21. CIE Technical Committee 8-03. Guidelines for the evaluation of gamut mapping algorithms. Technical Report 156, CIE (2003)

22. Dugay, F., Farup, I., Hardeberg, J.Y.: Perceptual evaluation of color gamut mapping algorithms. Color Research and Application 33(6), 470–476 (2008)

Enhancing Underexposed Images Preserving the Original Mood

Silvia Corchs and Francesca Gasparini

DISCo (Dipartimento di Informatica, Sistemistica e Comunicazione),
University of Milano-Bicocca, Viale Sarca 336, 20126 Milano, Italy
{corchs,gasparini}@disco.unimib.it

Abstract. In the present article we focus on enhancing the contrast of images with low illumination that present large underexposed regions. Most of these images represent night images. When applying standard contrast enhancement techniques, usually the night mood is modified, and also a noise over-enhancement within the darker regions is introduced. In a previous work we have described our local contrast correction algorithm designed to enhance images where both underexposed and overexposed regions are simultaneously present. Here we show how this algorithm is able to automatically enhance night images, preserving the original mood. To further improve the performance of our method we also propose here a denoising procedure where the strength of the smoothing is a function of an estimated level of noise and it is further weighted by a saliency map. The method has been applied to a proper database of outdoor and indoor underexposed images. Our results have been qualitatively compared with well know contrast correction methods.

Keywords: local contrast enhancement, underexposed images, night images.

1 Introduction

Global and local contrast correction algorithms have become very popular to improve the quality of the captured images (like those obtained with mobile devices among others) when underexposed and overexposed regions are simultaneously present within the image. In the literature, many algorithms have been proposed, from histogram equalization-type techniques [17], [2] to other types of methods like the Retinex model [6] or local contrast corrections methods, where non linear masking is used in order to perform the local processing [13], [16].

In the present article we focus on enhancing the contrast of images with low illumination that present important or large underexposed regions. Most of these images depict night scenes typically acquired outdoor, or indoor scenes acquired with very low level of illumination (for instance inside pubs and discoteques, during parties, etc.). In these particular cases, when applying standard contrast enhancement techniques, usually the original mood of the image changes, and also a noise over-enhancement within the darker regions can be introduced. For

R. Schettini, S. Tominaga, and A. Trémeau (Eds.): CCIW 2011, LNCS 6626, pp. 125–136, 2011.
© Springer-Verlag Berlin Heidelberg 2011

Fig. 1. Example of underexposed images. Left, an outdoor night image. Right, an indoor image.

images taken with digital cameras, darker regions will contain more noise than the brighter ones. In Figure 1 an example of a night image and an indoor underexposed image are shown.

A contrast correction strategy applied to these images should find a trade-off between enhancing the visibility of details and preserving the original mood of the image. Moreover, it is also desirable to control the noise level in the output image.

In a previous work, [16], we have described our local contrast correction algorithm designed to enhance images where both underexposed and overexposed regions are simoultaneously present. In this paper we show how our algorithm is able to enhance this kind of strongly underexposed images, preserving the original mood. We add to our method an automatic white balance algorithm [3], that is able to mimic the behaviour of our visual system discounting cast of low and middle intensity, while mantaining strong cast due to a particular light condition, such as in the case of images acquired in a discoteque with coloured lights (see for example the image on the right of Figure 1). To further improve the performance of our method, we also propose here a denoising procedure. The denoising problem has been widely addressed within the literature [4], [14], [15], [19].

Noise estimation is a difficult task and different approaches have been proposed [8] [18] [11] [1]. While it is often assumed that noise is additive and Gaussian, for the particular case of underexposed images we note that it is strongly dependent on the image intensity. Moreover, the noise in digital images is both chromatic and achromatic.

Thus in our method we propose to move to the YCbCr color space and estimate the noise level for each channel and apply different denoising strategies for each of them.

For the intensity channel Y, we propose to apply a modified version of the bilateral filter introduced by Tomasi and Manduchi, [19]. In order to obtain a selective denoise, the smoothing effect of the bilateral filter is weighted by a saliency map of the image. Saliency is a concept which states that there are regions in a scene that are more relevant than their neighbors and hence draw attention. Based on a biologically plausible architecture, several authors implemented a saliency map model mainly using color, intensity and orientation cues to predict salient regions,[9,12] The idea of performing different enhancing strategies with respect to the salience of the regions of an image where previously used by many authors, see for example Gasparini et al [7]. As the high frequencies are more visible in the intensity channel with respect to the chromatic ones, we apply for the latter ones the well known Wiener filter, instead of the bilateral filter.

The paper is organized as follows. In section 2 our local contrast correction algorithm is summarized, underlying its behaviour with respect to the images considered in this work. In section 3 the automatic white balance algorithm here applied is briefly described and some example images are reported. The concept of saliency and the saliency map here adopted are described in section 4, while in section 5 the denoise module here proposed, function of the estimated level of noise and weighted by a saliency map, is described. Finally in section 6 we present the experimental results, showing some images processed by our whole procedure and comparing qualitatively our outputs with well known methods such as Retinex and the local exponential correction introduced by Moroney. Section 7 summarizes the conclusions.

2   Local Contrast Correction Algorithm

The Local Contrast Correction (LCC) algorithm here adopted is based on a local and image dependent exponential correction [16]. This algorithm aims to correct images that simultaneously present overexposed and underexposed regions. The LCC algorithm is developed starting from Moroney's technique [13], where the exponent of a gamma correction like function is not a constant but depends on the point to be corrected, its neighbouring pixels and on the global characteristic of the image. The corrected image $I_c(i,j)$ is obtained as follows:

$$I_c(i,j) = I(i,j)^{\alpha^{\left(\frac{128 - mask(i,j)}{128}\right)}} \tag{1}$$

where α is a parameter depending on the image properties. For low contrast images, where a stronger correction is needed, α should be high, while for better contrasted images, α should diminish towards 1, which corresponds to no correction (See Schettini et al. [16] for more details). In equation 1, $mask(x,y)$ is an inverted low-pass version of the intensity of the input image. In the LCC method, instead of the Gaussian filter of the Moroney proposal, the bilateral filter of Tomasi and Manduchi is used [19]. Bilateral filtering smoothes images while preserving edges, by means of a nonlinear combination of nearby image values. The bilateral filter combines grey levels or colors based on both their geometric closeness and their photometric similarity, and prefers near values to distant values in both spatial and intensity domains. The idea developed by the bilateral filter is to combine domain and range Gaussian filtering (depending respectively on a spatial standard deviation σ_s and on a range standard deviation σ_r). In this way, both geometric and photometric locality are simultaneously enforced. The *mask* corresponding to the bilateral filter approach is defined over a window of size $(2K + 1)(2K + 1)$ and is given by:

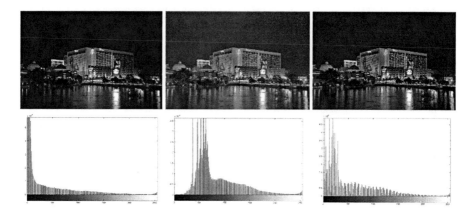

Fig. 2. Original image (left column); the result after applying the local esponential correction of equation 1 (middle column); the final enhanced image, after the stretching and clipping adjustement (right column). Corresponding histograms of the intensity channel are reported below the images.

$$mask(i,j) = \frac{1}{k(i,j)} \sum_{p=i-K}^{i+K} \sum_{q=j-K}^{j+K} exp\left\{-\frac{1}{2\sigma_s^2}\left[(i-p)^2 + (j-q)^2\right]\right\}$$

$$exp\left\{-\frac{1}{2\sigma_r^2}\left[I_{inv}(i,j) - I_{inv}(p,q)\right]^2\right\} I_{inv}(p,q) \qquad (2)$$

where $I_{inv}(i,j) = 255 - I(i,j)$ and $k(i,j)$ is a normalization factor:

$$k(i,j) = \sum_{p=i-K}^{i+K} \sum_{q=j-K}^{j+K} exp\left\{-\frac{1}{2\sigma_s^2}\left[(i-p)^2 + (j-q)^2\right]\right\}$$

$$exp\left\{-\frac{1}{2\sigma_r^2}\left[I_{inv}(i,j) - I_{inv}(p,q)\right]\right\} \qquad (3)$$

In the present implementation, working with color images, we apply the rule of equation 1 to the intensity component in the YCbCr color space. From a deeper analysis of the intensity histogram before and after the proposed local correction, it comes that, despite a better occupation of the grey levels, the overall contrast enhancement is not satisfying. In fact, the new histogram is more spread than the original but it is moved and concentrated around the middle values of the range. The effect that makes the processed image greyish is intrinsic in the mathematic formulation of equation 1 adopted for the local correction. To overcome this problem a further step of contrast enhancement, consisting of a stretching and clipping procedure, is added . To determine the strength of the stretching and thus the number of bins to be clipped, it is considered how the darker regions occupy the intensity histogram before and after the LCC algorithm. Pixels belonging to a dark area, such as a dark object, or a dark background (for example the sky during the night) usually occupy a narrow and peaked group of bins at the beginning of the intensity histogram. These pixels should populate more or less the same bins after a contrast enhancement algorithm. On the other hand, pixels of regions that create a more spread histogram peak, after the same algorithm must populate an even more spread region of the histogram. In Figure 2 left, an image with a dark background that shuold be preserved after the contrast enhancement procedure is shown; the same image after the esponential correction is depicted in the middle column, while the final image after the stretching step is shown on the right. The corresponding histograms are shown below the images. More details can be found in [16].

3   Automatic White Balance

The algorithm proposed uses both the chromaticity and the intensity of the image to estimate the illuminant, and performs the compensation by a diagonal transforms. In particular it combines a spatial segmentation process with empirical designed weighting functions aimed to select the scene objects containing more information for the light chromaticity estimation. The algorithm is a modified

Fig. 3. First row, left) an example of image with a dominant color that should be removed; right) corresponding color corrected output. Second row, left) an image whose dominant color characterizes the mood of the scene and thus should be preserved; right) corresponding output.

version of the traditional white patch algorithm. The main peculiarity of this color balancing lies in how it determines the region to be set at white, called white balancing region (WB region). Accordingly to wide accepted results that not all the pixels have the same significance in terms of information content of scene illuminant, it takes into account both chromaticity, intensity and spatial information of the image data. In particular it works by combining a spatial segmentation process and proper weighting profiles aimed to select the scene objects containing more information for the light chromaticity estimation. A particular charateristic of this algorithm is that it tries to simulate our visual system, discounting only low or middle intensity casts, that our visual system is ususally able to compensate, leaving unchanged the dominant color that is need to keep the mood of the acquired scene. In Figure 3 one image whose dominant color should be removed, and one image where the dominant color shold remain unchanged are reported in the first and second row respectively. The output of our automatic white balance algorithm is depicted near the corresponding original images. A detailed description of the method can be found in [3].

4   Saliency Map

Saliency is a concept which states that there are regions in a scene that are more relevant than their neighbors and hence draw attention. In the present work we use the contrast-based saliency map proposed by Ma and Zhang [12]. The basic algorithm divides the image into small rectangular tiles. At each tile, a contrast

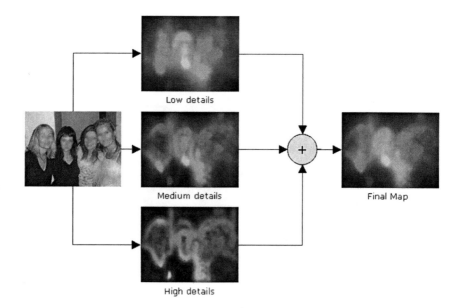

Fig. 4. Original image (left column), the three levels of saliency maps (middle column), the final multi-level saliency map (right column). Courtesy of Ciocca and Schettini [5].

Fig. 5. Example of the saliency map adopted in our method, obtained using only the high details

score is computed from the differences of average colors between the given tile and its neighbor's tiles. The contrast score expresses the saliency of the pixels in the tile. The contrast scores of all the tiles define the saliency map of the image. The size of the tiles, and the size of the neighborhoods determine the dimensions of the salient areas that can be detected. The basic, single scale algorithm has been extended by Ciocca and Schettini [5] to compute three different levels of saliency maps. Using neighborhoods of increasing size, each aimed at a particular level of detail (small, medium and large) a multi-level saliency map was formulated. In Figure 4 the original image, the corresponding three different levels of saliency maps and the final multi-level saliency map are shown.

In the present work we choose to use only the high-details saliency map. In this way for each pixel (x, y) of the contrasted image $I_c(x, y)$ the saliency map called $SalMap(x, y)$, is obtained. As an example, in Figure 5 an image of our database and the corresponding saliency map are shown.

5   Salience-Adaptive Denoising Module

For underexposed images, noise is not simply additive, but it is also strongly dependent on the image intensity level. Moreover, noise changes depending on the exposure setting and camera model and it can also vary within an individual image. Therefore, for the images we address in the present article, we ignore what type of noise is present in the image (addditive and/or multiplicative, chromatic and/or achromatic). For this reason, we are not interested here in estimating the noise level as a function of the image intensity. We are mainly interested in estimating noise within the darker regions. In these regions the original Signal to Noise Ratio (SNR) is significantly low and any contrast correction will increase the noise level, further reducing the initial SNR. We select as dark regions those corresponding to the first peak of the intensity histogram of the original image. The noise level will be estimated within these regions in the contrast corrected image, as we are interested in the noise increase due to the enhancement. As the

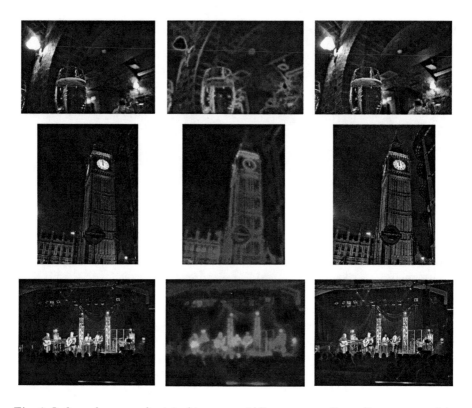

Fig. 6. Left: underexposed original images; middle: corresponding saliency maps; right: outputs of our whole method

noise in digital images is both chromatic and achromatic, we move to the YCbCr color space and we estimate noise for each channel, evaluating the corresponding standard deviations within the selected regions.

In our denoising module we apply different strategies to intensity and color channels. For the intensity channel Y we adopt a modified version of the bilateral filter introduced by Tomasi and Maduchi [19] and described in section 2. In our algorithm, the standard deviation σ_r of the Gaussian function in the range domain is related to the estimated intensity noise σ_{noise}. In particular, following the proposal of Liu et al [10] we set:

$$\sigma_r = 1.95\sigma_{noise} \tag{4}$$

Moreover, the strength of the filtering is weighted by the saliency map $SalMap(x, y)$ defined above, so that regions more visually salient are filtered less than region less significant. This effect is obtained making σ_r spatially varying, defining a new $\hat{\sigma}_r(x, y)$ as follows:

$$\hat{\sigma}_r(x, y) = \sigma_r(1 - SalMap(x, y)) \tag{5}$$

On the other hand, for each of the color channels Cb and Cr, we apply a Wiener filter, which is a filter adaptive with respect to the level of noise and specifically designed for additive noise. In our algorithm the reference value of noise for each channel is estimated as described above.

6 Results and Discussion

We have tested our method on a datasets of more than 40 images acquired with digital cameras of medium/high quality. Thus the images considered have dimension between 4 and 6 Mpixels. For these dimensions we have applied the rule of equation 4 to estimate the σ_r of the bilateral filter. We have noticed that the factor of this equation should be tuned with respect to the dimension of the processed images. How to tune this parameter will be object of a future work. In Figure 6 the results of the proposed method are shown for some example images. On the left the underexposed original images are shown, in the middle the corresponding saliency maps here adopted are reported, while the output of our whole method can be seen on the right.

In order to compare the results, it is not easy to define reliable no reference quality metrics with normalized range of values. Moreover, it is even more difficult

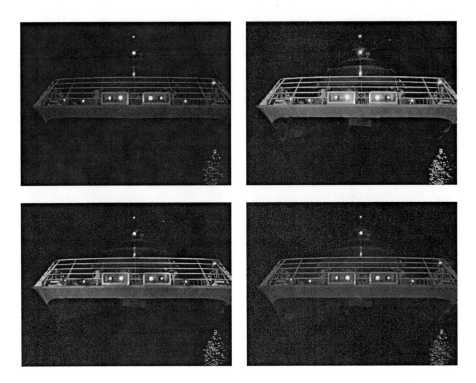

Fig. 7. Original image (top row, left). Image processed with our method (top row, right). Retinex and Moroney results respectively bottom row, left and right.

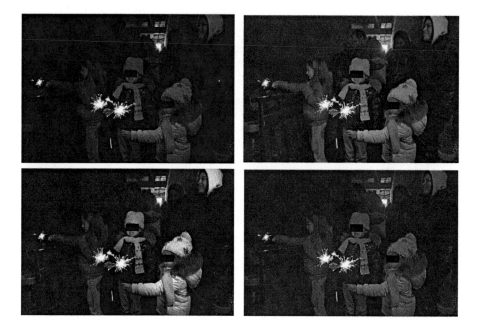

Fig. 8. Original image (top row, left). Image processed with our method (top row, right). Retinex and Moroney results respectively bottom row, left and right.

in the present case where the reduction of noise, the sharpness of the image and the color balancing should be simoultaneously taken into account. Therefore, we only report here qualitatively comparisons with well known methods available in the literature. In particular we have considered the Frankle and McCann version of Retinex [6], as an example of algorithm that not only increases the contrast but also performs a color balancing, and the local exponential correction of Moroney [13] as a typical example of local correction that shows good performance in case of low contrasted images with both under and over-exposed regions but that is not designed to enhanced images with a very low SNR in the darker regions. Two example sets of images are shown in Figures 7 and 8.

From a qualitative visual analysis we can note that for this kind of images the Retinex method can introduce color distortions, while the Moroney results show grayish appearance. Our method enhnaces the details, preserving the original mood and keeping the noise whitin an acceptable level from a perceptive point of view. A better analysis of the results requires also a subjective psychovisual test, with more images and contents, and involving in the tests a proper number of observers.

7   Conclusions

In this work we have presented an adaptive enhancement procedure especially suited for underexposed images, where the noise level of the darker regions usually increases significantly after common contrast processing. In particular we were not interested here in enhancing all the details of the underexposed images but instead we were interested in preserving the dark mood typical of night images or of indoor images acquired in particular light contitions (such as those acquired in pubs, discoteques, etc.). To further improve the quality of the processed images, our algorithm adds a proper denoising module after a local and image dependent contrast correction and automatic white balance procedure. This denoising module is 'salience-adaptive' as it is weighted by the saliency map of the image. Moreover, its strength is piloted by the noise level of the image. Experimental results and a visual comparison with well known methods, reveal that our method is able to preserve the original mood of the acquired scenes, keeping the noise level low.

References

1. Aja-Fernndez, S., Vegas-Snchez-Ferreroa, G., Martn-Fernndez, M., Alberola-Lpez, C.: Automatic noise estimation in images using local statistics. additive and multiplicative cases. Image and Vision Computing 27, 756–770 (2009)
2. Arici, T., Dikbas, S., Altunbasa, Y.: A histogram modification framework and its application for image contrast enhancement. IEEE Transactions on Image Processing 18, 1921–1935 (2009)
3. Bruna, A., Naccari, F., Gasparini, F., Schettini, R.: Multidomain pixel analysis for illuminant estimation. In: Proc. of SPIE Digital Photography II, vol. 6069, pp. 115–122 (2006)
4. Buades, A., Coll, B., Morel, J.M.: A review of image denoising algorithms, with a new one. Simul. 4, 490–530 (2005)
5. Ciocca, C., Schettini, R.: Multiple image thumbnailing. Proceedings of SPIE Digital Photography VI, vol. 7537, p. 75370S (2010)
6. Frankle, J., McCann, J.: Method and apparatus for lightness imaging. US Patent 4, 384, 386 (1983)
7. Gasparini, F., Corchs, S., Schettini, R.: Low quality image enhancement using visual attention. Optical Engineering letters 46, 040502 (2007)
8. Immerkaer, J.: Fast noise variance estimation. Computer Vision and Image Understanding 64, 300–302 (1996)
9. Itti, L., Koch, C.: A saliency-based search mechanism for overt and covert shifts of visual attention. Vision Research 40, 1489–1506 (2000)
10. Liu, C., Freeman, W., Szeliski, R., Kang, S.B.: Noise estimation from a single image. In: IEEE Computer Society Conference on Computer Vision and Pattern Recognition, 2006, vol. 1, pp. 901–908 (2006)
11. Liu, C., Szeliski, R., Kang, S.B., Zitnick, C.L., Freeman, W.T.: Automatic estimation and removal of noise from a single image. IEEE Transactions on Pattern Analysis and Machine Intelligence 30, 299–314 (2008)
12. Ma, Y., Zhang, H.J.: Contrast-based image attention analysis by using fuzzy growing. In: Proc. of the Eleventh ACM International Conference on Multimedia, pp. 374–381 (2003)
13. Moroney, N.: Local colour correction using non-linear masking. In: IS&T/SID Eighth Color Imaging Conference, pp. 108–111 (2000)
14. Perona, P., Malik, J.: Scale-space and edge detection using anisotropic diffusion. IEEE Trans. on Pattern Analysis and Machine Intelligence 12, 629–639 (1990)

15. Portilla, J., Strela, V., Wainwright, M.J., Simoncelli, E.P.: Image denoising using scale mixtures of Gaussians in the wavelet domain 12, 1338–1351 (2003)
16. Schettini, R., Gasparini, F., Corchs, S., Marini, F., Capra, A., Castorina, A.: A contrast image correction method. Journal of Electronic Imaging 19, 023005 (2010)
17. Stark, A.: Adaptive image contrast enhancement using generalizations of histogram equalization. IEEE Transactions on Image Processing 9, 889–896 (2000)
18. Tai, S., Yang, S.: A fast method for image noise estimation using laplacian operator and adaptive edge detection. In: Communications, Control and Signal Processing ISCCSP, pp. 1077–1081 (2008)
19. Tomasi, C., Manduchi, R.: Bilateral filtering for gray and color images. In: Proc. IEEE Int. Conf. Computer Vision, pp. 839–846 (1998)

On the Application of Structured Sparse Model Selection to JPEG Compressed Images

Giovanni Maria Farinella and Sebastiano Battiato

Image Processing Laboratory,
Dipartimento di Matematica e Informatica,
Università degli Studi di Catania,
Viale A. Doria 6 - 95125 Catania, Italia
{gfarinella,battiato}@dmi.unict.it
http://iplab.dmi.unict.it

Abstract. The representation model that considers an image as a sparse linear combination of few atoms of a predefined or learned dictionary has received considerable attention in recent years. Among the others, the Structured Sparse Model Selection (SSMS) was recently introduced. This model outperforms different state-of-the-art algorithms in a number of imaging tasks (e.g., denoising, deblurring, inpainting). Despite the high denoising performances achieved by SSMS have been demonstrated, the compression issues has been not considered during the evaluation. In this paper we study the performances of SSMS under lossy JPEG compression. Experiments have shown that the SSMS method is able to restore compressed noisy images with a significant margin, both in terms of PSNR and SSIM quality measure, even though the original framework is not tuned for the specific task of compression. Quantitative and qualitative results pointed out that SSMS is able to perform both denoising and compression artifacts reduction (e.g., deblocking), by demonstrating the promise of sparse coding methods in application where different computational engines are combined to generate a signal (e.g., Imaging Generation Pipeline of single sensor devices).

Keywords: Sparse Coding, Inverse Problems, Compression, Denoising, Image Enhancement, Image Restoration.

1 Introduction and Motivations

Many imaging issues require to solve an inverse problem, that is, the problem of estimating an image I from a degraded version J which has been obtained through a non-invertible linear degradation operator U, and further altered by an additive noise w:

$$J = UI + w \tag{1}$$

Typical inverse problems in the context of image enhancement and restoration are *Denoising* (where w is the Gaussian white noise and U is neglected), *Deblurring* (where U is a convolution operator and w is the noise),

R. Schettini, S. Tominaga, and A. Trémeau (Eds.): CCIW 2011, LNCS 6626, pp. 137–151, 2011.
© Springer-Verlag Berlin Heidelberg 2011

Inpainting[1] (where U is a binary mask on the image and w is typically neglected) and *Zooming* (where U is a subsampling operator on a uniform grid and w is typically neglected).

Among the methods used to address the above inverse problems [1–8], sparse coding has been receiving considerable attention as it has shown promising results [9–16]. Sparse coding is a method for modeling signals as sparse linear combinations of dictionary elements [17–19]. The basic assumption of this model is that natural images admit a sparse decomposition in some redundant basis (or so-called dictionary). Each image patch is considered as a discrete array of positive numbers that can be generated by linear combinations of overcomplete bases set, where the natural statistics are captured by the fact that the vector of coefficients is sparse, so that to generate the image patch only few bases contribute. Image enhancement and restoration is performed through estimation of the sparse coefficient vectors, related the overcomplete bases set under consideration, which are useful to approximate the original image patches from the degraded version.

Despite sparse coding have been tested on different image enhancement problems, literature lacks of studies on application of sparse coding in presence of lossy compression or in general when unknown (or partially known) degradation processes have been applied simultaneously. This motivates the study reported in here.

The lossy compression process (i.e., JPEG compression [20]) attempts to eliminate redundant or unnecessary information. High compression factor could badly influence the quality of the final images highlighting undesirable effects. Block-based coding, as in JPEG-compressed images, may produce a number of artifacts which give rise to undesirable visual patterns (e.g., blocking). A large number of approaches have been proposed in literature to reduce the undesirable effects of image compression at post-processing stage [21–23]. Some of them perform a post-filtering in shifted windows of image blocks analyzing the DCT or Wavelet domain during the smoothing procedure. The reduction of compression artifacts at post-processing stage is important to retain the benefits of the compression (for instance, lower transmission and storage costs). The big challenge is to obtain the best results in terms of standard quality measures with the smallest number of visual errors.

In this paper we present the results obtained employing the Structure Sparse Coding Model Selection (SSMS) [16] to restore compressed noisy images. SSMS has been demonstrated to be a powerful tool for different imaging issues (e.g., image denoising, deblurring and inpainting). Here we consider the problem of restoring gray and color images which have been altered by an additive Gaussian noise and further compressed with the lossy compression JPEG algorithm. The underlying ideas, that we start to address in this paper, is related to the fact that in presence of complex or unknown imaging pipelines, where different factors

---

[1] *Demosaicking* can be considered as a special case of the inpainting problem with regular subsampling on a specific uniform grid for each color channel, contaminated by an additive noise due to sensors characteristics.

contribute to the degradation of the original signal (e.g., CFA subsampling, noise, compression, etc.), sparse coding methods could be adopted to restore the original signals.

Experimental results performed on the standard Kodak dataset[2] show that the employed framework makes possible to recover information with a significant margin also in presence of high noise coupled with high compression factor, even though the original framework is not tuned for the specific task of compression. Quantitative and qualitative results pointed out that SSMS is able to perform both denoising and reduction of the blocking artifacts introduced by compression, by demonstrating the promise of sparse coding methods in the context under consideration.

The remainder of the paper is organized as follows: Section 2 introduces the sparse coding concepts, whereas Section 3 presents the SSMS framework for denoising. Section 4 reports the experiments and discusses the results obtained exploiting SSMS to restore compressed noisy images. Section 5 concludes the paper with avenues for further research.

2   Sparse Coding for Image Enhancement and Restoration

Sparse coding has emerged as powerful paradigm to describe signals based on the sparsity and redundancy of their representations [17–19]. For signals of a class $\Gamma \subset \Re^N$, this model suggests the existence of a dictionary $D \in \Re^{N \times K}$ which contains K prototype signals ($|\Gamma| \gg K \geq N$), also referred as atoms. The model assumes that for any signal $I \in \Gamma$ there exists a sparse linear combination of atoms from D that approximates it well. When $K > N$ the dictionary is said to be redundant or overcomplete. The dictionary employed to sparsely represent the signals is usually learned from a dataset [19].

The sparse coding model has been successfully exploited in the contexts of image enhancement and restoration [9–16], where it is considered the state-of-the-art in terms of both quantitative and qualitative results. In these contexts, images are decomposed into overlapping patches $I \in \Gamma$ of size $\sqrt{N} \times \sqrt{N}$. A patch is assumed to be sparsely represented in an overcomplete dictionary $D = \{d_1, \ldots, d_K\} \subset \Gamma$:

$$I = I_\Lambda + e = \sum_{m=1}^{M} a_m d_m^\Lambda + e \tag{2}$$

where $d_m^\Lambda \in \Lambda \subseteq D$, $M = |\Lambda| \leq K$ and the approximation error $\|e\|^2 \ll \|I\|^2$. A sparse approximation $\widetilde{I} = \sum_{m=1}^{M} \widetilde{a}_m d_m^\Lambda$ of I is obtained with a basis pursuit algorithm which minimizing a Lagrangian penalized by a sparse l^1 norm:

$$\widetilde{a} = \arg\min_{a} \|I - \sum_{k=1}^{K} a_k d_k\|^2 + \lambda \|a\|_1. \tag{3}$$

---

[2] The Kodak dataset is available at the http://r0k.us/graphics/kodak/

In a typical inverse problem the aim is to estimate I from a degraded version

$$J = UI + w \qquad (4)$$

which has been obtained through a non-invertible linear degradation operator U, and further altered by an additive noise w. Taking into account the Equation (2) the degraded image J can be written as

$$J = \sum_{m=1}^{M} a_m \, U d_m^{\Lambda} + e', \qquad (5)$$

with $e' = Ue + w$. This means that the degraded image J is well approximated by using the same coefficients a that are useful to sparsely approximate I in Equation (3) together with the transformed dictionary $UD = \{ Ud_1, \ldots, Ud_K \}$. The inverse problem of estimating an approximation of I from the degraded version J is hence solved by replacing the original dictionary D with the transformed one UD in the Equation (3).

3   Structured Sparse Model Selection

The degree of freedom in selecting the few atoms of the dictionary used to approximate I is exponentially large. This fact leads to unstable signal estimation. The Structured Sparse Model Selection (SSMS) put "structure" in sparsity to stabilize the estimation [16]. SSMS is defined with a dictionary D composed by H sub-dictionaries $B^1, \ldots, B^H$, each being an orthogonal basis. An image patch $I \in \Re^N$ is assumed to be well approximated in one of these sub-dictionaries:

$$I = \sum_{m=1}^{M} \langle I, b_m^{h_0} \rangle b_m^{h_0} + e^{h_0}, \qquad (6)$$

where h_0 is the index of the sub-dictionary that best approximate I in Equation (6). The best basis B^{h_0} is selected by maximizing the projection energy on $B^h = \{ b_1^h, b_2^h, \ldots, b_M^h \}$ over all the orthogonal bases $B^h \in D$:

$$h_0 = \arg \min_h \sum_{m=1}^{M} |\langle I, b_m^h \rangle|^2. \qquad (7)$$

In this model the sub-dictionaries are initialized with Principal Component Analysis (PCA) over syntetic edge patterns of size $\sqrt{N} \times \sqrt{N}$. The edge patterns are grouped taking into account various orientations (Figure 1). For each orientation, the PCA over the relative syntetic edge patterns is computed and a basis is obtained. For each basis only the first $\sqrt{N}$ eigenvectors are retained, whereas the others are discarded due their negligible corresponding eigenvalues. The first eigenvector is replaced with the DC component.

Fig. 1. Syntetic edge patterns with orientation 30°

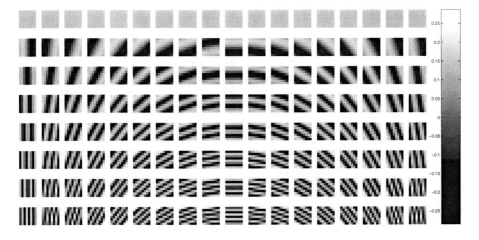

Fig. 2. The dictionary obtained through PCA on syntetic edge patterns grouped taking into account different orientations. Columns correspond to a specific sub-dictionary (one for each orientation). Each basis is composed by eight atoms (rows). The forth column is related the basis obtained considering the syntetic edge patterns in Figure 1.

Figure 2 shows the sub-dictionaries computed on the syntetic edge patterns of size 8×8 and 18 different orientations (from $0°$ to $170°$ with a step of $10°$). The sub-dictionaries are further adapted to the image of interest by applying the PCAs over the image patches, grouped following the model selection. First, the SSMS assign a model h to each image patch, then each basis $\boldsymbol{B}^h$ is adapted to the image by recalculating the PCA with all the image patch that have been assigned to the model h.

In case of denoising task, where images are degraded with Gaussian noise $\boldsymbol{w}$ of variance σ^2, the aim is to estimate $\boldsymbol{I}$ from the degraded patch $\boldsymbol{J} = \boldsymbol{I} + \boldsymbol{w}$. The final patch approximation computed by SSMS model is obtained with a thesholding estimator in the best basis $\boldsymbol{B}^{h_0}$:

$$\widetilde{\boldsymbol{I}} = \sum_{\boldsymbol{b}_m^{h_0} \in \Lambda} \langle \boldsymbol{J}, \boldsymbol{b}_m^{h_0} \rangle \boldsymbol{b}_m^{h_0}. \tag{8}$$

where $\Lambda = \{\boldsymbol{b}_m^{h_0} : |\langle \boldsymbol{J}, \boldsymbol{b}_m^{h_0} \rangle| > T\}$.

4   Experimental Results

Experiments on restoring compressed noisy images have been carried out with the 24 standard benchmark images of the Kodak database. Each test involved an image of the dataset considered in grayscale or color, corrupted with additive Gaussian noise ($\sigma = 5, 10, 20$), and finally compressed (compression quality = $Uncompressed, 100, 75, 50, 25, 15$) through the JPEG Matlab engine. The SSMS was employed with patches of size $N = 8 \times 8$, $H = 18$ sub-dictionary computed by considering syntetic edge patterns at different orientations (from $0°$ to $170°$ with a step of $10°$), size of each sub-dictionary $M = 8$, and threshold as suggested in [16] ($T = 3\sigma$). In practical use, a preliminary noise estimation phase ([25–27]) could help to properly set the threshold T.

The peak signal-to-noise ratio (PSNR) and the structural similarity index (SSIM) [24] are used as performance measure in our quantitative evaluation. The PSNR is considered to assess the quality of reconstruction of the lossy compressed noisy images, whereas SSIM index is useful to assess the quality taking into account the human eye perception.

Table 1 and Table 2 report the quantitative results considering the images in grayscale. For each couple of parameters (σ, compression quality), the reported PSNR and SSIM values are obtained averaging over the PSNR and SSIM results with respect to the 24 images of the Kodak dataset. Experiments point out that SSMS model leads to recover from 0.5545 dB ($\sigma = 5$, compression quality = 15) to 4.9879 dB ($\sigma = 20$, compression quality = $Uncompressed$) in terms of PSNR, with a gain from 0.0235 to 0.4299 in terms of SSIM. Visual inspection of the images reported in Figure 5 and Figure 6 is useful to assess the quality of the results. Note that in addition to the significant margin obtained in terms of PSNR and SSIM, visual results show that the model leads to remove some undesirable artifacts introduced by JPEG compression, even though the framework is not tuned for the specific task of compression.

Table 3 and Table 4 report the quantitative results obtained considering the images in the RGB color space. For each combination of parameters (color channel, compression quality and σ), the PSNR and SSIM values are obtained averaging over the PSNR and SSIM results related the 24 images of the Kodak dataset. The average gain in terms of PSNR and SSIM for each color channel at different σ and compression quality is reported in Figure 3 and Figure 4, whereas in Figure 7 and Figure 8 shown the original images and the restored ones.

Since JPEG compression is performed in YCbCr color domain, we have further tested the performance of SSMS to restore compressed noisy images taking into account that color space (without chromatic subsampling). In Table 5 and Table 6 are reported the results obtained restoring an image belonging to the test dataset under consideration, whereas in Figure 9 is shown a particular of both, the input image and the restored one.

Quantitative and qualitative results confirm that SSMS is able to perform denoising as well as compression artifacts reduction (i.e., deblocking), hence demonstrating the promise of sparse coding methods to restore signals which have been corrupted by different combined non-invertible factors.

Table 1. Quantitative evaluation through PSNR measure on the Kodak dataset considering images in grayscale

Average PSNR Gray Images		σ					
		5		10		20	
		Corrupted	Restored	Corrupted	Restored	Corrupted	Restored
Compression Quality	15	34.0468	34.6012	33.1735	34.4414	30.5417	33.5587
	25	34.8751	35.6358	33.1437	35.1633	30.3355	34.2415
	50	35.7431	37.0212	32.9187	35.9523	29.4379	33.9803
	75	36.4144	38.4877	31.9832	36.5222	29.1156	34.0308
	100	37.1075	40.7517	32.0141	36.9737	29.2979	34.2741
	Uncompressed	37.1645	40.7581	32.0392	36.9838	29.3047	34.2926

Table 2. Quantitative evaluation through SSIM measure on the Kodak dataset considering images in grayscale

Average SSIM Gray Images		σ					
		5		10		20	
		Corrupted	Restored	Corrupted	Restored	Corrupted	Restored
Compression Quality	15	0.8118	0.8352	0.7647	0.8256	0.5407	0.7812
	25	0.8498	0.8749	0.7512	0.8533	0.5687	0.8841
	50	0.8703	0.9098	0.7298	0.8794	0.4190	0.8041
	75	0.8766	0.9326	0.6627	0.8930	0.3779	0.8077
	100	0.8617	0.9526	0.6573	0.9018	0.4022	0.8186
	Uncompressed	0.8630	0.9524	0.6585	0.9017	0.4027	0.8187

Table 3. Quantitative evaluation through PSNR measure on the Kodak dataset considering images in the RGB color space

Average PSNR - Channel R		σ					
		5		10		20	
		Corrupted	Restored	Corrupted	Restored	Corrupted	Restored
Compression Quality	15	32.9902	33.3342	32.7338	33.3179	31.5153	32.8581
	25	34.2075	34.6793	33.6011	34.4384	31.4757	33.4783
	50	35.4551	36.1144	34.0996	35.4205	30.9785	33.7740
	75	36.6877	37.6297	34.0933	36.1304	30.2216	33.9218
	100	39.4043	40.5143	34.1726	36.7819	30.3628	34.0484
	Uncompressed	37.1565	40.6088	32.0294	36.8196	29.2926	34.0492

Average PSNR - Channel G		σ					
		5		10		20	
		Corrupted	Restored	Corrupted	Restored	Corrupted	Restored
Compression Quality	15	33.6942	34.1499	33.3616	34.0998	31.8656	33.4347
	25	34.7088	35.2838	34.0181	34.9745	31.6331	33.7891
	50	36.0809	36.8430	34.4845	35.9155	31.1180	34.0652
	75	37.3821	38.4397	34.4313	36.5933	30.2989	34.1409
	100	39.7078	40.9313	34.1405	36.9259	30.3353	34.1864
	Uncompressed	37.1648	40.6397	32.0526	36.8594	29.3193	34.1325

Average PSNR - Channel B		σ					
		5		10		20	
		Corrupted	Restored	Corrupted	Restored	Corrupted	Restored
Compression Quality	15	32.8844	33.2351	32.7255	33.3686	31.7672	33.3061
	25	33.9941	34.4873	33.5374	34.4881	31.7236	34.0112
	50	35.2433	35.9493	34.0432	35.5168	31.2101	34.3547
	75	36.5143	37.5120	34.1305	36.3551	30.4399	34.5442
	100	39.3584	40.4643	34.3871	37.0467	30.6662	34.6490
	Uncompressed	37.1969	40.6160	32.0970	36.9827	29.3793	34.5623

Table 4. Quantitative evaluation through SSIM measure on the Kodak dataset considering images in the RGB color space

Average SSIM - Channel R		σ					
		5		10		20	
		Corrupted	Restored	Corrupted	Restored	Corrupted	Restored
Compression Quality	15	0.7953	0.8155	0.7835	0.8106	0.6831	0.7757
	25	0.8431	0.8604	0.8119	0.8447	0.6556	0.7943
	50	0.8836	0.9009	0.8194	0.8743	0.6102	0.8085
	75	0.9059	0.9270	0.8059	0.8917	0.5334	0.8148
	100	0.9222	0.9527	0.7828	0.9013	0.5454	0.8173
	Uncompressed	0.8680	0.9528	0.6663	0.9028	0.4097	0.8196

Average SSIM - Channel G		σ					
		5		10		20	
		Corrupted	Restored	Corrupted	Restored	Corrupted	Restored
Compression Quality	15	0.8096	0.8306	0.7974	0.8249	0.6926	0.7859
	25	0.8552	0.8727	0.8228	0.8555	0.6619	0.8010
	50	0.8935	0.9103	0.8273	0.8816	0.6141	0.8126
	75	0.9139	0.9341	0.8117	0.8967	0.5347	0.8166
	100	0.9212	0.9533	0.7759	0.9010	0.5348	0.8172
	Uncompressed	0.8665	0.9523	0.6641	0.9018	0.4089	0.8188

Average SSIM - Channel B		σ					
		5		10		20	
		Corrupted	Restored	Corrupted	Restored	Corrupted	Restored
Compression Quality	15	0.7733	0.7955	0.7614	0.7927	0.6610	0.7622
	25	0.8233	0.8434	0.7916	0.8304	0.6364	0.7828
	50	0.8669	0.8872	0.8022	0.8624	0.5931	0.7966
	75	0.8917	0.9157	0.7907	0.8811	0.5185	0.8014
	100	0.9164	0.9449	0.7761	0.8896	0.5373	0.7992
	Uncompressed	0.8604	0.9458	0.6514	0.8901	0.3949	0.8009

Table 5. Average channels' PSNR obtained by considering the image in the YCbCr color space

Average Channels' PSNR (Kodim04)		σ					
		5		10		20	
		Corrupted	Restored	Corrupted	Restored	Corrupted	Restored
Compression Quality	15	34.1606	34.8368	33.9226	35.0148	32.4425	34.5508
	25	35.6912	36.4566	34.9614	36.2366	32.1483	35.2412
	50	37.2455	38.2577	35.3904	37.5269	31.4054	35.7042
	75	38.4669	39.9343	35.0356	38.2294	30.4014	35.9062
	100	39.7016	42.5318	34.3084	38.9809	30.4972	36.1308

Table 6. Average channels' SSIM obtained by considering the image in the YCbCr color space

Average Channels' SSIM (Kodim04)		σ					
		5		10		20	
		Corrupted	Restored	Corrupted	Restored	Corrupted	Restored
Compression Quality	15	0.8620	0.8897	0.8476	0.8920	0.7175	0.8639
	25	0.8976	0.9198	0.8596	0.9123	0.6586	0.8790
	50	0.9195	0.9426	0.8382	0.9294	0.5883	0.8904
	75	0.9249	0.9557	0.8019	0.9358	0.4937	0.8927
	100	0.9071	0.9681	0.7476	0.9417	0.5007	0.8960

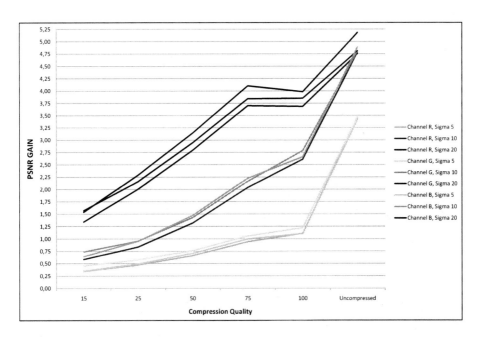

Fig. 3. Average gain in terms of PSNR considering the Kodak dataset in the RGB color space

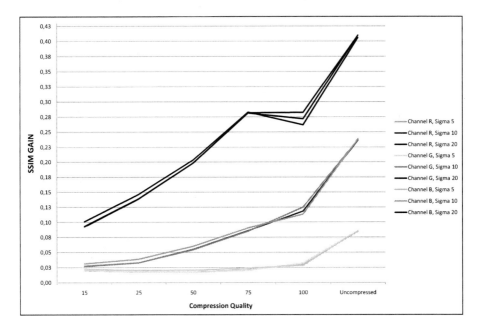

Fig. 4. Average gain in terms of SSIM considering the Kodak dataset in the RGB color space

Fig. 5. Qualitative evaluation on grayscale images. The original image is shown at the top. Images altered by an additive Gaussian noise are shown in the odd columns (from left to right: $\sigma = 10, 20$), whereas even columns correspond to the restored images. Rows are related the compression quality applied to the noisy image (from top to bottom: $75, 50, 25, 15$). The details are better seen by zooming on a computer screen.

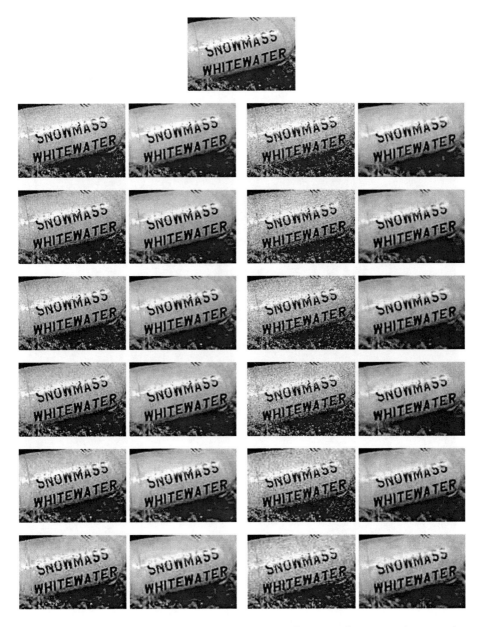

Fig. 6. Qualitative evaluation on grayscale images. The original image is shown at the top. Images altered by an additive Gaussian noise are shown in the odd columns (from left to right: $\sigma = 10, 20$), whereas even columns correspond to the restored images. Rows are related the compression quality applied to the noisy image (from top to bottom: *Uncompressed*, 100, 75, 50, 25, 15). The details are better seen by zooming on a computer screen.

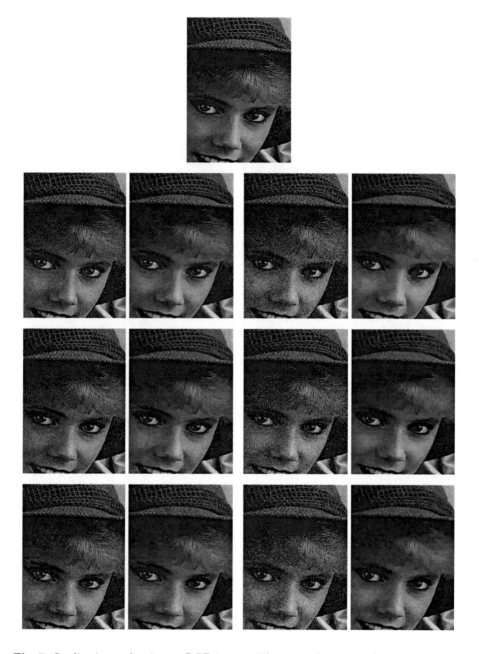

Fig. 7. Qualitative evaluation on RGB images. The original image is shown at the top. Images altered by an additive Gaussian noise are shown in the odd columns (from left to right: $\sigma = 10, 20$), whereas even columns correspond to the restored images. Rows are related the compression quality applied to the noisy image (from top to bottom: $50, 25, 15$). The details are better seen by zooming on a computer screen.

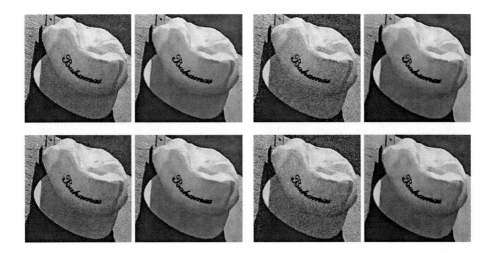

Fig. 8. Qualitative evaluation on RGB images. Images altered by an additive Gaussian noise are shown in the odd columns (from left to right: $\sigma = 10, 20$), whereas even columns correspond to the restored images. Rows are related the compression quality applied to the noisy image (from top to bottom: $50, 25$). The details are better seen by zooming on a computer screen.

Fig. 9. Qualitative evaluation on YCbCr images. Left: corrupted image ($\sigma = 20$, Compression Quality $= 50$). Right: restored image. The details are better seen by zooming on a computer screen.

5   Conclusion and Future Works

Sparse Coding has received considerable attention in recent years as model useful in different imaging problems. In this paper we have considered the problem of restoring information from lossy compressed noisy images by employing the Structured Sparse Model Selection (SSMS) approach. Although the method was not tuned for the specific task of compression, the experiments have shown that it is able to recover significant information obtaining good quantitative and qualitative performances. These preliminary results lead to push our future research in studying sparse coding methods which take into account the compression operator in modeling the representation of the image. Ad-hoc quality measures to assess the deblocking properties [28] should be taken into account in future works.

References

1. Bertalmío, M., Sapiro, G., Caselles, V., Ballester, C.: Image Inpainting. In: SIG-GRAPH (2000)
2. Li, X., Orchard, M.T.: New edge-directed interpolation. IEEE Transactions on Image Processing 10(10), 1521–1527 (2001)
3. Battiato, S., Gallo, G., Stanco, F.: A Locally-Adaptive Zooming Algorithm for Digital Images. Image Vision and Computing Journal 11(20), 805–812 (2002)
4. Buades, A., Coll, B., Morel, J.-M.: A Non-Local Algorithm for Image Denoising. In: IEEE Computer Society Conference on Computer Vision and Pattern Recognition (2005)
5. Buades, A., Coll, B., Morel, J.M.: A review of image denoising algorithms, with a new one. Multiscale Modeling and Simulation 4(2), 490–530 (2006)
6. Battiato, S., Bosco, A., Bruna, A.R., Rizzo, R.: Noise Reduction for CFA Image Sensors Exploiting HVS behavior. Sensors Journal - MDPI Open Access - Special Issue on Integrated High-Performance Imagers 3(9), 1692–1713 (2009)
7. Joshi, N., Zitnick, C.L., Szeliski, R., Kriegman, D.J.: Image deblurring and denoising using color priors. In: Computer Vision and Pattern Recognition (2009)
8. Battiato, S., Guarnera, M., Messina, G., Tomaselli, V.: Recent patents on color demosaicing. Recent Patents on Computer Science 1(2), 194–207 (2008)
9. Aharon, M., Elad, M., Bruckstein, A.: K-SVD: An algorithm for designing overcomplete dictionaries for sparse representation. IEEE Transaction on Signal Processing 54(11), 4311–4322 (2006)
10. Elad, M., Aharon, M.: Image denoising via sparse and redundant representations over learned dictionaries. IEEE Transactions on Image Processing 54(12), 3736–3745 (2006)
11. Mairal, J., Elad, M., Sapiro, G.: Sparse representation for color image restoration. IEEE Transactions on Image Processing 17(1), 53–69 (2008)
12. Mairal, J., Bach, F., Ponce, J., Sapiro, G., Zisserman, A.: Discriminative Learned Dictionaries for Local Image Analysis. In: IEEE International Conference on Computer Vision and Pattern Recognition (2008)
13. Mairal, J., Bach, F., Ponce, J., Sapiro, G., Zisserman, A.: Non-local sparse models for image restoration. In: International Conference on Computer Vision (2009)

14. Lou, Y., Bertozzi, A., Soatto, S.: Direct sparse deblurring. Technical Report, CAM-UCLA (2009)
15. Fadili, M.J., Starck, J.L., Murtagh, F.: Inpainting and zooming using sparse representations. The Computer Journal 52(1) (2009)
16. Yu, G., Sapiro, G., Mallat, S.: Image Modeling and Enhancement via Structured Sparse Model Selection. In: IEEE International Conference on Image Processing (2010)
17. Olshausen, B.A., Field, D.J.: Sparse coding with an overcomplete basis set: A strategy employed by V1? Vision Research 37, 3311–3325 (1997)
18. Olshausen, B.A., Field, D.J.: Sparse Coding of Sensory Inputs. Current Opinion in Neurobiology 14, 481–487 (2004)
19. Mairal, J., Bach, F., Ponce, J., Sapiro, G.: Online dictionary learning for sparse coding. In: International Conference on Machine Learning (2009)
20. Wallace, G.K.: The JPEG still picture compression standard. Communications of the ACM 34(4) (1991)
21. Zhai, G., Zhang, W., Yang, X., Lin, W.: Efficient Image Deblocking Based on Post filtering in Shifted Windows. IEEE Transactions on Circuits and Systems for Video Technology 18(1), 122–126 (2008)
22. Zhai, G., Zhang, W., Yang, X., Lin, W., Xu, Y.: Efficient Deblocking With Co-efficient Regularization, Shape-Adaptive Filtering, and Quantization Constraint. IEEE Transactions on Multimedia 10(5), 735–745 (2008)
23. Kim, J.: Adaptive Blocking Artifact Reduction using Wavelet-Based Block Analysis. IEEE Transactions on Consumer Electronics (55), 2 (2009)
24. Wang, Z., Bovik, A.C., Sheikh, H.R., Simoncelli, E.P.: Image quality assessment: From error visibility to structural similarity. IEEE Transactions on Image Processing 13(4), 600–612 (2004)
25. Foi, A., Trimeche, M., Katkovnik, V., Egiazarian, K.O.: Practical Poissonian-Gaussian Noise Modeling and Fitting for Single-Image Raw- Data. IEEE Transactions on Image Processing 17(10), 1737–1754 (2008)
26. Kim, Y.-H., Lee, J.: Image feature and noise detection based on statistical hypothesis tests and their applications in noise reduction. IEEE Transactions on Consumer Electronics 51(4), 1367–1378 (2005)
27. Bosco, A., Bruna, A., Giacalone, D., Battiato, S., Rizzo R.: Signal-Dependent Raw Image Denoising Using Image Sensor Characterization Via Multiple Acquisitions. In: SPIE Electronic Imaging 2010 - Digital Photography VI (2010)
28. Yim, C., Bovik, A.: Quality Assessment of De-blocked Images. IEEE Transaction on Image Processing 20(1), 88–98 (2011)

Material Classification for Printed Circuit Boards by Kernel Fisher Discriminant Analysis

Takahiko Horiuchi, Yuhei Suzuki, and Shoji Tominaga

Graduate School of Advanced Integration Science, Chiba University, Japan
{horiuchi@faculty,suzukiyuhei@graduate,shoji@faculty}.chiba-u.jp

Abstract. This paper proposes an approach to a reliable material classification for printed circuit boards by kernel Fisher discriminant analysis. The proposed approach uses only three dimensional features of the surface-spectral reflectance reduced from the high-dimensional spectral imaging data for effectively classifying the surface material on each pixel point into several elements such as substrate, metal, resist, footprint, and silk-screen paint. We show that a linear classification of these elements does not work well, because the feature distribution is not well separated in the three dimensional feature space. In this paper, a kernel technique is used to constructs a subspace where the class separability is maximized in a high-dimensional feature space. The performance of the proposed method is compared with the previous algorithms using the high-dimensional spectral data.

Keywords: Material classification, printed circuit board, spectral reflectance, region segmentation, kernel discriminant analysis.

1 Introduction

Automatic visual inspection (AVI) has become crucial to improve quality in printed circuit board (PCB) manufacture. A PCB is one of the most complicated minute objects to understand from the observed image in a variety of industries. The raw PCB, i.e. boards without components, may have defects such as: hairline, pin-hole, wrong size hole, open circuit, and breakout. Many researchers (e.g., see the references in [1]) repeatedly emphasized the importance of developing techniques and algorithms for an automatic inspection system in the electronic industry. Consequently, a wide range of defect detection techniques and algorithms have been reported and implemented in AVI systems [2-6]. Most of them were based on binary or gray-scale images to find board defects. A raw PCB surface layer is composed of various elements, which are a mixture of different materials, and the area of each element is very small. These features make the machine inspection difficult by using binary, gray-scale images, or even by using general color imaging systems based on only three spectral bands of RGB. The segmentation of a PCB image enables us to transform the original problem of inspecting a complex PCB image to a simpler problem of inspecting a well-defined segmented image. The surface of the raw PCB is partitioned into small areas of different materials such as metal, resist, footprint,

R. Schettini, S. Tominaga, and A. Trémeau (Eds.): CCIW 2011, LNCS 6626, pp. 152–164, 2011.

substrate, and print areas. These materials are difficult to be classified accurately based on binary, gray-scale or RGB images.

In order to solve the problems, in our previous works, a material classification algorithm was proposed based on surface-spectral reflectance [7-10]. Those techniques can produce higher classification accuracy comparing with grayscale-based or RGB-based approaches. However, the analysis faces the problem of data storage requirement and high-computation cost, because of high-dimension of spectral data. Dimensional reduction of spectral data is important for improving the high-computation cost.

The present paper proposes an approach to a reliable material classification for PCBs by kernel Fisher discriminant analysis. The proposed approach uses only 3-channel signals of the surface spectral reflectance selected from the high-dimensional spectral imaging data for effectively classifying the surface material on each pixel point into several elements. The performance of our spectral image segmentation algorithm is compared with the previous segmentation algorithms using high-dimensional spectral imaging data. Experimental results from a number of raw PCBs have shown the effectiveness of the developed method for classification of complicated images.

2   Imaging System

2.1   Spectral Camera System

Figure 1 shows the constructed spectral imaging system for capturing raw PCBs. The camera system consists of a monochromatic CCD camera (Retiga 1300) with 12-bit dynamic range and Peltier cooling, a macro lens of C-mount connected directly to the camera, VariSpec™ Liquid Crystal Tunable Filter (LCTF), IR-cut filter and a personal computer. The LCTF is convenient for spectral imaging because the wavelength band can be changed easily and electronically. The LCTF used in this study has the spectral properties of narrow band filtration of 10nm and wavelength range [400-700 nm]. The XY stage helps to easily control the camera system distance and position. The rotating stage controls rotation and position of the measured object. The imaging system automatically captures and saves spectral images with arbitrary number of bands and shutter speeds. The actual measurement time required for capturing one spectral image with size 1280×1024 pixels for the area 35mm×30mm and 31-bands is 4.75 seconds. The viewing direction of the camera is always perpendicular to the board surface as shown in Fig. 1.

2.2   Observation Condition

Suitable lighting and viewing conditions can facilitate inspections, avoiding the needs for complex image processing algorithms. In this study, we use multiple light sources of 300W incandescent lamps. Figure 2 shows the observation geometry with two light sources for effective surface illumination. In order to avoid large fluctuation of pixel values between highlight area and matte area, we control the illumination from two directions [left and right]. The light sources illuminate the same surface alternatively from one of the two directions that are mirrored about the viewing direction. Each light source is carefully set to illuminate the surface of the PCB uniformly. We investigated a proper illumination angle for observing PCB materials. We found that the minimum illumination angle is 20-degrees and this is because of the camera shadow on the board. Decreasing the incident angle to less than 25-degrees makes strong specular highlight on the board especially on metal parts, and increasing this angle to more than 25-degrees makes metal parts more noisy and difficult to classify. The illumination angles were determined empirically as 25-degrees to the surface normal of the board. The viewing direction of the camera was perpendicular to the board surface. The board is placed a few cm apart from the front of the camera system.

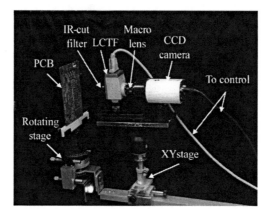

Fig. 1. Imaging system

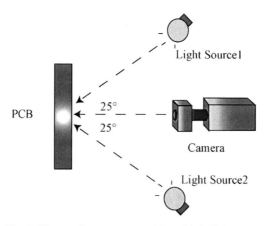

Fig. 2. Observation geometry with multiple light sources

2.3   Reflection Properties of Printed Circuit Board

The observed surface reflection depends not only on the material composition, but also on the geometry of observation. For instance, the metal surface includes strong specular highlight, depending on viewing and lighting angles. Sharp edges of metal flakes and holes produce specular highlight effect on one side and shadowing effect on the other side. In addition, the footprint is a sort of metal composed of solder. This object surface is rough, and gloss appears on the surface at some angles of viewing and lighting. These properties lead to large fluctuation of pixel values between highlight area and matte area. Therefore our acquisition system with different illumination directions is useful for discriminating the surface appearances. Figure 3 illustrates a part of printed circuit board captured by our system and contains the elements of metal, substrate (base material of the board), print (silk-screen print), footprint (gray metallic footprint), and resist (metals coated with photo-resist).

While the camera system dynamic range of 12-bits is adequate for most parts of circuit board surfaces, it is often needed to acquire HDR images for some parts including specular highlights such as metal. Three pictures of the same scene are automatically taken with different shutter speeds (different exposures), and the multiple images are combined into a single image to extend the dynamic range of the camera to 14-bits. Thus we can capture the spectral data of minute printed circuit board objects from the HDR images at different illumination directions.

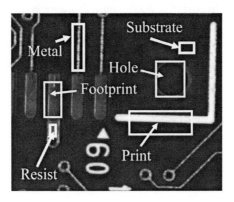

Fig. 3. Partial image of a raw circuit board

2.4   Estimation of Surface-Spectral Reflectance

We use a straightforward way for obtaining reliable estimates of the surface-spectral reflectance function from the camera outputs under narrow band filtration. Let $\lambda_1, \lambda_2, ..., \lambda_p$ be p wavelengths of filtration, usually corresponding to 400, 410,...,700nm, and let $S(\lambda)$ be the surface-spectral reflectance. In our measurement system, $p = 31$ at 10nm interval. The spectral reflectance can be estimated from the sensor outputs O_k as

$$S(\lambda_k) = \frac{O_k}{\int_{400}^{700} E(\lambda) R_k(\lambda) d\lambda}, \quad (k = 1, 2, ..., p) \tag{1}$$

where $E(\lambda)$ is the illuminant spectral-power distribution of an incandescent lamp, and $R_k(\lambda)$ is the k-th sensor spectral sensitivity function. The reflectance image without specular highlight and shadow are needed for material classification of raw circuit boards. That is, a light source illuminates the same surface alternatively from two directions [left and right]. We then unify the spectral reflectance data to produce only one spectral reflectance image from the captured images by the algorithm in Refs. [9-10].

3 Classification Algorithm with Dimensional Reduction

We consider dimension reduction for classification based on Fisher discriminant analysis.

3.1 Fisher Discriminant Analysis

The Fisher linear discriminant analysis (FLDA) is known as effective feature extraction and class discrimination analysis for 2-class or multi-class problem in pattern recognition and data analysis. In the following we first apply Fisher's discriminant to the PCB classification.

Let $\mathbf{s}_i = \{S(\lambda_1), S(\lambda_2), S(\lambda_3)\}_i$ be a three-dimensional surface reflectance vector which is properly sampled from ρ-dimensional estimated reflectance in Eq.(1). A collection of training samples $\{\mathbf{s}_i\}$ is denoted as $\chi = \{\mathbf{s}_1, \mathbf{s}_2, \cdots, \mathbf{s}_n\}$. Suppose that the sample $\mathbf{s}_i$ belong to the l_i-th class, $l_i \in \{1, 2, \cdots, L\}$ and n_l is the number of samples belonging to the l-th class. In this paper, $L=5$ (substrate, metal, resist, footprint, and paint).

Given a three-dimensional surface reflectance vector $\mathbf{s}$, the Fisher's linear discriminant is then obtained by a new feature vector $\mathbf{w} = \mathbf{A}^T \mathbf{s}$ which maximizes

$$J(\mathbf{w}) = \frac{\mathbf{w}^T \Sigma_B \mathbf{w}}{\mathbf{w}^T \Sigma_W \mathbf{w}}, \tag{2}$$

where $\mathbf{A} = [a_{ij}]$ is a coefficient matrix. The matrix Σ_W and Σ_B are the within-class covariance matrix and the between-class covariance matrix of the input feature vectors $\mathbf{s}$, which are computed as

$$\Sigma_W = \sum_{i=1}^{n} \alpha_{l_i} \left(\mathbf{s}_i - \overline{\mathbf{s}}_{l_i}\right)\left(\mathbf{s}_i - \overline{\mathbf{s}}_{l_i}\right)^T, \tag{3}$$

$$\Sigma_B = \sum_{l=1}^{L} \alpha_l \left(\overline{\mathbf{s}}_l - \overline{\mathbf{s}}_T\right)\left(\overline{\mathbf{s}}_l - \overline{\mathbf{s}}_T\right)^T, \tag{4}$$

where $\alpha_l, \bar{s}_l$ and $\bar{s}_T$ denote *a priori* probability of class-*l*, the mean vector of the mapped samples belonging to the class-*l*, and the mean vector of all mapped samples, respectively.

The optimal coefficient matrix **A** is then given by solving the following eigen-equation

$$\Sigma_B \mathbf{A} = \Sigma_W \mathbf{A}\Lambda, \quad \left(\mathbf{A}^T \Sigma_W \mathbf{A} = \mathbf{I}\right), \tag{5}$$

where Λ is a diagonal matrix of eigenvalues and **I** denotes the unit matrix. The *j*-th column of **A** is the eigenvector corresponding to the *j*-th largest eigenvalue. Thus, importance of each element of the new features **w** are evaluated by the corresponding eigenvalues.

We applied FLDA to the PCB classification. However, linear classification did not work well in this case. Figure 4 shows an example of feature distribution when $\lambda_1 = 450$nm, $\lambda_2 = 550$nm and $\lambda_3 = 650$nm. We can find specific characteristics for the average reflectance of each element. For example, λ_1, λ_2 and λ_3 are high reflectance for the print, and λ_2 and λ_3 are high reflectance but λ_1 is low reflectance for the metal. However, those three dimensional features are distributed and mixed by the low reflectance part. Therefore, clearly we cannot classify the overlapped clusters. If we transform the feature distribution into a higher dimensional space, linear classification can be possible. Linear classification in a higher dimensional feature space is developed with low-computational cost by using a kernel trick technique in the next section.

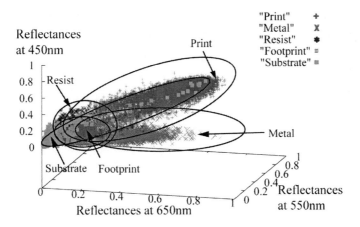

Fig. 4. Feature distribution in three dimensional feature space

3.2   Classification by Kernel Fisher Discriminant Analysis

Let $\phi: \mathbf{s} \in \chi \rightarrow \phi(\mathbf{s}) \in F$ be a nonlinear mapping from the original input space to a higher dimensional feature space F.

The main idea of Kernel Fisher discriminant analysis (KFDA) is to apply the Fisher criterion in the higher dimensional feature space. So the criterion for KFDA algorithm can be given by the new feature vector ψ which maximizes

$$J(\psi) = \frac{\psi^T \Sigma_B^{(K)} \psi}{\psi^T \Sigma_W^{(K)} \psi}, \tag{6}$$

$$\psi \in span\{\phi(s_i), i = 1, \cdots, n\} \subset F, \quad \psi = \sum_{i=1}^{n} a_i \phi(s_i), \tag{7}$$

where a_i is the coefficient for the i-th kernel base. Clearly, if F is very high- or even infinite dimensional, this will be impossible to solve directly. To overcome this limitation, dot-products $(\phi(\omega) \cdot \phi(s))$ of the training patterns are used instead of mapping the data explicitly. As we are then able to compute these dot-products efficiently, we can solve the original problem without ever mapping explicitly to F. This can be achieved Mercer kernels. These kernels $K(\omega, s)$ compute a dot-product in some feature space F, i.e. $K(\omega \cdot s) = (\phi(\omega) \cdot \phi(s))$. Then the Eq.(7) can be written as

$$\psi = \sum_{i=1}^{n} a_i K(\omega_i, s), \tag{8}$$

where a_i is the coefficient vector for the i-th kernel base.

Let $K(s) = (K(\omega_1, s), \cdots, K(\omega_n, s))^T$ be a vector of kernel bases for a feature vector s. Then the Eq.(8) can be written as

$$\psi = A^{(K)^T} K(s), \tag{9}$$

where $A^{(K)^T} = [a_1, \cdots, a_n]$ is the coefficient matrix. As a kernel function, in this paper, an isotropic Gaussian function $K(\omega_i, s) = \exp\left[-\|\omega_i - s\|^2 / 2\sigma^2\right]$ is typically used. The location of the kernel base ω_i is fixed to each of the training samples and the number of kernel n equals to the number of the training samples. Moreover the matrix $\Sigma_W^{(K)}$ and $\Sigma_B^{(K)}$ are the within-class covariance matrix and the between-class covariance matrix of the kernel vectors $K(s)$, which are computed as

$$\Sigma_W^{(K)} = \sum_{i=1}^{n} \alpha_{l_i} \left(K(s_i) - \overline{K(s_{l_i})} \right) \left(K(s_i) - \overline{K(s_{l_i})} \right)^T, \tag{10}$$

$$\Sigma_B^{(K)} = \sum_{l=1}^{L} \alpha_l \left(\overline{K(s_l)} - \overline{K(s_T)} \right) \left(\overline{K(s_l)} - \overline{K(s_T)} \right)^T, \tag{11}$$

where $\overline{K(s_l)}$ and $\overline{K(s_T)}$ denote the mean vector of the mapped samples belonging to the class-l, and the mean vector of all mapped samples, respectively.

The optimal coefficient matrix $\mathbf{A}^{(K)}$ is then given by solving the following eigen-equation

$$\Sigma_B^{(K)}\mathbf{A}^{(K)} = \Sigma_W^{(K)}\mathbf{A}\Lambda, \quad \left(\mathbf{A}^{(K)T}\Sigma_W^{(K)}\mathbf{A}^{(K)} = \mathbf{I}\right). \tag{12}$$

Figure 5 shows two examples of new feature vector ψ and projected features in Fig.4. To show in the figure easily, a binary relation is plotted. By the linear classification in the high-dimensional space, each element can be classified appropriately.

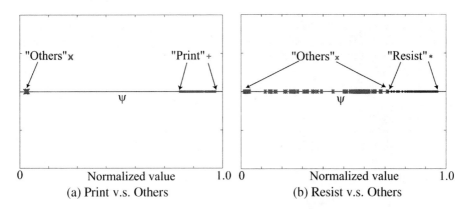

Fig. 5. Projected features on the new feature vector ψ in the high-dimensional space

4 Experiments

We have examined the performance of the proposed method in experiments using real samples of raw PCBs. In our experiments, we used three surface reflectance values at $\lambda_1 = 450nm$ in blue region, $\lambda_2 = 550nm$ in green region, and $\lambda_3 = 650nm$ in red region as three-dimensional features. In our preliminary experiment, we examined various order of the classification such as simultaneous classification (L=5) and serious binary classification (L=2). As a result we selected the binary classification by classifying one by one. Concretely, we classified the PCB elements in order of metal, print, resist, footprint and substrate. As training samples χ for designing classifier, we selected 100 samples from the target element and 100 samples from other elements at random. Therefore, in the present experiment, we set n=200 and L=2 for each classification process. The standard deviations of Gaussian kernel were set σ=0.2 for print and metal, σ=0.4 for footprint and σ=0.8 for resist. The influence of these parameters to the classification result is discussed in Sec. 6.

The scene of a raw circuit board in Fig. 3 was captured with the present spectral imaging system under incandescent lamps. The image size was 1137×867 pixels. Two data sets of surface-spectral reflectances were estimated from the two spectral images at two different light sources. We combined these reflectance images into one reflectance image by comparing the corresponding reflectances at the same pixel point and applying the above rules to all pixels. Fig. 6(a) shows the typical spectral reflectance image obtained for the PCB in Fig. 3. Next, the proposed classification algorithm was executed for the spectral reflectance image. Figure 6(b) shows the classification results by using the three-dimensional data. In the figure, the segmented are painted in different colors, such as white for print, yellow for metal, green for resist-coated metal, black for substrate and grey for footprint. It should be note that the observed PCB image is clearly classified into five material regions and through-holes.

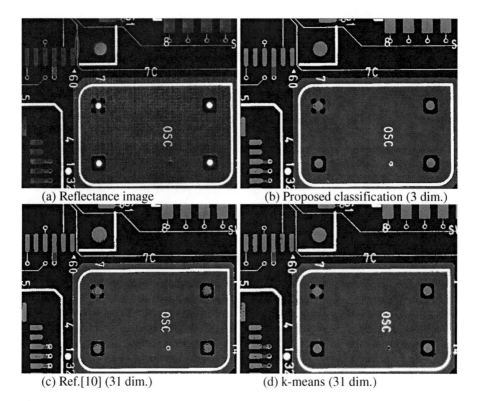

(a) Reflectance image   (b) Proposed classification (3 dim.)

(c) Ref.[10] (31 dim.)   (d) k-means (31 dim.)

Fig. 6. Material classification results for a part of the raw PCB (1137×867)

For comparison with the previous algorithms using high-dimensional spectral features, we choose the normalized cut [10] and the traditional k-means algorithm. Those algorithms do not need training samples, but they require expensive computational cost and memory requirements for large size images. The final segmentation results for all algorithms are summarized in Fig. 6. Figs. 6(c) and (d) show the segmentation results by the normalized cut algorithm and k-means clustering, respectively. We changed the initial seed points for k-means many times but we obtained almost the same result. Figures 7(a)-(d) show close-up images of Figs.6(a)-(d) at a thin metal line in the red-circle region in Fig. 6(a). It is obvious in the close-up view that the proposed method provides better classification even in thin lines than the other methods. Note that a lot of thin metal lines were classified correctly by the proposed method.

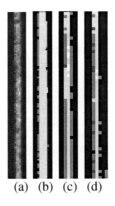

(a) (b) (c) (d)

Fig. 7. Close-up images of a thin metal line of Fig.6

The accuracy of material classification is demonstrated by comparing the classification results with the ground truth of each circuit board. Table 1 lists the accuracy of the algorithms used in comparison. The classification by the respective methods was repeated with different parameter settings. The table shows the best classification results for comparison. The classification quality for the whole regions is calculated numerically using

$$\text{Quality rate} = \frac{\text{Correct classified pixels}}{\text{Total number of pixels}}. \tag{13}$$

As in Table 1, the accuracy of the proposed supervised algorithm with three-dimensional features has almost the same quality as our previous unsupervised algorithm with 31-dimensional features.

Table 1. Comparison of the accuracy for the compared methods

Method	Proposed method	Previous method [10]	31dim. k-means
Quality rate	96.4%	96.3%	93.5%

5 Discussion

The accuracy can depend on the number of training samples, the size of the PCBs, the standard deviation of kernel functions, and the feature selection. By changing these parameters, we have investigated the performance of the proposed algorithm.

5.1 The Number of Samples

Figure 8 shows the relationship between the number of training samples and the quality rate. The training samples were selected at random from the data set, and the same experiment was performed ten times in the number of each sample. The other experimental conditions were the same as Sec. 4. The result shows that high quality rate around 95% can be obtained even by ten samples if the samples are appropriately given. However, the quality rate is greatly influenced with the training sample. The results are unstable when using a small number of training samples. In other words, more than 50 samples are needed for high quality.

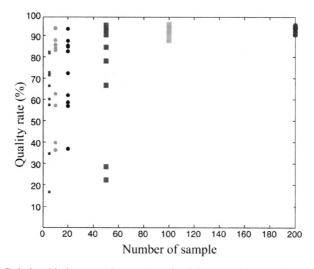

Fig. 8. Relationship between the number of training samples and the quality rate

5.2 Size of PCBs

Figure 9 shows the relationship between the size of PCB and the quality rate. The training samples were selected at random from the data set, and the same experiment was performed ten times in each size. The other experimental conditions were the same as Sec. 4. The result suggests that the quality rate is independent of the size of the PCB.

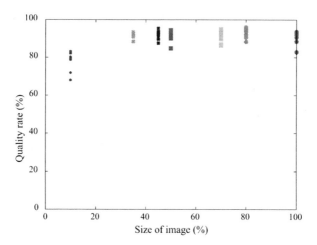

Fig. 9. Relationship between the PCB size and the quality rate

5.3 Standard Deviation of Gaussian Kernel

In a Gaussian kernel function, the standard deviation that corresponds to the kernel width is a parameter related to the generalization ability. Figure 10 shows the relationship between the standard deviation and the quality rate. The number of training samples was 100 samples for each element. The standard deviation σ at $\sigma \in [0, 2]$ gives relatively stable quality rate to each element though metal line slightly changes.

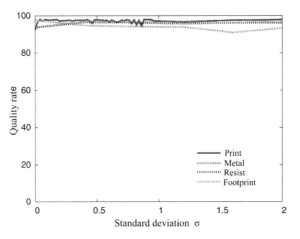

Fig. 10. Relationship between the standard deviation of the Gaussian kernel and the quality rate

5.4 Feature Selection

Table 2 shows change of the quality rate for the three channels selected at different wavelengths. Little change of the quality rate is recognized when selecting the channel in the visible range almost evenly. However, the result suggested that the best wavelength combination is (450nm, 550nm, 650nm).

Table 2. Quality rate for the three channels selected at different wavelengths

λ_1 (nm)	λ_2 (nm)	λ_3 (nm)	Quality rate
430	530	630	92.4%
430	570	670	95.5%
440	530	630	93.3%
450	570	670	93.2%
450	550	650	96.4%
460	530	630	96.4%
470	530	630	95.3%

6 Conclusion

This paper has proposed an approach to a reliable material classification for PCBs by the kernel Fisher discriminant analysis. In this approach, reflectance values at only three different wavelengths reduced from the high-dimensional spectral imaging data were used for effectively classifying the surface material on each pixel point into several elements. We developed a kernel technique which constructs a subspace to maximize the class separability in a high-dimensional feature space. The performance of the proposed method was compared with the previous algorithms using the high-dimensional spectral data. The goodness was shown in experiments, where the classification accuracy was compared with the unsupervised classification algorithms with high-dimensional features. Our algorithm could be applied directly to the material classification problem in a variety of raw PCBs.

Since the proposed algorithm uses only three-spectral channels, a color camera with narrow bands would be used as an imaging device. Selection of the best wavelength bands in the visible range remains as a future problem.

References

1. Moganti, F., Ercal, F., Dagli, C.H., Tsunekawa, S.: Automatic PCB Inspection Algorithms: A Survey. Computer Vision and Image Understanding 63(2), 287–313 (1996)
2. Chang, P.C., Chen, L.Y., Fan, C.Y.: A Case-based Evolutionary Model for Defect Classification of Printed Circuit Board Images. J. Intell. Manuf. 19, 203–214 (2008)
3. Tsai, D.M., Yang, R.H.: An Eigenvalue-based Similarity Measure and Its Application in Defect Detection. Image and Vision Computing 23(12), 1094–1101 (2005)
4. Ibrahim, Z., Al-Attas, S.A.R.: Wavelet-based Printed Circuit Board Inspection Algorithm. Integrated Computer-Aided Engineering 12, 201–213 (2005)
5. Huang, S.Y., Mao, C.W., Cheng, K.S.: Contour-Based Window Extraction Algorithm for Bare Printed Circuit Board Inspection. IEICE Trans. 88-D, 2802–2810 (2005)
6. Leta, F.R., Feliciano, F.F., Martins, F.P.R.: Computer Vision System for Printed Circuit Board Inspection. In: ABCM Symp. Series in Mechatronics, vol. 3, pp. 623–632 (2008)
7. Tominaga, S.: Material Identification via Multi-Spectral Imaging and Its Application to Circuit Boards. In: 10th Color Imaging Conference, Color Science, Systems and Applications, Scottsdale, Arizona, pp. 217–222 (2002)
8. Tominaga, S., Okamoto, S.: Reflectance-Based Material Classification for Printed Circuit Boards. In: 12th Int. Conf. on Image Analysis and Processing, Italy, pp. 238–243 (2003)
9. Ibrahim, A., Tominaga, S., Horiuchi, T.: Material Classification for Printed Circuit Boards by Spectral Imaging System. In: Trémeau, A., Schettini, R., Tominaga, S. (eds.) CCIW 2009. LNCS, vol. 5646, pp. 216–225. Springer, Heidelberg (2009)
10. Ibrahim, A., Tominaga, S., Horiuchi, T.: A Spectral Imaging Method for Material Classification and Inspection of Printed Circuit Boards. Optical Engineering 49(5), 057201-1–057201-10 (2010)

Color Correction: A Novel Weighted Von Kries Model Based on Memory Colors

Alejandro Moreno*, Basura Fernando, Bismillah Kani,
Sajib Saha, and Sezer Karaoglu

Color in Informatics and Media Technology (CIMET)
{alejandro.moreno,sezer.karaoglu,sajib.saha}@hig.no,
{bismillahkani,basuraf}@gmail.com
http://www.master-erasmusmundus-color.eu/

Abstract. In this paper we present an automatic color correction framework based on memory colors. Memory colors for 3 different objects: grass, snow and sky are obtained using psychophysical experiments under different illumination levels and later modeled statistically. While supervised image segmentation method detects memory color objects, a luminance level predictor classifies images as dark, dim or bright. This information along with the best memory color model that fits to the data is used to do the color correction using a novel weighted Von Kries formula. Finally, a visual experiment is conducted to evaluate color corrected images. Experimental results suggest that the proposed weighted von Kries model is an appropriate color correction model for natural images.

Keywords: Color Correction, Memory Color, Von Kries Model, Multi-spectral Images.

1 Introduction

Memory colors can be understood as a phenomenon in which an object's characteristic color influences our perception of its color. According to Fairchild, memory colors can be considered a phenomenon where, in our minds, a particular object has a particular color associated to it. This happens even though the actual color is often different from what we remember [2]. Research shows that memory colors are usually located in a compact area within the chromaticity space [11]; having a narrow range of hue values, even for different people. This conveys that memory colors can be generalized, and although they can change depending on several factors related to culture [4] [12], the fact that people perceive certain objects irremediably associated to particular colors cannot be overlooked.

---

* This work is part of CIMET project contest organized by Nokia Corporation and CIMET. Special thanks to University of Eastern Finland and Gjovik University College, Norway.

R. Schettini, S. Tominaga, and A. Trémeau (Eds.): CCIW 2011, LNCS 6626, pp. 165–175, 2011.

These characteristics of memory color objects have inspired new trends in research to analyze the cognitive effects and cultural dependencies of memory colors, the definition of new memory color categories and ways in which to apply this information in higher level image analysis and processing stages. In [3] memory color has been used for image segmentation and classification. Zhang and Quan use 3 memory color categories to determine different illuminants present in an image by clustering pixels based on memory color information [15]. In [10] Aitao Lu et al. show that memory colors play a key role in early perceptual processes for object recognition.

Kaiqi et al. [13] propose the use of object recognition for automatic color constancy, but their approach requires one or more of the training objects to be present in the analyzed image. The use of visual object categories was also considered in [14], but the estimation method they present is based solely on utilizing the mean color values of the categories without any further analysis in the chromaticity domain. Moreover the evaluation method introduced is rather expensive to compute.

One of the most recent and interesting works based on memory colors was done by Esa Rahtu et al. in [11], where data of memory color objects present in an image was used to shift the color values for automatic color correction. Since most of the work done in color correction is based on low-level image information, the use of high level information such as memory color objects and semantic content of images to perform such task proves to be novel and highly interesting. Nonetheless, it still presents some shortcomings: the model claims to provide visually pleasing images but no psychopshysical experiment was carried out to prove this. Also, the model works for only one memory color object present in each image, thus the presence of several memory color objects forces the model to choose one of them to perform the correction.

This paper solves these 2 shortcomings while addressing some new and interesting questions about memory colors. First, an analysis to find out the difference, if any, of memory colors under different lighting conditions was carried out. Two different experiments were performed, one where users were asked to recall memory colors without any visual aid and another were images were used to provide context information. Second, a novel color correction formula based on a weighted Von Kries model is proposed. The model works for any number of memory color objects present simultaneously in the image. Third, a pioneer approach to collect memory color data by using multispectral images in the psychophysical experiments is used. The paper is structured as follows: The proposed framework is described in section 2; section 3 explains memory color data acquisition process; section 4 describes the proposed color correction model; section 5 illustrates the experimental results and finally the conclusion in section 6.

2   Proposed Framework

The proposed framework is two fold, (1) memory color data acquisition and modeling (2) color correction process. The overall process is represented in Fig. 1 and Fig. 2.

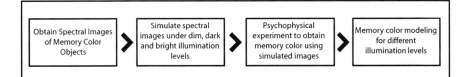

Fig. 1. Memory color data acquisition and modeling process

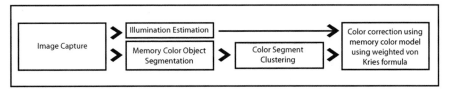

Fig. 2. Color correction process

First, memory color spectral images were captured and simulated for three different illumination levels: dark, dim and bright. Memory color objects were grayed out of the images and shown to 19 observers, whom were asked to vote for the most preferable memory color under a given illumination level for each object (memory colors obtained using images as visual aid will be called preferable memory colors). Afterwards, a second experiment was performed to obtain memory colors based solely on the recall of the subjects. The selected memory color patches were measured in CIE XYZ coordinates using a colorimeter considering the surround illumination. For each memory color object, reported colors were modeled using an ellipsoid in CIELab space for each illumination level.

The color correction process started by estimating the image illumination and segmenting the memory color objects. Knowing the illumination level, finding the most suitable model for a given memory color was possible. The image was segmented into several memory color regions and each memory color was partitioned into two clusters using K-means to reduce intra class variability and discarding outliers. After this, the weighted von Kries color correction model was applied based on the closest memory color for the selected model and the mean of the color cluster. In all the experiments and models sky, grass and snow were used as memory color objects however, the proposed framework and model can be extended to other memory color objects too.

3   Memory Color Data

3.1   Multispectral Image Acquisition

The advantage of using multi-spectral images is that it is possible to simulate the exact same image under known luminance levels and light sources.The spectral images were captured using the Nuance liquid crystal tunable filter (LCTF)

spectral camera (Fig. 3) that works on visible range. The model is Nuance FX. Spectral data with the dynamic of 12 bits was acquired using optimal integration times for each measured channel with the imaging software (Nuance 2.4) and the data was further analyzed with a custom-made MATLAB program. CIEXYZ color coordinates were calculated using 1931 human observer color matching function and the illuminant chosen was 'D65'. The standard reference white was placed in the image area and acquired along with the image which was later used to correct the raw spectral reflectance data. Images were simulated for three luminance levels selected as reflective values of 20%, 50% and 100%.

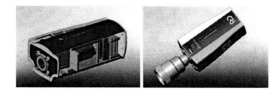

Fig. 3. Nuance liquid crystal tunable filter (LCTF) spectral camera

3.2   Memory Color Experiment

Nineteen observers volunteered for the memory color experiment: 14 males and 5 females; all with normal color vision, as confirmed by the Ishihara test plates screening method [6]. The mean age for all the observers was 24.6 (range 21 to 27). A matte white lighting cabinet with diffuse illumination was used to simulate each of the three different lighting condition levels: bright, dim and dark. Mean luminance levels of 2230 lux, 650 lux and 170 lux were used to simulate each lighting condition. The patches used for color selection were taken from the printed Munsell Chart.

Each observer participated in two short sessions. In the first session users were asked to recall the color of sky, grass and snow under a particular illumination and then select the Munsell patch that most closely resembled the color in his memory. Afterwards, the illumination level was changed and after the user had adapted, he was asked to repeat the procedure. This was done for the three luminance levels and the colors obtained through this method were called memory colors.

In the second session the procedure was the same but instead of recalling the color, the spectral images simulated under different illumination were displayed to the user. In these images, the memory color object was grayed out. The user was asked to select the color he would like to give to the memory color object using the Munsell patches once they had adapted to the different lighting conditions. These colors were called preferable memory colors.

In each session intra observer variability was taken into consideration by showing the color patches in random order 3 times for each observer.

Fig. 4. Memory color visual experiments

3.3 Memory Color Modeling

The obtained memory color data was modeled as ellipses, for each lighting level and memory color object [11]. Instead of representing the memory color in linear RGB space, the use of L*a*b* color space was proposed. L*a*b* color space is device independent and is developed for color difference measurements. Mean vector m and covariance matrix C were calculated for each instance of memory color obtained from visual experiments. Afterwards, the memory color ellipses were modeled using the following equation.

$$r_m^2 = (x - m)^T C^{-1} (x - m).$$

(1)

Here r_m is a parameter of the model. Given a data point x, x will be included in the ellipse, if corresponding r_m value is greater than some threshold.

4 Color Correction Model

4.1 Memory Color Segmentation

The main goal of memory color object detection and segmentation was to assist the color correction based on the memory color objects present in the image. To recognize memory color objects, a simple and fast supervised machine learning approach is proposed in this paper. 38 images which contain sky, grass and snow were collected; 18 of them were used for training and 20 for testing. First, patches that contain sky, grass and snow in the training images were manually labeled. Afterwards all images were transformed into L*a*b* opponent color space and for each pixel a 3D color histogram consisting of eight bins for each channel was computed for a local neighborhood of size 7x7. Afterwards the 512 bin histogram is transformed into 1-D histogram using concatenation. This local color descriptor was used as a feature vector. To reduce the dimensionality PCA was applied on all training samples until 90% of the energy remained in the signal. For training, Random Forest classifier [1] was used with 8 random features and 20 trees. 200000 samples were selected randomly to learn about grass, snow and sky. The test set was also labeled for grass, snow and sky to measure the classification accuracy. A 93% classification rate is reported using Random Forest [1] classifier. The Random Forest classifier is an ensemble classifier consists decision trees and outputs the class that is the mode of the class's output by individual trees. It is a very fast classifier compared to many other classification algorithms.

4.2 Illumination Estimation

The estimation of the lighting condition of an image still poses a series of difficulties. Even if an image is taken in broad daylight, if using only color analysis, dark color and shadows might lead to a misclassification or a bad estimation of the lighting condition. Currently there are algorithms that are able to obtain the lighting information accurately by applying complex and computationally expensive algorithms. In [9], not only the lighting condition of an image is obtained with a high accuracy but also the light sources and positions. Nonetheless, a representative object in the input image needs to be manually outlined to be able to perform the analysis. This and similar approaches while effective cannot be applied in the proposed system since low to mid power devices are targeted and their computation becomes prohibitive. Also, the input images can not undergo any kind of manual preprocessing.

Taking into consideration these restrictions, a more simple yet precise approach had to be considered. In [8] the authors propose a novel algorithm for image enhancement based on a multi-scale wavelet transform and a statistical approach to image representation proposed by Jobson in [7]. The statistical approach provided a simple, fast and effective method to classify the images without modifying them. Jobson states that good visual representation of images converge to some statistical characteristics. Based on this fact, 25 randomly selected images from the internet were analyzed under 3 different lighting conditions, same as the multispectral data analyzed previously: bright, dim and dark. Working with the RGB values would be the most common practice, however this color space has some undesirable properties like correlation between color channels. Hence, the use of the iHLS color space [5] was preferred due to the separation of chromaticity information from lightness information, and its brightness channel independence from the saturation channel. The overall lightness was obtained by taking the mean of the lightness values of the whole image. Afterwards K-Means clustering was performed to obtain the values which were used to classify the input images. Three well defined clusters were obtained, one for each lighting condition as seen in Fig 5. An 89% classification accuracy is obtained for our test set.

4.3 Color Correction

Let us consider a set of memory color objects R. Color correction is done using weighted von Kries [2] model after the image has been segmented into $|R|$ number of memory color regions using supervised segmentation. Weights of each component are determined by two factors. First, the distance to the closest memory

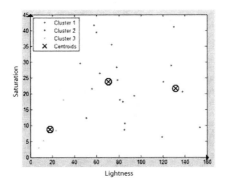

Fig. 5. Lightness clusters for the train images

color in the memory color model. Second, the normalized area of the memory color region in the segmented image. Each memory color segment in the image was represented by one representative p by taking the mean color of memory color segment, or multiple representatives by applying K-means algorithm.

Using the elliptic model x of the memory color object r $(r \in R)$ at the classified lighting level, and the memory color segment representative p in the image, the distance between them is calculated as follows:

$$d_r = minD\left(x, p\right). \tag{2}$$

where D is ΔE or the color difference formula in a given color space. The normalized area of a given memory color segment $r, (r \in R)$ is denoted by A_r $(0 \leq A_r \leq 1)$. The weight factor for a given memory color segment r is defined as follows.

$$w_r = \frac{A_r}{d_r}. \tag{3}$$

The normalized weight factor W_r is defined as follows.

$$W_r = \frac{w_r}{\Sigma_{\forall i \in R} w_i}. \tag{4}$$

Suppose the ith memory color closest vector to the model is represented by m_i and $m_i = [\ m_i^r, m_i^g, m_i^b\ ]$ where rgb is the cone response color space. Suppose in the image the corresponding memory color object representative vector is given by $p_i = [\ p_i^r, p_i^g, p_i^b\ ]$. The color correction for an input pixel having intensity [R,G,B] is corrected to $[R_c, G_c, B_c]$ using the following weighted von Kries formula.

$$R_c = \left(\Sigma_i W_i \frac{p_i^r}{m_i^r}\right) \times R. \tag{5}$$

$$G_c = \left(\Sigma_i W_i \frac{p_i^g}{m_i^g}\right) \times G. \tag{6}$$

$$B_c = \left(\Sigma_i W_i \frac{p_i^b}{m_i^b} \right) \times B. \tag{7}$$

The same color correction can be represented in matrix form as follows.

$$\begin{vmatrix} R_c \\ G_c \\ B_c \end{vmatrix} = \begin{vmatrix} \frac{p_i^r}{m_i^r} & \frac{p_{i+1}^r}{m_{i+1}^r} & \frac{p_{i+2}^r}{m_{i+2}^r} \\ \frac{p_i^g}{m_i^g} & \frac{p_{i+1}^g}{m_{i+1}^g} & \frac{p_{i+2}^g}{m_{i+2}^g} \\ \frac{p_i^b}{m_i^b} & \frac{p_{i+1}^b}{m_{i+1}^b} & \frac{p_{i+2}^b}{m_{i+2}^b} \end{vmatrix} \otimes \begin{vmatrix} W_i \\ W_{i+1} \\ W_{i+2} \end{vmatrix} \odot \begin{vmatrix} R & G & B \end{vmatrix}^T. \tag{8}$$

A better representation of the memory color segments in an image is achieved using multiple representatives through a clustering algorithm to reduce the intra class color variability. The proposed method uses K-means algorithm but it is also possible to use any density based clustering algorithm such as mean-shift or mixture of Gaussians. The experimental results show that two clusters are sufficient to represent accurately memory color segments in an image and to successfully apply color correction. Applying color correction using 2 representatives for the 3 memory color categories result in 8 color corrected images. Visual experiments were carried out to find the best results. Experimental results suggest that memory color varies a lot from one observer to another. Color correction solely based on memory color data may not be the most suitable. Therefore preferable memory colors for grass, sky and snow were collected. These colors were also used in the color correction process using the same framework. In the next section a comparison study of these color correction methods is carried out.

5 Experimental Results

The summary of the experimental results obtained in visual experiments for memory color acquisition is shown in table 1 and table 2. isual experiment to analyze the performance of our algorithm was also carried out. Two color correction datasets were developed: one based on the memory color model and the other based on preferable color model. Each model generated nine color corrected images. Users were shown eight color corrected images along with the original image and were not aware of the presence of the original image. 235 observers participated in the experiment which consisted in choosing the most preferable or pleasing image. When preferable memory color model based correction was used, 23% of the users liked the original image while 77% preferred the color corrected image. On the other hand, 40% preferred the original image when memory color based correction was used. In overall, 30% of the users preferred the original image while 70% preferred the color corrected images.

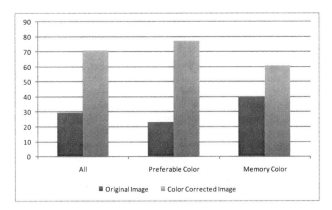

Fig. 6. Acceptability percentage for original image vs. color corrected image. Statistics for models, using preferable color and memory color.

Fig. 7. Sample of online visual experiment. The 8 color corrected images are shown together with the original one. The original image is number 1.

Fig. 8. Differences between some of the proposed color corrected images

Table 1. L*a*b* values of the memory colors without context information

Lighting	Object	Mean			Variance			Max			Min		
		L*	a*	b*	L*	a*	b*	L*	a*	b*	L*	a*	b*
Dark	Grass	73.93	-31.21	45.05	3.03	230.81	208.03	75.74	-6.6	59.89	71.63	-56.39	23.51
	Sky	63.27	-17.63	-8.73	4.91	47.13	96.81	65.38	-10.11	2.77	59.64	-31.94	-23.14
	Snow	67.22	0.18	16.43	0.02	0.04	0.73	67.64	0.53	18.94	67.1	-0.02	15.62
Dim	Grass	73.98	-32.57	44.6	3.33	135.63	233.73	76.08	-10.25	60.22	71.6	-46.52	22.94
	Sky	63.5	-18.36	-8.08	3.09	60.08	59.86	65.2	-9.55	0.9434	59.3	-29.6	-24.25
	Snow	67.27	-0.24	16.7	0.02	0.05	0.64	67.33	0.5	17.09	66.93	-0.19	14.75
Bright	Grass	74.05	-30	47.23	4.7	248.15	297.34	76.17	-5.7	62.24	70.18	-50.6	21.47
	Sky	63.84	-22.16	-7.86	1.55	42.72	22.22	65.55	-12.62	-3.79	61.19	-34.31	-16.53
	Snow	67.61	-1.9	17.68	0.04	0.06	1.19	68.09	-1.67	20.53	67.47	-2.18	17.01

Table 2. L*a*b* values of the prefereable memory colors using images

Lighting	Object	Mean			Variance			Max			Min		
		L*	a*	b*	L*	a*	b*	L*	a*	b*	L*	a*	b*
Dark	Grass	73.2	-30.63	40.08	5.68	229	229	76.17	-1.93	59.89	69.37	-58.85	23.23
	Sky	64.84	-11.14	0.24	2.05	53.76	69.83	66.49	-1.5	11.19	61.56	-21	-15.03
	Snow	67.17	5.33	20.19	-0.03	323.31	195.09	67.64	62.42	64.43	66.93	-0.29	14.75
Dim	Grass	73.4	-26.94	43.08	4.26	183.57	159.43	76.12	-6.32	60	69.36	-59.21	18.28
	Sky	63.92	-11.81	-4.21	3.35	33.35	81.36	66.51	1.27	11.88	59.31	-24.28	-24.25
	Snow	67.31	-2.91	15.82	0.03	116.77	16.4	67.75	0.5	19.63	67.09	-37.22	3.35
Bright	Grass	73.97	-27.03	47.36	3.26	111.47	174.54	76.17	-14.76	63.49	70.91	-52.41	25.26
	Sky	64.21	-17.58	-4.7	2.06	55.76	63.14	67.23	-6.2	13.74	62.18	-31.16	-14.8
	Snow	67.54	-2.01	17.8	0.02	0.06	0.34	67.72	-1.67	18.23	67.47	-2.18	17.01

6   Conclusion

A novel color correction process based on a weighted Von Kries model and a new approach to acquire memory color data by exploiting the advantages of multi-spectral imaging is presented in this paper. Proposed color correction process utilizes multiple memory color objects present in the image to generate pleasing color corrections. The results reveal that 70% of the users preferred the color corrected images. It must be noted that color preferences are very subjective, hence it becomes difficult to propose one type of correction that will suit all observers. Nonetheless, the proposed model is capable of providing pleasant color corrections which suits the majority of the observers.

References

1. Breiman, L.: Random forests. Machine Learning 45, 5–32 (2001), 10.1023/A:1010933404324
2. Fairchild, M.D.: Color Appearance Models, 2nd edn. Wiley-IS&T, UK (2005)
3. Fredembach, C., Estrada, F., Süsstrunk, S.: Memory colour segmentation and classification using class-specific eigenregions. Journal of the Society for Information Display 17, 921–931 (2009)
4. Gage, J.: Color and Culture: Practice and Meaning from Antiquity to Abstraction. Thames & Hudson, UK (1993)
5. Hanbury, A.: A 3D-polar coordinate colour representation well adapted to image analysis. In: Bigun, J., Gustavsson, T. (eds.) SCIA 2003. LNCS, vol. 2749, pp. 804–811. Springer, Heidelberg (2003)
6. Ishihara, S.: Tests for colour blindness (1917)
7. Jobson, D.J., Rahman, Z., Woodell, G.A.: Statistics of visual representation, vol. 4736, pp. 25–35. SPIE, Bellingham (2002)
8. Kaiqi, H., Zhenyang, W., Qiao, W.: Image enhancement based on the statistics of visual representation. Image and Vision Computing 23(1), 51–57 (2005)
9. Lopez-Moreno, J., Hadap, S., Reinhard, E., Gutierrez, D.: Compositing images through light source detection. Computers & Graphics 34(6), 698–707 (2010); Graphics for Serious Games; Computer Graphics in Spain: a Selection of Papers from CEIG 2009; Selected Papers from the SIGGRAPH Asia Education Program
10. Lu, A., Xu, G., Jin, H., Mo, L., Zhang, J., Zhang, J.X.: Electrophysiological evidence for effects of color knowledge in object recognition. Neuroscience Letters 469(3), 405–410 (2010)
11. Rahtu, E., Nikkanen, J., Kannala, J., Lepistö, L., Heikkilä, J.: Applying visual object categorization and memory colors for automatic color constancy. In: Foggia, P., Sansone, C., Vento, M. (eds.) ICIAP 2009. LNCS, vol. 5716, pp. 873–882. Springer, Heidelberg (2009)
12. Roberson, D., Davidoff, J., Davies, I.R.L., Shapiro, L.R.: Color categories: Evidence for the cultural relativity hypothesis. Cognitive Psychology 50, 378–411 (2005)
13. Stepan, O., Jiri, M., Ondrej, C.: On the interaction between object recognition and colour constancy, vol. 45, pp. 5–32. IEEE Computer Society, Los Alamitos (2003)
14. van de Weijer, J., Schmid, C., Verbeek, J.: Using high-level visual information for color constancy. In: IEEE 11th International Conference on Computer Vision, ICCV 2007, pp. 1 –8 (2007)
15. Zhang, H., Quan, S.: Memory color assisted illuminant estimation through pixel clustering, vol. 7537, p. 75370J. SPIE, Bellingham (2010)

Fast Color-Weakness Compensation with Discrimination Threshold Matching

Rika Mochizuki[1,2], Satoshi Oshima[2], and Jinhui Chao[2]

[1] NTT Cyber Solutions Laboratories, 1-1 Hikarinooka, Yokosuka-shi, Kanagawa,
239-0847 Japan
[2] Chuo University, 1-13-27 Kasuga, Bunkyo-ku, Tokyo, 112-8551 Japan

Abstract. We present a method to compensate color-weak vision along the confusion lines, based on matching between discrimination thresholds of the color-weak observer and of color-normals. The compensation and simulation map preserve color-differences of every pair of colors between color-normals and the color-weak observer. We developed an explicit formula for compensation and simulation of color-weak vision in closed form. The method is easy to implement and fast.

1 Introduction

The adaptation of color information for color-weak observers is one of the most important subjects in universal design and barrier-free IT technology. Currently used methods either enhance color contrast between symbols and background or need to define criteria to satisfy certain, often conflicting, visual restrictions. The former approach therefore do not apply to natural images, the latters obtain compensation colors by optimization and the solutions are not unique and difficult to justify. Besides, since these approaches avoid colors which are hard to see for color-weak observers and replace these colors with those easier for them to see, the compensated images could have unnatural color distributions or even artifacts.

There are two major open problems related to compensation of color-weak vision. The first one is that no objective criterion of compensation is available since color perception of an individual is not directly observable or measurable. The second problem is that the degree and characteristics of color-weakness vary widely among individuals and different color stimuli. In order to overcome these difficulties, we proposed earlier a new criterion for color-weakness compensation based on matching between discrimination thresholds of the color-weak observer and of average color-normals. This criterion uses the global theory of Riemann geometry on distance-preserving maps (called isometries) or color-difference-preserving maps. Our target is to compensate such that subjective color differences between every pairs of colors in an image are kept the same for both the color-weak observer and the normal observers.

R. Schettini, S. Tominaga, and A. Trémeau (Eds.): CCIW 2011, LNCS 6626, pp. 176–187, 2011.

The condition in the criterion, taking into account individual characteristics, provides such an isometry between the color spaces of color-normals and described color-weak observer. An implementation of such compensation using local affine transforms is described in [9]. A different approach using geodesic coordinates or Riemann normal coordinates is found in [10] and [11]. These compensation methods need many local computations e.g., linear algebraic computation in the first and solution of ODEs in the second approach. One of the reasons is that it is usually hard to express the compensation color explicitly and in a closed form.

In this paper, by applying this criterion to Brettel's color-blind model, we derive a color-weak map for simulation and compensation of color-weak observers along the confusion lines. This isometry map can be described by a parameter called color-blind index, which is defined as the ratio of lengths of discrimination thresholds between the color-weak observer and average color-normals along the confusion line direction. In particular, we obtain an explicit formula of the color-weak map for the simulation and also its inverse map for compensation in closed forms. Therefore the implementation is straightforward and fast. The proposed methods are evaluated by psychological experiments based on the Semantic Differential (SD) method.

2   Compensation Criterion

2.1   Discrimination Thresholds and Color Spaces as Riemann Spaces

We know that one of the few objectively measurable quantities in color science is the just-noticeable-difference or discrimination thresholds data. Well known examples are the so-called MacAdam ellipses. They define the most important perceptual characteristics of small or local color-differences. At the same time, the discrimination thresholds also provide an excellent representation of individual characteristics for color vision. In fact, these color discrimination thresholds provide the color space with a rich geometric structure which allows us to apply the powerful tools of Riemann geometry.

First of all, the discrimination thresholds provide at every point in a color space a measure of local distance in color space in the following way.

Denote a test color as x and choose it as the origin, for a color vector y in the neighborhood of x with respect to the origin, the discrimination threshold at x can be represented as ellipses(ellipsoids) centered at the test color x:

$$y^T R(x)y = 1. \tag{1}$$

Here the positive definite matrix $R(x)$, varying smoothly with the location of the test color x, is uniquely determined by the ellipses (ellipsoids) and vice versa.

With such a matrix $R(x)$ defined at every x, the local distance around x can be expressed as

$$\| \, dx \, \|^2 = dx^T R(x) dx \qquad (2)$$

Such a space with a smoothly defined local distance or the matrix $R(x)$ is called a Riemann space, and $R(x)$ defines the Riemann metric[6]. In fact, it has been known since Helmholtz that a color space is a Riemann space which is not Euclidean. Understanding the geometry of this Riemann space and its applications has been an important research fields e.g. [5]. If existing researches mainly used local geometry such as metric tensors, our approach tries to explore the global structure of color spaces.

2.2   Color Difference Preserving Map and New Criterion of Compensation

In a Riemann space, the local distance around a point x is defined by the metric $R(x)$, which corresponds to small color difference on a color space. On the other hand, the distance between any two points x_1, x_2 is defined as the length of the shortest curve connecting the two points. The shortest curve between the two points is called the geodesic.

Consider a map f between two color spaces C_1 and C_2. Let $R_1(x)$ and $R_1(y)$ be the Riemann metrics of C_1 at x and of C_2 at y,

$$f : C_1 \longrightarrow C_2; \qquad y = f(x)$$

We wish to preserve the color difference between C_1 and C_2, in particular, the distance between any pair x_1 and x_2 in C_1 should be equal to the distance between their images $y_1 = f(x_1)$ and $y_2 = f(x_2)$ in C_2.

In Riemann geometry, a local color-difference preserving map at every point is called a local isometry. A map preserving large color-differences between any pair of colors is a global isometry. In fact, to obtain a local isometry is easy, one only needs to check that the metric $R_1(x)$ at every point x is mapped to the metric $R_2(y)$ at $y = f(x)$. The global isometry however is hard to deal with, just as large color differences are.

However, it turned out that these two isometries are in fact the same thing. So as soon as one can construct a local isometry, a global one in obtained at the same time.

Assume two color spaces C_1, C_2 describe color-normal observers and a color-weak observer. If we can match the thresholds at every corresponding color pair, such that the small color differences are adjusted to be always the same for every pair, then the large color difference between any corresponding pair of colors is also identical.

Thus, we propose as the criterion of color-weak compensation to transform the color space of the color-weak observer so that it has the same geometry, and therefore the same color differences, as the color space of color-normal observers. The details is given below.

2.3 Discrimination Threshold Matching Condition[9][11]

We define a color-weak map w which transforms the color space C_w of the color-weak observer to C_n of color-normal observers as

$$w : C_w \longrightarrow C_n : \qquad y = w(x)$$

This map is a local isometry or small color difference preserving if the Jacobian D_w of w satisfies the following condition for all x and $y = f(x)$.

$$R_n(y) = D_w^T R_w(x) D_w \tag{3}$$

We also call this equation the threshold matching condition.

Now the compensation map can be defined as the inverse map of the color-weak map w, and its local linear approximation is $(D_w)^{-1}$. Applying w^{-1} to the input color image and showing it to color-weak observers will provide them the same experience as the color-normal observer.

3 Measurement and Estimation of Discrimination Thresholds

The discrimination thresholds of both the color-normal observers and the color-weak observers are measured using a vision-field-splitting display. The observer sees a square area of 14 cm $\times$14 cm from a distance of 80cm by using 10 degrees field of vision. Discrimination threshold data were measured from 45 college students (37 male, 8 female, 2 color-weak observers) in CIEXYZ coordinates.

We choose 10 points uniformly sampled within the gamut of the monitor as test colors, and measured thresholds in 14 directions from each test color in CIEXYZ color space. The step-size of the color variation is randomly chosen from $1 \times 10^{-5} \sim 9 \times 10^{-5}$.

To estimate the equations of ellipsoids from these thresholds, we choose the center of the ellipsoid as the origin to eliminate linear terms. Then the 14 sampling points $\mathbf{x}_i = (x_i, y_i, z_i), i = 1 \cdots 14$ on the surface of the ellipsoid are substituted into the defining equation. The coefficients in the equation are obtained by least squares fitting.

3.1 Measurement Results

The average of thresholds of color-normals and the threshold of the first color-weak observer are shown in Fig.1 and Fig.2. Both ellipses are shown in the u'v' plane Fig.3. It can be observed that the latter is always wider and lie outside of the former, which confirms the reduced sensibility of the color-weak observer. Similar thresholds data of the second color-weak observer are also shown in Fig.4, Fig.5.

The discrimination threshold along the confusion lines of protanopia in xy plane, of the protanopic color-weak observer and average of color-normal observers are shown in Fig.6.

4   Compensation Along Confusion Lines

In the following we apply the method from Section 2 to Brettel's color blind model[1].

This model describes color-blind vision as a projection in LMS space along the L axis for protanopia and the M axis for deuteranopia, those axes are in correspondence to the confusion lines. This model consists of the two planes which are spanned by three invariant hues which are perceived equally by both color-normal and color-blind observers.

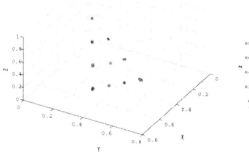

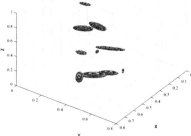

Fig. 1. Threshold ellipsoids of color-normals

Fig. 2. Threshold ellipsoids of the first color-weak

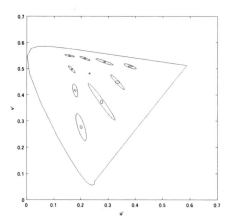

Fig. 3. Ellipses of color-normals and the first color-weak observers on $u'v'$ plane

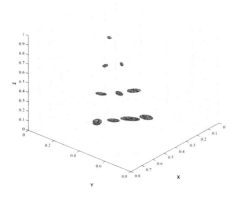

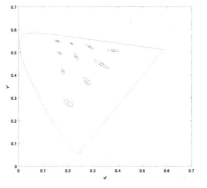

Fig. 4. Threshold ellipsoids of the second color-weak

Fig. 5. Ellipsis of the second color-weak on $u'v'$ plane

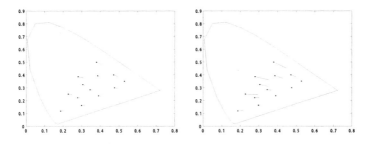

Fig. 6. Thresholds along directions of confusion lines

4.1   Color-Weak Map and Linear Approximation

We first consider a linear color-weak model and compensation shown in Fig.7. It is easy to implement and also serves as an intuitive explanation of the rigorous model shown in section 4.2.

In Fig.7, Q, Q' denote the color stimuli perceived by an average color-normal and the color-blind observer. Q' is the projection of Q onto the color-blind planes, along L axis for protanopia and M axis for deutanopia, corresponding to the confusion lines. Since Q' is determined uniquely from Q, we use the following notations. For a 3D vector R, a scalar R will be used to express position of R on the confusion line passing through it, in term of the distance from Q' to R.

Linear Color-Weak Map. The color-weak map w maps every stimulus Q toward the color blind plane without reaching it. If we assume w is a linear map, the perception of a color-weak observer defined as Q'' will be in the form of

$$Q'' = w(Q) = \omega Q' + (1 - \omega)Q \qquad (0 \leq \omega < 1) \qquad (4)$$

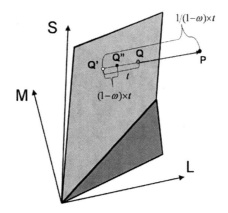

Fig. 7. Linear color-weak model and compensation

Here the parameter w, which indicates the degree of color-weakness, is called the color-weak index. The observer is completely color-blind if $w = 1$ and a color-normal if $w = 0$. Every stimuli Q is mapped along the confusion line to a point Q'' between Q and color-blind stimulus Q', and the distance $Q' - Q$ marked as t in Fig.7 is reduced by a factor of w at the stop position.

$$Q'' = w(Q) = Q + \omega(Q' - Q) \tag{5}$$

On the other hand, Q moved to Q'' the reduced distance $(Q' - Q)$ by a factor $1 - \omega$.

$$Q'' = w(Q) = Q' + (1 - \omega)(Q - Q') \tag{6}$$

Linear Color-Weak Compensation. The color weak map w simulates color-weak vision when applied to the original image. The compensation map is the inverse map w^{-1}, which preprocesses the original image as follows.

$$P = w^{-1}(Q) = Q' + \frac{1}{(1 - \omega)}(Q - Q') \tag{7}$$

Substituting the compensated color P into eq.(4) one can confirm that the color-weak observer actually perceives the same color as color-normals.

Estimation of Color-Weak Index. In order to obtain the color-weak map one needs to estimate the color-weak index ω, which is however not directly observable . In fact, ω can be uniquely determined by the threshold matching condition in section 2.3. First, the Jacobian of color-weak map w is

$$D_w = 1 - \omega \tag{8}$$

Denote the thresholds of color-normal and of the color-weak observer along the confusion line as α_n and α_w. Here the local isometry criterion (3) becomes (9),thus the color-weak index ω can be defined as (10).

$$\alpha_n = (1 - w)\alpha_w \tag{9}$$

$$1 - w := \frac{\alpha_n}{\alpha_w} \tag{10}$$

Notice the statement on linearity of the color-weak map is equivalent to that the color-weak index w is a constant on a confusion line. This assumption could be used in implementation to obtain w by taking the ratio of the mean on each confusion line of the thresholds of color-normals and of the color-weak observer.

4.2   Rigorous Definition of Color-Weak Map

Generally, color-weakness has large variations among different observers and different color stimuli as well. Therefore the color-weak map is not a linear map and w is not a constant (see fig.9). Below we show a rigorous definition of the color-weak map and compensation.

First, the 1D color spaces C_n for color-normals and C_w for the color-weak observer on a confusion line, and the color-weak map w are shown in Fig.8.

According to the threshold matching criterion in the section 2.3, we define the Jacobian of the color-weak map using the color-weak index as follows, here $w(Q)$ is the color-weak index at Q.

$$D_w(Q) = \frac{\alpha_n(Q'')}{\alpha_w(Q)} =: 1 - w(Q) \tag{11}$$

The color-weak map is then defined by the integral of Jacobian in C_w:

$$Q'' = w(Q) = Q' + \int_{Q'}^{Q} (1 - w(x))dx \tag{12}$$

It can be observed to be an extension of (6).

On the other hand, the compensation map can be defined by an integral in C_n, which is an extension of (7).

$$P = w^{-1}(Q) = Q' + \int_{Q'}^{Q} \frac{1}{1 - w(y)}dy \tag{13}$$

In fact, one can obtain an exact correspondence between two color spaces of the color-weak observer and color-normals by using the color-weak map (12) and its inverse map (13).

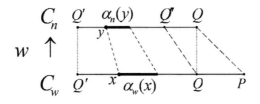

Fig. 8. Rigorous definition of color-weak map

4.3   Implementation

The distribution of the color-weak index ω on the $u'v'$ plane is shown in Fig.9. To obtain the color-weak map and the compensation map from the observed discrimination threshold data, we first define the sampling points $\{x_0, x_1, x_2, ...\}$ on the confusion line in C_w as follows:

$$x_0 = Q', \qquad x_{i+1} = x_i + \alpha_w^{(i)}$$

Here, $\alpha_w^{(i)} := \alpha_w(x_i), i = 1, 2, ...$ are the discrimination thresholds at sampled points $\{x_i\}$.

Similarly, the sampling points $\{y_0, y_1, y_2, ...\}$ on the confusion line of C_n are defined using the discrimination threshold data $\alpha_n^{(j)} := \alpha_n(y_j), j = 1, 2, ...$ as follows:

$$y_0 = Q', \qquad y_{j+1} = y_j + \alpha_n^{(j)}$$

Then under the color-weak map, one has a precise correspondence between x_i and y_j.

$$w(x_k) = Q' + \int_{Q'}^{x_k} (1 - \omega(x))dx = x_0 + \sum_{i=0}^{k-1} \int_{x_i}^{x_{i+1}} (1 - \omega(x))dx$$

$$= y_0 + \sum_{i=0}^{k-1} \alpha_n^{(i)} = y_k$$

Thus $y_k = w(x_k), k = 0, 1, 2, ...$, and the color weak index at the k-th interval ω_k is defined by using the discrimination threshold of color-normals $\alpha_n^{(k)}$ and of the color-weak observer $\alpha_w^{(k)}$.

$$\omega_k := 1 - \frac{\alpha_n^{(k)}}{\alpha_w^{(k)}} \tag{14}$$

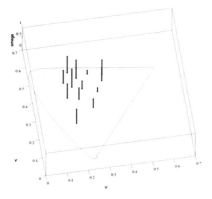

Fig. 9. Distribution of color-weak index

Assume that $x_I \leq Q < x_{I+1}$ in C_w and $y_J \leq Q < y_{J+1}$ in C_n.

Assume that the discrimination threshold $\alpha_w(x), x \in [x_{k-1}, x_k]$ in the k-th interval in C_w is a constant equal to that on the right end of the interval $\alpha_w^{(k)}$ and the discrimination threshold in k-th interval in C_n is a constant equal to $\alpha_n^{(k)}$, then the color-weak map and the compensation map can be realized by a sum of the discrimination thresholds on the confusion line:

$$Q'' = \sum_{i=0}^{I}(1 - \omega_i)(x_{i+1} - x_i) = \sum_{i=0}^{I} \alpha_n^{(i)} \tag{15}$$

$$P = \sum_{j=0}^{J} \frac{1}{1 - \omega_j}(y_{j+1} - y_j) = \sum_{j=0}^{J} \alpha_w^{(j)} \tag{16}$$

5   Simulation

The color-weak map is applied for the natural image in Fig.11, The color-weak simulated image is shown in Fig.10, the compensated image in Fig.12. Fig.13 and Fig.14 show the change of color distributions in the image before/after compensation in u'v' color space for color-weak observer. It can be observed that for the color-weak observer the distributions have been enlarged. In addition, the area of color distribution is enlarged 1.403 times.

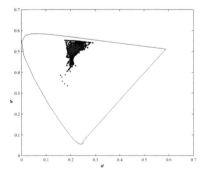
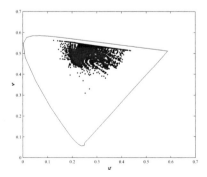

Fig. 10. Simulation   **Fig. 11.** Original image   **Fig. 12.** Compensation

Fig. 13. Color distribution of color-weak simulation image

Fig. 14. Color distribution of compensated image

6   Evaluation

We evaluated the compensated images and color-weak simulation images using the semantic differentiation (SD) test. This method is a standard culture-independent procedure to quantitatively evaluate subjective impressions. The questionnaire about the impression of each image is evaluated using 7 ranks for 8 pairs of opposite adjectives in Fig.15. These 8 pairs of adjectives are selected by another group of 4 color-normals, who are shown 12 images in the SD test and asked their impression in terms of adjectives. The 8 most often mentioned adjective pairs from their answers are chosen as the question adjective pairs in SD test.

Fig.16 shows the original image evaluated by color-normals and the compensated image by the color-weak observer, Fig.17 is the color-weak simulation evaluated by the color-weak observer and the original image evaluated by the color-normal. These comparisons show that the color-weak observer has quite similar impressions from the compensated image as the color-normals from the original image.

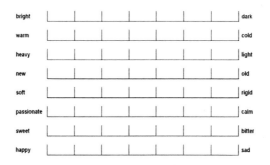

Fig. 15. Questionnaire paper for SD method

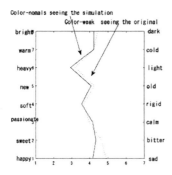
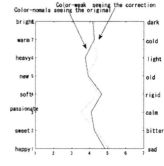

Fig. 16. SD scores before compensation   **Fig. 17.** SD scores after compensation

7 Conclusions

We propose a fast algorithm for color-weak compensation along confusion lines. The compensation is based on the criterion to match discrimination thresholds everywhere between color-normal observers and the color-weak observer. Comparing with previous implementations of compensation with the same criterion, we obtained explicit formulae for color-weak simulation and compensation in a closed form. Hence the new approach is simpler and easier to implement therefore hopefully useful in practice.

Acknowledgement. The authors are grateful to Dr. Reiner Lenz of Linköping Univeristy, Sweden for helpful comments to improve the early version of this paper.

References

1. Brettel, H., Vienot, F., Mollon, J.D.: Computerized simulation of color appearance for dichromats. Journal of Optical Society of America 14(10), 2647–2655 (1997)
2. Ichikawa, M., Tanaka, K., Kondo, S., Hiroshima, K., Ichikawa, K., Tanabe, S., Fukami, K.: Preliminary Study on Color Modification for Still Images to Realize Barrier-Free Color Vision. In: Proc. IEEE International Conference on Systems, Man and Cybernetics, SMC 2004 (2004)
3. Troiano, L., Birtolo, C., Italiane, P.: Adapting Palettes to Color Vision Deficiencies by Genetic Algorithm. In: Proc. 10th Genetic and Evolutionary Computation Conference in CD-ROM (2008)
4. MacAdam, D.L.: Visual sensitivities to color differences in daylight. Journal of Optical Society of America 32(5), 247–274 (1942)
5. Wyszecki, G., Stiles, W.S.: Color Science, 2nd edn. Wiley Classics Library (2000)
6. do Carmo, M.P.: Riemannian Geometry. Birkhauser, Basel (1992)
7. Chao, J., Osugi, I., Suzuki, M.: On definitions and construction of uniform color space. In: Proceedings of CGIV 2004, The Second European Conference on Colour in Graphics, Imaging and Vision, Aachen, Germany, April 5-8, pp. 55–60 (2004)
8. Regan, B.C., Reffin, J.P., Mollon, J.D.: Luminance noise and the rapid determination of discrimination ellipses in colour deficiency. Vision Research 34(10), 1279–1299 (1994)
9. Mochizuki, R., Nakamura, T., Chao, J., Lenz, R.: Color-weak correction by discrimination threshold matching. In: Proceedings of CGIV 2008, 4th European Conference on Color in Graphics, Imaging, and Vision, Terrassa, Spain, June 9-13, pp. 208–213 (2008)
10. Chao, J., Lenz, R., Matsumoto, D., Nakamura, T.: Riemann geometry for color characterization and mapping. In: Proceedings of CGIV 2008, Proceedings of 4th European Conference on Color in Graphics, Imaging, and Vision, June 9-13, pp. 277–282 (2008)
11. Ohshima, S., Mochizuki, R., Chao, J., Lenz, R.: Color reproduction using riemann normal coordinates. In: Trémeau, A., Schettini, R., Tominaga, S. (eds.) CCIW 2009. LNCS, vol. 5646, pp. 140–149. Springer, Heidelberg (2009)

Video-Based Illumination Estimation

Ning Wang[1,2], Brian Funt[2], Congyan Lang[1], and De Xu[1]

[1] School of Computer Science and Infromation Technology,
Beijing Jiaotong University, Beijing, China
[2] School of Computing Science, Simon Fraser University,
8888 University Drive, Burnaby, B.C, Canada
wangauss@gmail.com, funt@sfu.ca

Abstract. One possible solution to estimating the illumination for color constancy and white balance in video sequences would be to apply one of the many existing illumination-estimation algorithms independently to each video frame. However, the frames in a video are generally highly correlated, so we propose a video-based illumination-estimation algorithm that takes advantage of the related information between adjacent frames. The main idea of the method is to cut the video clip into different 'scenes.' Assuming all the frames in one scene are under the same (or similar) illuminant, we combine the information from them to calculate the chromaticity of the scene illumination. The experimental results showed that the proposed method is effective and outperforms the original single-frame methods on which it is based.

Keywords: color constancy, illumination estimation, scene cutting.

1 Introduction

Images recorded by a camera depend on three factors: the physical content of the scene, the illumination incident on the scene, and the sensitivity functions of the camera. The ability of a vision system to remove the effect of the illumination and recognize colors of objects independent of the light source is called color constancy [1]. The difficult problem in obtaining color constancy is to correctly estimate the chromaticity of the scene illumination. Once the scene illumination is determined, it can be used to transform the image so that it appears to be taken under a 'canonical', often white, light source. However, it is an ill-posed problem to determine the illumination chromaticity from the digital counts of an image. So only if additional assumptions are made, can the problem be solved. One such assumption is the Grayworld assumption, namely, that the average reflectance in the scene is achromatic. Under the Grayworld assumption, the illumination color is computed as the average RGB value of the image. The MaxRGB method makes a different assumption, namely, that the maximum digital count from each of the color channels taken separately represents the illumination color. Recent tests of this assumption indicate that it holds quite well [2]. A generalization of these two methods, called Shades of Gray [3], combines them using the Minkowski norm function. Other approaches based on more complex statistics of the image chromaticity distributions

R. Schettini, S. Tominaga, and A. Trémeau (Eds.): CCIW 2011, LNCS 6626, pp. 188–198, 2011.
© Springer-Verlag Berlin Heidelberg 2011

include the neural network approach [4], color by correlation [5], and the Bayesian approach [6]. All these algorithms are based on the zero-order structure of images, which means using the statistical distributions of the original pixel values to estimate the light source color of the image. In contrast, Van de Weijer et al. [7] have introduced a method based on the Grayedge hypothesis that uses higher-order structures (image derivatives) as the basis for illumination estimation.

These algorithms, however, are all designed in the context of still images. Although any one of them could be used on video by applying it on every single frame, no use would be made of the information from nearby frames. Since a video clip contains a series of still images that are related in time and, generally, in scene content as well, we propose a video-based illumination-estimation algorithm that takes advantage of the related information between adjacent frames. The main idea of the method is to cut the video clip into different 'scenes,' and then assuming that all the frames in the scene were taken under the same (or similar) illuminant, we combine the information from them to calculate the chromaticity of the scene illumination. It is reasonable to expect that combining the information across frames might improve performance since it is well known that the accuracy of most illumination-estimation algorithms improves as the number of distinctly colored surfaces increases [8]. Tests described below show that the video-based method is better than the frame-based approaches on which it relies.

The paper is organized as follows. In Section 2, the color image formation process is reviewed. In Section 3, a video-based illumination estimation algorithm is proposed. In Sections 4 and 5, the experimental results and the conclusions are presented.

2   Color Image Formation

The image digital counts, $\mathbf{f} = (R, G, B)^T$, for a Lambertian surface are the integral products of the illumination spectra $e(\lambda)$, the surface reflectance spectra $s(\lambda, \mathbf{x})$ and the camera sensitivity functions $\mathbf{r}(\lambda) = (R(\lambda), G(\lambda), B(\lambda))$,

$$\mathbf{f}(\mathbf{x}) = \int_{\omega} e(\lambda) s(\lambda, \mathbf{x}) \mathbf{r}(\lambda) d\lambda , \tag{1}$$

where $\mathbf{x}$ is the spatial coordinate in the image, λ is the wavelength, and ω is the visible spectrum range. The goal of an illumination-estimation algorithm is to determine the illumination chromaticity (i.e., $r = R / (R + G + B)$, $g = G / (R + G + B)$, and $b = B / (R + G + B)$) from the image values. This, however, is an ill-posed problem that cannot be solved without further assumptions. Grayworld, MaxRGB, Shades of Gray and Grayedge each make somewhat different assumptions, but they are all designed to solve for the illumination using only a single image frame as input. We will refer to them as frame-based (FB) methods. In contrast, we are proposing to use multiple frames from a video stream as input, which will refer to it as a video-based (VB) method.

3 Proposed Method

An overview of the proposed video-based illumination-estimation algorithm is shown
in Fig.1. There are four main steps. First of all, the illumination is estimated for each
frame individually using one of the standard FB algorithms. Then using a scene-
cutting method, the video frames are sorted into different 'scenes.' Under the
assumption that all frames within a single scene are lit by the same (or similar)
illuminant, the information from them is combined to produce an estimate of the
illuminant for the scene as a whole. This estimate is then also assigned to the scene's
individual frames. The details of each step are discussed below.

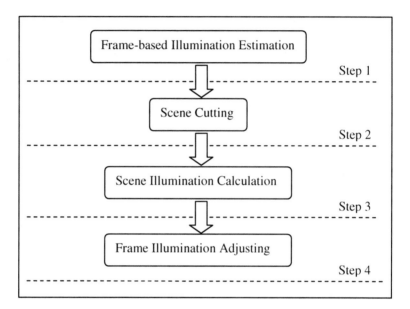

Fig. 1. Overview of video-based illumination estimation. See text for details.

Step 1. Frame-Based Illumination Estimation

For each frame, an FB algorithm is used to estimate its frame illumination color. Five
commonly used FB methods—Grayworld (GW), MaxRGB, Shades of Gray (SoG), 1st
and 2nd order Grayedge (GE)—were tried. These particular methods are simple,
unsupervised, fast, and sufficiently accurate to form a basis for the subsequent VB
estimate. Of course, almost any other FB algorithm could be used instead.

The generalized edge-based framework proposed by van de Weijer et al. [7] is
based on the Minkowski norm of the spatial image derivatives. The rgb color $\mathbf{e}^{n,p,\sigma}$ of
the illumination is estimated as

$$\left(\int_\Omega \left| \frac{\partial^n \mathbf{f}^\sigma(\mathbf{x})}{\partial \mathbf{x}^n} \right|^p d\mathbf{x} \right)^{1/p} = k\mathbf{e}^{n,p,\sigma} , \tag{2}$$

where $n=1$ or 2 indicates the 1st or 2nd order of the spatial derivative of the image; $p \in [1,\infty)$ is the Minkowski norm; σ is the standard deviation of a Gaussian filter; $k \in [0,1]$ is a scaling constant. An FB algorithm based on this equation assumes that the pth Minkowski norm of the derivative of the reflectance in a scene is achromatic. The five FB methods mentioned above can be viewed as special cases of this equation: $e^{0,1,0}$ is Grayworld, $e^{0,\infty,0}$ is MaxRGB, $e^{0,p,0}$ is Shades of Gray, $e^{1,p,\sigma}$ and $e^{2,p,\sigma}$ are the 1st and 2nd order Grayedge algorithms.

Implementation details related to the FB algorithms are as follows. MaxRGB is the new version proposed by Funt et al. [2], which removes clipped pixels and applies a median filter to the image before computing the maxima of the color channels. For Shades of Gray and Grayedge, the choice of parameters is based on the results reported by van de Weijer et al. [7]. For every frame, the frame illumination color **Fe** is computed using equation (2).

Step 2. Scene Cutting

The VB algorithm must determine which frames are under the same (or similar) illuminant as accurately as possible, or in other words, to determine the point at which the scene illumination changes. Ideally, the scene cutting would be based on the true illumination chromaticity, but then, of course, the illumination-estimation problem would have already been solved. Alternatively, the less-than-perfect FB estimate of the illumination in each frame is used to determine when the illumination has changed significantly. Change is measured in terms of the angular difference between the illumination chromaticity estimated for the current frame and the overall scene illumination estimated from the preceding frames. The angular difference θ computed as

$$\theta(t) = \cos^{-1}(\mathbf{Fe}_t \cdot \mathbf{Se}_s) \ , \tag{3}$$

where $\mathbf{Fe}_t$ is the FB estimated illumination chromaticity of frame t and $\mathbf{Se}_s$ is the scene illumination chromaticity calculated from past frames that are contained in scene s. Given an angular threshold θ_{Thres}, if $\theta(t) > \theta_{Thres}$, then $t\text{-}1$ is the end frame of the scene s and t is the first frame of next scene $s+1$. This will be called Angular Difference (AD) cutting.

Clearly, this method of scene cutting will fail when the FB estimate is unreliable. As an alternative, we also considered scene cutting based on measuring the change in scene content from frame to frame. The assumption is that sequential frames with similar content are likely lit by the same illuminant. This is implemented in terms of color histograms [10] with large changes in the histogram between frames used as an indication that the scene has changed. The histograms were defined in RGB color space of size 8x8x8. The difference δ between color histograms is defined in terms of the Bhattacharyya [11] coefficient (a measure of their similarity) as:

$$\delta(t) = 1 - \sum_{x \in X} \sqrt{h_t(x)h_{t+1}(x)} \ , \tag{4}$$

where $h_t(x)$ is the color histogram of frame t, and X is the set of histogram bins. Given a threshold δ_{Thres}, if $\delta(t) > \delta_{Thres}$, then t is the last frame of the scene. This method is called color Histogram Difference (HD) cutting.

Of course, HD-based scene cutting also may fail at times so a third alternative is to combine the AD and HD methods in what will be termed Combined Difference (CD) cutting in the tables below. CD cuts a scene wherever either AD or HD or both would cut it.

Step3. Scene Illumination Calculation

Given a scene cut from a complete video along with the FB illumination estimate for each of its frames, the next step is the calculation of the overall scene illumination from the individual frame illuminations. This is done simply using either the mean or median of the frame estimates. The scene illumination for scene s, $\mathbf{Se}_s$, is calculated therefore either as

$$\mathbf{Se}_s = mean(\{\mathbf{Fe}_t\}_s)/\left|mean(\{\mathbf{Fe}_t\}_s)\right| , \tag{5}$$

or

$$\mathbf{Se}_s = median(\{\mathbf{Fe}_t\}_s)/\left|median(\{\mathbf{Fe}_t\}_s)\right| , \tag{6}$$

where $\{\mathbf{Fe}\}$ is the set of the FB illumination estimates for all frames in the scene, s the index of the scene and t is the index of the frame.

Step 4. Frame Illumination Adjusting

The last step of the VB algorithm is to replace the illumination estimate for each of the scene's frames with the newly calculated scene illumination:

$$\mathbf{Fe}'_t = \mathbf{Se}_s , \tag{7}$$

where $\mathbf{Se}_s$ is the scene illumination of scene s and $\mathbf{Fe}'_t$ is the adjusted frame illumination of frame t. Based on $\mathbf{Fe}'$, all the frames in the video clip could then be color balanced for the canonical illuminant using the von Kries coefficient rule.

4   Testing the Video-Based Illumination-Estimation Method

The video-based scene illumination method described above is tested on the gray-ball dataset presented by Ciurea and Funt [9]. This set contains 11,346 images extracted from about two hours digital video recorded with a Sony VX-2000 digital video camera. For each image, the ground-truth illumination is measured in terms of the RGB values of the pixels on a small gray ball attached in front of the camera (see Fig. 2 for example). The original images are 360x240 but are cropped to 240x240 in order to eliminate the gray ball. The dataset was originally presented as a test set for FB illumination-estimation methods, and as such the frames are at least 1/3 second apart.   Fortunately, the ordering of frames in the dataset corresponds to their original ordering in the video. Hence, sequences of the still frames represent a

3-frame-per-second movie. In addition to having the ground-truth illumination available for every frame, this dataset has the advantage that it has been widely used in testing FB algorithms, thereby making comparison to these algorithms straightforward. The FB algorithms we compared here include the five methods mentioned in Section 3, Grayworld (GW), MaxRGB, Shades of Gray (SoG), and 1st and 2nd order Grayedge (GE).

For a single frame, the angular error between the ground-truth illumination chromaticity $\mathbf{e}_a = (r_a, g_a, b_a)$ and the estimated illumination chromaticity $\mathbf{e}_t = (r_t, g_t, b_t)$ is computed as

$$error = \cos^{-1}(\mathbf{e}_a \cdot \mathbf{e}_t) \ . \tag{8}$$

Note that chromaticities are necessarily unit vectors. For the dataset as a whole, the median, mean, RMS and maximum angular errors computed across all frames is reported as well.

For the VB algorithm, there are three choices of cutting method (AD, HD, or CD) in Step 2, and two choices of combination method (mean versus median) in Step 3. In order to determine the best combination of choices, we first compare the use of mean versus median in Section 4.1, and then incorporate the better one with each of the three scene-cutting methods in Section 4.2. Finally, the performance of the VB algorithm using the optimal set of choices is compared to that of the FB algorithms in Section 4.3.

Fig. 2. Sample 3-frame-per-second image sequences from the 11,346 set [9]

4.1 Comparison of Methods for Combining FB Estimates

To test whether the using the mean or the median is better in terms of combining the estimates across a scene, and also to determine what the best possible result would be given a perfect scene cutting algorithm, we used the ground-truth illumination provided by the gray ball as the basis for scene cutting. For ground-truth illumination cutting, we computed the ground-truth illumination angular differences ϕ between neighboring frames,

$$\phi(i) = \cos^{-1}(\mathbf{T}\mathbf{e}_i \cdot \mathbf{T}\mathbf{e}_{i+1}) \ , \tag{9}$$

where **Te** is the ground-truth illumination and i is the frame index. As with the other cutting methods, given an angular threshold ϕ_{Thres}, if $\phi(i) > \phi_{Thres}$, then i-1 is the end frame of the scene s and i is the first frame of next scene $s+1$. The ground-truth illumination angular differences for all pairs of neighboring frames are shown in Fig. 3 (*left*), and their histogram is shown in Fig. 3 (*right*).

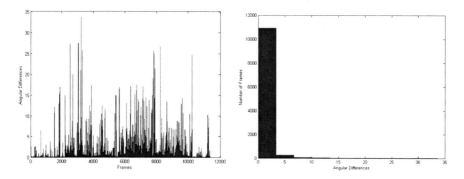

Fig. 3. (*Left*) Angular differences of ground-truth illumination between all pairs of neighboring frames. (*Right*) Corresponding histogram of the angular differences.

From Fig. 3 we can see that most of the angular differences are in the range [0, 5], and therefore select $\phi_{Thres} = 5$ as the threshold. With this value, the 11,346 dataset is divided into about 380 scenes, which is close to what manual cutting produces. The VB algorithm's performance on the 11,346 set is listed in Table 1 as a function of the different FB methods with the FB results combined using either the mean or median. From this table, it is clear that generally the mean is slightly superior to the median as a combination strategy. Therefore, the mean is used in all subsequent tests.

Table 1. Comparison of mean versus median for combining FB estimates tested on the 11,346 dataset

FB Methods	Scene Illumination Calculation Methods	Angular Error			
		Median	Mean	RMS	Max
GW	Mean	**4.57**	**5.96**	**7.46**	**33.26**
	Median	4.74	6.17	7.80	33.75
MaxRGB	Mean	5.06	**6.49**	**8.36**	**24.46**
	Median	**4.99**	6.69	8.62	24.83
SoG	Mean	4.10	**5.06**	**6.19**	**29.66**
	Median	**3.99**	5.13	6.23	29.91
1st GE	Mean	**3.76**	**4.90**	**6.09**	**27.27**
	Median	3.88	4.94	6.12	29.53
2nd GE	Mean	**3.86**	**5.05**	**6.22**	**26.57**
	Median	3.97	5.08	6.22	26.70

4.2 Scene Cutting Methods Comparison

As there are 15 images taken places in the 11346 set, we divided them into two non-overlap subsets, one is for training and the other is for testing. In our experiments, we have 5618 images in the training set and 5728 images in the testing set. The training set is used to find out the optimal threshold values and the testing set is used to test.

The three scene cutting methods (AD, HD, CD) described above were tested in terms of the effect each has on the average VB angular error measure. In order to get the best value for the threshold for AD, we tested the VB algorithm with θ_{Thres} ranging from 0 to 40. The results are shown in Fig. 4 from which an appropriate threshold value for AD for each FB method can be determined. The thresholds chosen are: $\theta_{Thres} = 20$ for Grayworld, $\theta_{Thres} = 8$ for MaxRGB, $\theta_{Thres} = 20$ for Shades of Gray, $\theta_{Thres} = 12$ for 1st and 2nd order Grayedge.

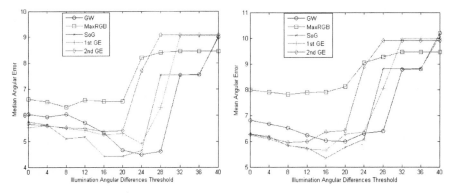

Fig. 4. Angular error as a function of threshold value used by AD for scene cutting tested on the training set. The threshold value is varied from 0 to 40. Threshold=0 corresponds to every frame being a separate scene and therefore equivalent to FB. Left: median angular error. Right: mean angular error.

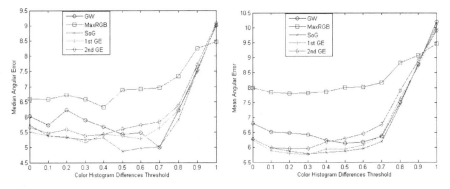

Fig. 5. The relationship between angular error and the threshold of HD on the training set. The threshold value is from 0 to 1. Threshold=1 is equivalent to the corresponding FB method. Left: median angular error. Right: mean angular error.

A similar test was conducted to determine the threshold values for optimal HD scene cutting. VB performance with δ_{Thres} ranging from 0 to 1 was evaluated, and the results are shown in Fig. 5. Based on these plots, the threshold values chosen were: $\delta_{Thres} = 0.6$ for Grayworld, MaxRGB, Shades of Gray and 2nd order Grayedge, and $\delta_{Thres} = 0.5$ for 1st order Grayedge.

Table 2 compares the performance of the VB algorithm as a function of both the scene-cutting and the FB methods being used on the testing set. Although the differences are not large, Table 2 shows that overall CD performs as well or better than either AD or HD applied separately. In the following tests, CD will be used as the scene cutting method.

Table 2. Video-Based performance on the testing dataset as a function of the scene-cutting method (angular difference, histogram difference, combined difference) and the FB (Greyworld, MaxRGB, Shades of Gray, Greyedge) method used

FB Methods	Scene Cutting Methods	Angular Error			
		Median	Mean	RMS	Max
GW	AD: $\theta_{Thres} = 20$	5.30	**6.78**	8.67	36.21
	HD: $\delta_{Thres} = 0.6$	5.33	7.06	9.01	**35.15**
	CD: $\theta_{Thres} = 20, \delta_{Thres} = 0.6$	**5.29**	6.99	**8.65**	35.96
MaxRGB	AD: $\theta_{Thres} = 8$	3.46	**5.43**	7.20	**28.01**
	HD: $\delta_{Thres} = 0.6$	3.66	6.00	7.76	22.62
	CD: $\theta_{Thres} = 8, \delta_{Thres} = 0.6$	**3.43**	5.48	**7.19**	**28.01**
SoG	AD: $\theta_{Thres} = 20$	4.89	5.85	7.08	**27.64**
	HD: $\delta_{Thres} = 0.6$	4.93	5.96	7.40	28.81
	CD: $\theta_{Thres} = 20, \delta_{Thres} = 0.6$	**4.76**	**5.66**	**6.83**	28.81
1st GE	AD: $\theta_{Thres} = 12$	3.80	5.29	6.86	32.09
	HD: $\delta_{Thres} = 0.5$	3.68	5.29	6.61	**27.89**
	CD: $\theta_{Thres} = 12, \delta_{Thres} = 0.5$	**3.66**	**5.23**	**6.55**	32.09
2nd GE	AD: $\theta_{Thres} = 12$	3.61	4.99	6.47	26.39
	HD: $\delta_{Thres} = 0.6$	3.74	5.52	7.03	26.43
	CD: $\theta_{Thres} = 12, \delta_{Thres} = 0.6$	**3.60**	**4.89**	**6.33**	**26.38**

4.3 Comparing to FB Existing Algorithms

Based on the tests in Sections 4.1 and 4.2, the VB algorithm should be based on combining the mean of the FB results across scenes cut using the CD (combine difference method using both inter-frame illumination and color histogram differences). The remaining question is the extent to which VB improves upon the FB result for each of the FB methods. Table 3 compares the results of VB employing each of the 5 FB algorithms. From this table, we can see that when using the VB algorithm for illumination-estimation, all the error measures—median, mean, RMS and maximum—decreased, in some cases by as much as 20%. Table 3 shows that video-based illumination-estimation, which makes use of information from multiple frames within a scene, although simple, is quite effective.

Table 3. Comparison of the VB and FB methods on the 11,346 set

Methods		Angular Error			
		Median	Mean	RMS	Max
GW	FB	6.34	7.36	8.99	43.82
	VB	5.08(-19.9%)	6.24(-15.2%)	7.78(-13.5%)	34.33(-21.7%)
MaxRGB	FB	5.30	6.85	8.78	28.38
	VB	4.86(-8.3%)	6.60(-3.6%)	8.62(-1.8%)	28.01(-1.3%)
SoG	FB	5.33	6.17	7.51	36.04
	VB	4.19(-21.4%)	5.30(-14.1%)	6.50(-13.4%)	28.18(-21.8%)
1st GE	FB	5.12	6.09	7.54	34.14
	VB	4.44(-13.3%)	5.51(-9.5%)	6.87(-8.9%)	32.09(-6.0%)
2nd GE	FB	5.11	5.98	7.33	32.15
	VB	4.11(-19.6%)	5.38(-10.0%)	6.71(-8.5%)	26.78(-16.7%)

5 Conclusion

By utilizing the information available from a contiguous set of frames from a video sequence, video-based estimates of the chromaticity of the scene illumination improved by as much as 20% over estimates based on single frames in isolation. The video-based method simply averages the illumination estimates of the frames taken individually. However, it is crucial to be able to determine when in the video sequence the scene illumination scene has changed such that the subsequent frames should not be included in the average. Scene cutting based on measuring both change in the frame-based illumination estimates and change in scene content quantified in terms of color histograms proved effective.

Acknowledgment

This work is supported by National Nature Science Foundation of China (60803072) and (61033013), and the Natural Sciences and Engineering Research Council of Canada.

References

1. Forsyth, D.A.: A Novel Algorithm for Color Constancy. International Journal of Computer Vision 5(1), 5–36 (1990)
2. Funt, B., Shi, L.: The Rehabilitation of MaxRGB. In: Proc. IS&T Eighteenth Color Imaging Conference, San Antonio (2010)
3. Finlayson, G.D., Trezzi, E.: Shades of gray and colour constancy. In: Color Imaging Conference, IS&T - The Society for Imaging Science and Technology, pp. 37–41 (2004)

4. Cardei, V.C., Funt, B., Barnard, K.: Estimating the scene illumination chromaticity by using a neural network. J. Opt. Soc. Am. A. 19(12), 2374–2386 (2002)
5. Finlayson, G.D., Hordley, S.D., Hubel, P.M.: Color by correlation: A simple, unifying framework for color constancy. IEEE Trans. Pattern Analysis and Machine Intelligence 23(11), 1209–1221 (2001)
6. Brainard, D.H., Longère, P., Delahunt, P.B., Freeman, W.T., Kraft, J.M., Xiao, B.: Bayesian model of human color constancy. Journal of Vision 6, 1267–1281 (2006)
7. van de Weijer, J., Gevers, T., Gijsenij, A.: Edge-based color constancy. IEEE Trans. Image Proc. 16(9), 2207–2214 (2007)
8. Barnard, K., Martin, L., Coath, A., Funt, B.: A comparison of computational color constancy algorithms - part ii: Experiments with image data. IEEE Trans. Image Proc. 11(9), 985–996 (2002)
9. Ciurea. F., Funt, B.: A Large Image Database for Color Constancy Research. In: Proc. Eleventh Color Imaging Conference, pp. 160–164. The Society for Imaging Science and Technology (2003)
10. Swain, M.J., Ballard, D.H.: Color indexing. Int. J. Comput. Vision, 11–32 (1991)
11. Djouadi, A., Snorrason, O., Garber, F.D.: The Quality of Training Sample Estimates of the Bhattacharyya Coefficient. IEEE Trans. Pattern Anal. Mach. Intell., 92–97 (1990)

Effective Color Image Retrieval Based on the Gaussian Mixture Model

Maria Luszczkiewicz-Piatek[1] and Bogdan Smolka[2,*]

[1] University of Lodz, Faculty of Mathematics and Computer Science,
Department of Applied Computer Science, Banacha 22, 90-238 Lodz, Poland
`mluszczkiewicz@math.uni.lodz.pl`
[2] Silesian University of Technology, Department of Automatic Control,
Akademicka 16 Str, 44-100 Gliwice, Poland
`bogdan.smolka@polsl.pl`

Abstract. The main problem addressed in this paper is as follows: a system applying the proposed framework should retrieve all images whose color structure is similar to that of the given query image, independently on the applied lossy coding. We propose an approach based on the color histogram approximation using the Gaussian Mixture Model. The proposed method incorporates the information on the spatial distribution of the color image pixels utilizing the bilateral filtering scheme. The retrieval results were evaluated on large databases of natural color images and the usefulness of the proposed technique was compared with some commonly known retrieval methods operating on color histograms.

Keywords: color image retrieval, lossy compression, Gaussian mixture.

1 Introduction

Over the recent years, many spectacular technological achievements have revolutionized the way information is acquired and handled. Nowadays, more than ever, there is an exponentially growing number of images being captured, stored and made available on the Internet. However, managing this huge amount of visual information for retrieval purposes, especially when a very specific retrieval criterion is set, still remains a challenging task and therefore there are many attempts to address it [1, 2].

Spatial organization of colors has been recently explored in form of spatial statistics between color pixels, such correlograms or some filter responses [3, 4, 5, 6]. Related approaches use points of interest similarly to classic object recognition methods [7] and many other retrieval methods rely on segmentation as a basis for image indexing [8,9,10,11]. Mutual arrangements of regions in images are also the basis of the retrieval, however the representation of the relationship can be non-symbolic [12].

The idea of parametric color image description is used in many image analysis solutions. Although several proposed image retrieval techniques utilize the *Gaussian Mixture Model* (GMM) [13, 14] as color distribution descriptor [15, 16], the aspect of the distortions caused by the lossy compression was not taken into account. These methods simply index all images in the database by fitting GMM to the data, according to some predefined rules.

---

* Corresponding author.

R. Schettini, S. Tominaga, and A. Trémeau (Eds.): CCIW 2011, LNCS 6626, pp. 199–213, 2011.

The lossy compression significantly corrupts the color distribution of an image and a lack of the application of any refinement techniques may lead to the high rate of false negative results, as images stored in lossy formats are considered as dissimilar on the basis of their corrupted color palette. The solutions proposed in this work aim to to overcome these difficulties through the modifications of the GMM procedure [17, 18, 19, 20, 21]. In details, in the proposed method the GMM is used as a descriptor of the image color distribution. Its advantage is that it overcomes the problems connected with high dimensionality of standard color histograms. However, the very important aspect is the fact that the proposed method, based on weighted two-dimensional Gaussians is robust to distortions introduced by lossy compression techniques and therefore it can be used for the retrieval of images contained in the Web based databases, which very often store images in lossy compression formats, like JPG.

The second group of issues analyzed in this paper is related to the important problem of the construction of a histogram sensitive to the color image composition. The drawback of various kinds of standard color histograms is that they do not take into account the spatial image structure, which is crucial in many applications such as object recognition and image categorization. Moreover, the proposed solution can be useful in retrieving images of the same content but differently arranged within the image as a result of the changes in image scene between capture moments. Therefore, images with the same color proportions, but with different color arrangements, have the same chromaticity histogram. Thus, the goal is to take into account the spatial arrangement of the image pixels. Therefore, we propose to use the weighting coefficients provided by the *Bilateral Filter* (BF) [22, 23], which considers the chromatic and topological similarity of neighboring image pixels.

The paper is organized as follows. The details of the new technique are described in Section 2. Section 3 presents the experimental setup of the retrieval, based on the proposed solution. The comparison of the experimental results for various compression schemes is also presented. In this section we also focus on the spatial arrangement of the color pixels within the scene depicted in the image. The comparison with other methods operating on color histograms is presented in Section 4. Finally, Section 5 concludes the concepts and results presented in this paper.

2   Gaussian Mixture Modeling

The first and very important decision concerning the color image data modeling is the choice of the color space suitable for the retrieval experiments [24]. In this paper we are using mainly the normalized rgb space (independent on the color intensity) and the results were also evaluated for the CIE Lab color space [25].

The first step in applying the proposed methodology is to construct the histogram $H(x, y)$ in the rg chromaticity space defined as $H(x, y) = N^{-1} \sharp \{r_{i,j} = x, g_{i,j} = y\}$, where $H(x, y)$ denotes a specified bin of a two-dimensional histogram with r component equal to x and g component equal to y, the symbol $\sharp$ denotes the number of samples in a bin and N is the number of color image pixels.

The next stage of the presented technique is the modeling of the color histogram using the Gaussian Mixture Models (GMM) and utilizing the Expectation-Maximization (EM) algorithm for the model parameters estimation as described in details in [13, 26].

The input data are realizations of a variable X, which are the (r, g) or (a, b) pairs (referring to rgb or CIE Lab) of the color image pixels: $X = (x_{1,1}, ..., x_{n_1,n_2})$, where n_1, n_2 denote image sizes. The probability density function $p(X|\Theta)$ of color data is governed by a set of parameters Θ. The GMM parameters are the mean and covariance matrix for each Gaussian function. We assume that the data items are independent and identically distributed and the resulting distribution density p of the data samples is $p(X|\Theta) = \prod_{i=1}^{N} p(x_i|\Theta) = \mathcal{L}(\Theta|X)$. The function $\mathcal{L}(\Theta|X)$ is a likelihood function or likelihood of the parameters given the data. The goal of the estimation procedure is to find Θ^* which maximizes $\mathcal{L}$: $\Theta^* = \arg\max_\Theta \mathcal{L}(\Theta|X)$. Usually we maximize $\log \mathcal{L}(\Theta|\mathcal{X})$ as it is analytically more convenient.

Let us assume the following probabilistic model:

$$p(x|\Theta) = \sum_{m=1}^{M} \alpha_m p_m(x|\theta_m), \tag{1}$$

which is composed of M components and its parameters are defined as:
$\Theta = (\alpha_1, \ldots \alpha_M, \theta_1, \ldots, \theta_M)$, with $\sum_{m=1}^{M} \alpha_m = 1$. Moreover, each p_m is a function of the probability density function which is parameterized by θ_m. Thus, the analyzed model consists of M components with M weighting coefficients α_m.

Finally after derivations shown in [26] the model parameters are defined as:

$$\alpha_m^{k+1} = N^{-1} \sum_{i=1}^{N} p(m|x_i, \Theta^k), \quad \mu_m^{k+1} = \frac{\sum_{i=1}^{N} x_i \cdot p(m|x_i, \Theta^k)}{\sum_{i=1}^{N} p(m|x_i, \Theta^k)}, \tag{2}$$

$$\upsilon_m^{k+1} = \frac{\sum_{i=1}^{N} p(m|x_i, \Theta^k)(x_i - \mu_m^{k+1})(x_i - \mu_m^{k+1})^T}{\sum_{i=1}^{N} p(m|x_i, \Theta^k)}, \tag{3}$$

where μ and υ denote the mean and variance, m is the index of the model component and k is the iteration number. The E (Expectation) and M (Maximization) steps are performed simultaneously, according to (2) and (3) and in each iteration, as the input data we use parameters obtained in the previous one.

The main idea of the application of the GMM technique lies in the highly desirable properties of this approach. The inherent feature of the GMM enables to approximate the distorted color histogram of the color image subjected to lossy compression. The analyzed test image shown in Fig.1 a, was compressed to 15% of it's file size using JPG method. The lossy compression causes a loss of color information resulting in discontinuities in the chromaticity histogram (Figs. 1c and 1d). The proposed methodology counteracts this effect by smoothing the histogram in order to reconstruct its original shape (Figs. 1e-h), which is a basis for the effective image retrieval.

In the classical approach to the construction of the chromaticity histograms, the spatial arrangement of the color pixels in an image is not considered, and therefore e.g. two images of distinctly different content, but the same color palette, are recognized as very similar and related to the same query. This is illustrated by an example in Fig. 2. Each of the query images is composed of the same number of colors in the same proportions, but these colors are arranged in different spatial structures and each of these images has exactly the same chromaticity histogram. The perceptual difference perceived by

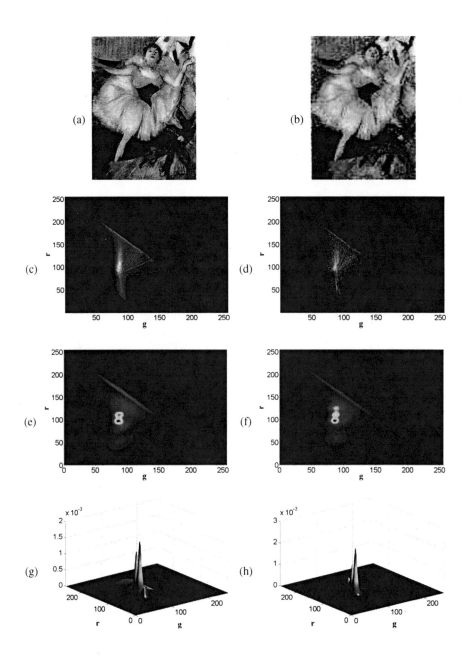

Fig. 1. Comparison of test rg histograms and their GMM models for an original image (a) and its JPG version (b). The second row (c, d) shows the rg histograms and the third row depicts the 2D visualizations of GMM of original image (e) and its JPG version (f). The bottom row presents the 3D visualizations of the GMM for analyzed images (g, h).

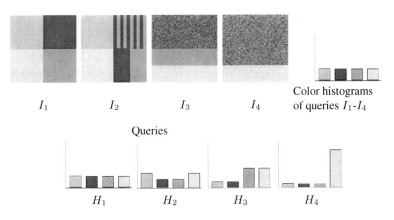

I_1 I_2 I_3 I_4

Color histograms
of queries I_1-I_4

Queries

H_1 H_2 H_3 H_4

Desired chromaticity histograms

Fig. 2. The color histogram evaluated without taking into account the spatial arrangement of the colors contained in the query image does not allow to discriminate between images of various color arrangements (upper row). The desired histogram construction should reflect the spatial arrangement of the colors contained in the images (lower row).

an observer is not reflected by their common color histogram. To describe these differences, the procedure of color histogram construction must be modified to report more accurately the differences between these images.

Thus, in order to reflect the differences in image content and also to improve the retrieval efficiency of the proposed retrieval scheme the concept of *Bilateral Filtering* (BF) [22, 23], was incorporated. Its use provides a possibility to emphasize in the rg color histogram all the pixels belonging to homogenous color areas. In general, its construction reflects two factors related with topological *closeness* and color *similarity* of image pixels.

Using the concept of BF, each pixel of the original image is taken into the rg histogram with the weight evaluated on the basis of the closeness to its neighbors and their color similarity. Thus, chromaticity histogram is in fact a histogram of weights associated to color pixels. Each bin value is the sum of the weights of the pixels of the particular $r - g$ or $a - b$ values.

In details, the weights assigned to the pixel at position (x, y) are computed according to the following scheme:

$$w_{x,y} = \frac{1}{n} \sum_{(i,j) \in W} \exp\left(-\frac{\| \, c_{x,y} - c_{i,j} \, \|}{h}\right)^{k_1} \cdot \exp\left(-\frac{d_{i,j}}{\delta}\right)^{k_2}, \qquad (4)$$

where $c_{i,j}$ and $c_{x,y}$ denote the color pixels at positions (i, j) and (x, y) respectively, h is the color difference scaling parameter, $d_{i,j}$ is the Euclidean distance between the pixel at position (i, j) and (x, y), which is the center of the filtering window W and δ is a spatial normalizing parameter equal to the diameter of the square filtering window. The number of pixels n in W was set to be equal to 10% of the total number of pixels in the image and we assumed $k_1 = k_2$.

2.1 Initial Conditions of the GMM

conditions on the basis of the clustering algorithms such as the *k-means* method [14]. Other approaches specify the starting values and randomly divide data to M classes and assign them to M groups corresponding to M model components. In practice, it is equivalent to the randomly generated set of integers from the range $(1, M)$ corresponding to each of the observation x_i.

The proposed variation of a random start, suitable for the presented methodology, comprises the random generation of independent mean values $\mu_i^{(0)}$ derived from normal distribution, denoted as G: $\mu_1^{(0)}, \dots, \mu_m^{(0)}$, $G(\bar{x}, \Sigma)$, where $\bar{x}$ is the mean of the analyzed samples of the data and Σ is the sample covariance matrix.

For the purposes of the histogram comparisons, several distance measures were used (denoted as d) and computed between the histogram of the evaluated image (denoted as H) and the 2D surface generated by the GMM model of its histogram, (denoted as C):

- L_1D : $d(H, C) = \sum_{i=1}^{\eta} \sum_{j=1}^{\eta} |H_{i,j} - C_{i,j}|,$

- L_2D : $d(H, C) = \left(\sum_{i=1}^{\eta} \sum_{j=1}^{\eta} |H_{i,j} - C_{i,j}|^2 \right)^{\frac{1}{2}},$

- Bhattacharyya Distance, (BD): $d(H, C) = \sum_{i=1}^{\eta} \sum_{j=1}^{\eta} \sqrt{H_{i,j} \cdot C_{i,j}}$

Extensive experiments lead to the conclusion that 7 components are sufficient to approximate the structure of a color histogram of lossy compressed images, and thus this number of components is adequate to reconstruct the original histogram structure with no prior knowledge about its construction. Figure 3a illustrates the exemplary modeling of lossy compressed images. It can be noticed that the increase of model complexity does not result in significant fitness improvement of the data derived from the model to uncorrupted data.

Additional experiments were conducted in order to estimate the number of necessary iterations of the EM algorithm. For each histogram structure 31 experiments were evaluated, for 7 model components, setting various starting conditions of the algorithm. The coefficients α were assigned randomly and drawn from uniform probability density function.

The obtained results (see Fig. 3b) lead to the conclusion that small number of iterations, such as 75, (in some cases even 50) are fairly enough to reflect the histogram structure independently on the used compression scheme. The further increase of the number of iterations will not significantly ameliorate the fitness of the data derived from the model to original color information.

For validating the accuracy of the modeling, the original test images were subjected to various compression techniques, such as JPG and JPG2000, and modeled using the GMM of 7 components with 75 iterations of the EM algorithm. For each of the images, fitting was done for 31 random initial values. The evaluated results in the form of the box plots are shown in Fig 3c. It can be noticed that the obtained results are in general comparable for all tested compression schemes.

3   Experimental Setup for GMM Based Image Retrieval

The experiments were performed in the following manner. The GMM parameters associated with all of the images in the chosen database were computed and saved in advance, so that only a similarity matrix is used for retrieving the most similar answers to the given query among all the candidate images in the database. The estimation of the GMM was done for 7 components with 75 iterations.

Having models parameters computed, a comparison between the histogram of the query image and of those belonging to the image database was performed and the images were ordered according to the values of the previously described L_1D, L_2D and BD distance measures. Due to the fact that L_2D produced irrelevant retrieval results it was excluded from the further experiments.

For the evaluation of the difference between two histograms we also used the the *Earth Mover's Distance* (EMD) similarity measure. The EMD is based on the assumption that one of the histograms reflects "hills" and the second represents "holes" in the ground of a histogram. The measured distance is defined as a minimum amount of work needed to transform one histogram into the other using a "soil" of the first histogram. As this method operates on signatures and their weights using GMM, we assigned as signature values the *mean* of each component and for the *signature weight* the weighting coefficient of each Gaussian in the model. The EMD computations were evaluated using the Y. Rubner algorithm implementation [27].

As can be seen in Fig. 4 the proposed method enables efficient retrieval of lossy compressed images. The results evaluated for images represented by their rg histogram, illustrate that the proposed method can successfully counteract the loss of color information. The suitability of the proposed method is especially visible when, for demonstration purposes, the GIF compression scheme, which severely distorts the color information was applied.

As it was mentioned before, the best solution to the problems addressed in this paper should be based on the perceptual similarity of colors which are related to their distance in a given space. Moreover, the color similarity measure should preferably offer compact color description. Therefore, the CIE Lab color space combined with the Earth Mover's distance promises to fulfil such a requirement.

Figure 5 illustrates the comparison between retrieval results evaluated for exemplary images of the Wang database using GMM approximation of color histograms evaluated in CIE Lab and rgb color spaces. Those results were compared to a set of candidate images produced by the retrieval system based only on color histograms which were not subjected to GMM modeling mixture (last rows in Fig. 5). The results show that the described methodology overcomes the drawbacks of the method based on histograms derived for images represented in rgb color space. Additionally, the application of the CIE Lab color space enables to fully utilize the qualities of the EMD measure providing accurate results even for highly compressed color images.

For the illustration of the proposed method, the Webmuseum and our database was chosen. Figure 6 shows the retrieval results evaluated for various settings of the BF parameters. The choice of the best set is rather a subjective matter as each of the shown

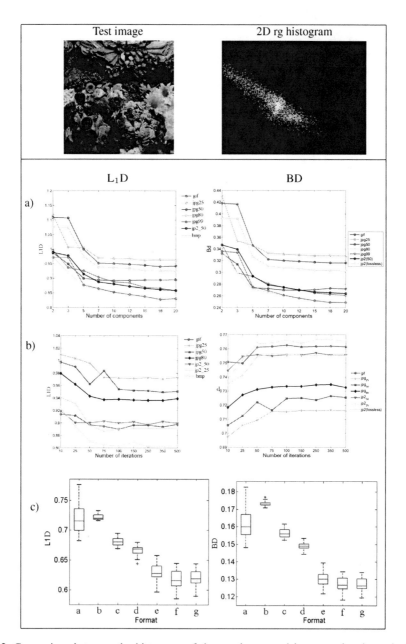

Fig. 3. Comparison between the histogram of the test image and its approximations obtained through the GMM using L_1D and BD distances for various number of model components (a) and iterations (b) of the estimation process performed by the EM algorithm. The bottom row (c) illustrates the statistical description of the modeling when using 7 components and 75 iterations of EM for various compression formats.

sets of candidate images is satisfactory. This example also illustrates the ability of the proposed technique to not only retrieve images of the same overall color palette, but also to promote images with homogenous color regions.

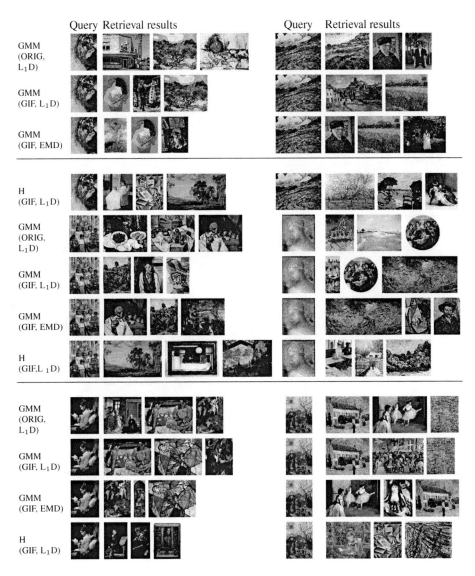

Fig. 4. Retrieval results for exemplary original images (denoted as ORIG) chosen from the database of Webmuseum and its color palette decreased versions. The GIF technique was applied as it facilitates the illustration of the changes caused by color information loss. Retrieval process was evaluated according to L_1 metric as a distance measure in rgb color space. For each query (left) three highest ranked images are shown.

208   M. Luszczkiewicz-Piatek and B. Smolka

GIF
(EMD, rgb)

GIF
(EMD, Lab)

JPG_{50}
(EMD, Lab)

BMP
(EMD, Lab)

H
(GIF, L_1D,rgb)

GIF
(EMD, rgb)

GIF
(EMD, Lab)

JPG_{50}
(EMD, Lab)

BMP
(EMD, Lab)

H
(GIF, L_1D,rgb)

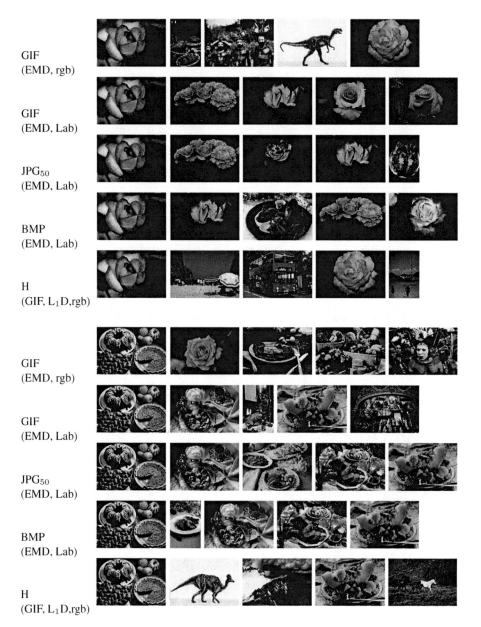

Fig. 5. Illustration of the retrieval results evaluated for images in GIF and JPG formats taken from the database of Wang using the rgb and Lab color space

Fig. 6. Comparison of retrieval results using the Webmuseum and our database obtained for various retrieval parameters: GMM for ab histogram derived from CIE Lab with no additional weighting, using EMD as similarity measure (a), $k_{1,2} = 1, h = 0.3$ (b), $k_{1,2} = 0.3, h = 1$ (c), $k_{1,2} = 2, h = 0.3$ (d), direct rg histogram comparison using L_1D metric (e)

Fig. 7. The comparison of the retrieval results performed on our database obtained for various retrieval methods: GMM with no additional weighting applied for the images represented in the CIE Lab color space (a) CEDD [29] (b) FCTH [30] (c), MPEG-7 SCD [31] (d), Tamura histogram [32] (e), Haar wavelet (f). The results were evaluated for images transformed to JPG_{25}, JPG_{15} and GIF.

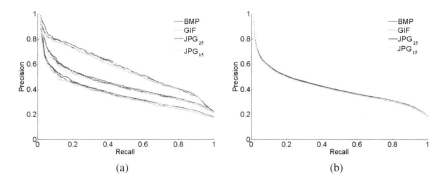

Fig. 8. Summary of the retrieval efficiency of the proposed method using the CIE Lab color space, evaluated for the database of Wang [8]. Plot (a) illustrates the retrieval power evaluated for three exemplary sets of 31 randomly chosen images. Plot (b) shows the retrieval results evaluated for the entire database of Wang.

4   Evaluation of the Proposed Method Efficiency

In order to test the proposed methodology we compared the retrieval results with those proposed by two well known, freely accessible image retrieval applications: img (Rummager) [28] and imgSeek, (www.imgseek.net). The first system comprises several methods among which the following were chosen: 60 bin histogram (CEDD) [29], 192 bin histogram (FCTH) [30], MPEG-7 [31] and Tamura [32] 16 bin directional histogram.

For the evaluation of results obtained using the GMM based technique we used the EMD method and the L_1 metric for comparisons of the distance between the histograms. As can be seen in Fig. 7 only the CEDD [31] and FCTH methods yield similar results. The candidate images retrieved by the more sophisticated techniques (Fig. 7d-f) present distinctively different color palettes than that of the query and therefore they seem to be unsuitable for the purpose of the retrieval of lossy compressed images.

It is worth underlining that although the proposed solution outperforms, when lossy compressed images are analyzed, the other approaches discussed above, it is crucial to prove that it also yields valuable and comparable results for images of various levels of information loss. Thus, Fig. 8 depicts the robustness of the proposed method to the distortions introduced during compression process through *Recall* and *Precision* plots using the database of Wang. Independently on the applied compression scheme, the retrieval power is comparable with that when original images were subjected to retrieval process. In these experiments the criterion of the successful retrieval was the membership to the same thematic group as the query. Therefore, the main aim of the presented plots is to show that proposed technique can produce meaningful results regardlessly to the rate of information loss associated with various compression methods.

5   Summary

Many retrieval system rely on the color composition of the analyzed images. Although, this approach seems to be generally correct and effective, one must be aware of the problem of accurately managing the vast amount of visual information. The methods operating on chromaticity histograms could be severely disabled as color palettes of lossy compressed images can differ, providing misleading conclusions. As shown in this paper, such a comparison produces incorrect results when the retrieval process is evaluated not on the original images but on their compressed versions. Thus, there is an urgent need for the evaluation of techniques overcoming that undesirable phenomenon. Such a method is described in this paper.

The main contribution of this work is the adaptation of the concept of the Gaussian Mixture Models and the application of the Bilateral Filtering for the purposes of the distorted chromaticity histogram approximation. The proposed scheme enables the retrieval system not only to take into account the overall image color palette but also to consider the the color dispersion understood as spatial arrangement of image colors .

The satisfactory retrieval results were achieved independently on the applied compression scheme. Therefore, the presented results proved the hypothesis that the loss of color information caused by lossy coding can be efficiently counteracted providing successful retrieval results.

Acknowledgments. This work has been supported by the Polish Ministry of Science and Higher Education under R&D grant no. N N516 374736 from the Science Budget 2009-2011.

References

1. Datta, R., Joshi, D., Li, J., Wang, J.Z.: Image Retrieval: Ideas, Influences, and Trends of the New Age. ACM Computing Surveys 40(2), 1–60 (2008)
2. Zhou, X.S., Rui, Y., Huang, T.S.: Exploration of Visual Data. Kluwer, Dordrecht (2003)
3. Pass, G., Zabih, R.: Comparing images using joint histograms. Journal of Multimedia Systems 7(3), 234–240 (1999)
4. Ciocca, G., Schettini, L., Cinque, L.: Image Indexing and Retrieval Using Spatial Chromatic Histograms and Signatures. In: Proc. of CGIV, pp. 255–258 (2002)
5. Lambert, P., Harvey, N., Grecu, H.: Image Retrieval Using Spatial Chromatic Histograms. In: Proc. of CGIV, pp. 343–347 (2004)
6. Hartut, T., Gousseau, Y., Schmitt, F.: Adaptive Image Retrieval Based on the Spatial Organization of Colors. Computer Vision and Image Understanding 112, 101–113 (2008)
7. Heidemann, G.: Combining Spatial and Colour Information For Content Based Image Retrieval. Computer Vision and Image Understanding 94, 234–270 (2004)
8. Wang, J.Z., Li, J., Wiederhold, G.: SIMPLIcity: Semantics-Sensitive Integrated Matching for Picture Libraries. IEEE Trans. Patt. Anal. Mach. Intel. 9, 947–963 (2001)
9. Rugna, J.D., Konik, H.: Color Coarse Segmentation and Regions Selection for Similar Images Retrieval. In: Proc. of CGIV, pp. 241–244 (2002)
10. Dvir, G., Greenspan, H., Rubner, Y.: Context-Based Image Modelling. In: Proc. of ICPR, pp. 162–165 (2002)
11. Jing, F., Li, M., Zhang, H.J.: An Effective Region-Based Image Retrieval Framework. IEEE Trans. on Image Processing 13(5), 699–709 (2004)
12. Berretti, A., Del Bimbo, E.: Weighted Walktroughs Between Extended Entities for Retrieval by Spatial Arrangement. IEEE Trans. on Multimedia 3(1), 52–70 (2002)

13. Dempster, A., Laird, N., Rubin, D.: Maximum Likelihood from incomplete data. J. Royal Stat. Soc. 39B, 1–38 (1977)
14. McLachlan, G., Peel, D.: Finite Mixtures Models. John Wiley & Sons, Chichester (2000)
15. Kuo, W.-J., Chang, R.-F.: Approximating the Statistical Distribution of Color Histogram for Content-based Image Retrieval. In: Proc. of ICASP, vol. 4, pp. 2007–2010 (2000)
16. Jeong, S.: Image Retrieval Using Color Histograms Generated by Gauss Mixture Vector Quantization. Comp. Vis. Image Understanding 94(1-3), 44–66 (2004)
17. Luszczkiewicz, M., Smolka, B.: Gaussian Mixture Model Based Retrieval Technique for Lossy Compressed Color Images. In: Kamel, M.S., Campilho, A. (eds.) ICIAR 2007. LNCS, vol. 4633, pp. 662–673. Springer, Heidelberg (2007)
18. Luszczkiewicz, M., Smolka, B.: A Robust Indexing and Retrieval Method for Lossy Compressed Color Images. In: Proc. of IEEE International Symposium on Image and Signal, Processing and Analysis, pp. 304–309 (2007)
19. Luszczkiewicz, M., Smolka, B.: Spatial Color Distribution Based Indexing and Retrieval Scheme. Advances in Soft Computing 59, 419–427 (2009)
20. Luszczkiewicz, M., Smolka, B.: Application of Bilateral Filtering and Gaussian Mixture Modeling for the Retrieval of Paintings. In: Proc. of ICIP, pp. 77–80 (2009)
21. Smolka, B., Szczepanski, M., Lukac, R., Venetsanoloulos, A.N.: Robust Color Image Retrieval for the World Wide Web. In: Proc. of ICASSP, pp. 461–464 (2004)
22. Elad, M.: On the Origin of the Bilateral Filter and Ways to Improve It. IEEE Trans. on Image Processing 11(10), 1141–1151 (2002)
23. Paris, S., Durand, F.: A Fast Approximation of the Bilateral Filter Using a Signal Processing Approach. Int. J. Comput. Vision 39B, 1–38 (2007)
24. Alata, O., Quintard, L.: Is There a Best Color Space for Color Image Characteriation or Representation Based on Multivariate Gaussian Mixture Model? Comp. Vis. Image Understanding 113, 867–877 (2009)
25. Kuehni, R.G.: Color Space and Its Divisions. John Wiley & Sons, Chichester (2003)
26. Bilmes, J.: A Gentle Tutorial on the EM Algorithm and its Application to Parameter Estimation for Gaussian Mixture and Hidden Markov Models. University of Berkeley, ICSI-TR-97-021 (1997)
27. Rubner, Y., Tomasi, C., Guibas, L.J.: A Metric for Distributions with Applications to Image Databases. In: Proc. of ICCV, pp. 59–66 (1998)
28. Chatzichristofis, S.A., Boutalis, Y.S., Lux M.: IMG(RUMMAGER): An Interactive Content Based Image Retrieval System. In: Proc. of the 2nd International Workshop on Similarity Search and Applications (SISAP), pp. 151–153 (2009)
29. Chatzichristofis, S.A., Boutalis, Y.S., Lux, M.: EDD: Color and Edge Directivity Descriptor, a Compact Descriptor for Image Indexing and Retrieval. In: Gasteratos, A., Vincze, M., Tsotsos, J.K. (eds.) ICVS 2008. LNCS, vol. 5008, pp. 312–322. Springer, Heidelberg (2008)
30. Chatzichristofis, S.A., Boutalis, Y.S., Lux, M.: FCTH: Fuzzy Color and Texture Histogram - a Low Level Feature for Accurate Image Retrieval. In: Proc. of the 9th International Workshop on Image Analysis for Multimedia Interactive Services (WIAMIS), pp. 191–196 (2008)
31. Manjunath, B.S., Ohm, J.R., Vasudevan, V., Yamada, A.: Color and Texture Descriptors. IEEE Trans. Cir. Sys. Video Technology 11, 703–715 (1998)
32. Tamura, S.M.H., Yamawaki, T.: Textural Features Corresponding to Visual Perception. IEEE Trans. Syst. Man Cybern. 8(6), 460–472 (1978)

Detecting Text in Natural Scenes Based on a Reduction of Photometric Effects: Problem of Color Invariance

Alain Trémeau[1], Christoph Godau[2], Sezer Karaoglu[2], and Damien Muselet[1]

[1] Laboratoire Hubert Curien, Batiment E, 18 rue Benoit Lauras, University Jean Monnet, 42000 Saint Etienne, France
{alain.tremeau, daminen.muselet}@univ-st-etienne
[2] Erasmus Mundus CIMET Master, University Jean Monnet, Batiment B, 18 rue Benoit Lauras, 42000 Saint Etienne, France

Abstract. In this paper, we propose a novel method for detecting and segmenting text layers in complex images. This method is robust against degradations such as shadows, non-uniform illumination, low-contrast, large signal-dependent noise, smear and strain. The proposed method first uses a geodesic transform based on a morphological reconstruction technique to remove dark/light structures connected to the borders of the image and to emphasize on objects in center of the image. Next uses a method based on difference of gamma functions approximated by the Generalized Extreme Value Distribution (GEVD) to find a correct threshold for binarization. The main function of this GEVD is to find the optimum threshold value for image binarization relatively to a significance level. The significance levels are defined in function of the background complexity. In this paper, we show that this method is much simpler than other methods for text binarization and produces better text extraction results on degraded documents and natural scene images.

Keywords: Text binarization, Contrast enhancement, Gamma function, Photometric invariants, Color invariants.

1 Introduction

One of the most challenging tasks for any computer vision system is to recognize the changes in an image which are due to a change in the underlying imaged surfaces from changes which are due to the effects of the scene illumination. The interaction between light and surface is complex and introduces unwanted artifacts into an image [1]. For example, shading, shadows, specularities and inter-reflections, as well as change to local variation in the intensity of color of the illumination all make it more difficult to achieve basic visual tasks such as text extraction (see Fig. 1) or background extraction (see Fig. 2 and 3). Fig. 2 demonstrates that the colors distribution of the background of image (c) of Fig. 1 is not homogeneous and that in the background there is strong chrominance variations. Fig. 3 demonstrates that the colors distribution of the background of image (d) of Fig. 1 is also not homogeneous and that in this region there is greater chrominance variations than in Fig. 1 (c). In order to attenuate

R. Schettini, S. Tominaga, and A. Trémeau (Eds.): CCIW 2011, LNCS 6626, pp. 214–229, 2011.

these effects illuminant-invariant models have been proposed. Several studies have shown that these models greatly attenuate most of effects described above. In this paper, in section 2, we show that these models suffer from limitations and do not perform well when addressing complex illumination conditions, such as those illustrated by image of Fig. 1 (d).

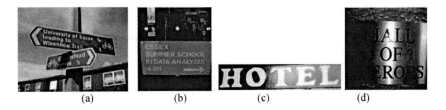

(a)   (b)   (c)   (d)

Fig. 1. Color changes due to shading (a), local variation in the intensity of the illumination (b), specularities (c), and specularities and inter-reflections (d)

Another challenging task is to enhance the image so that result is more suitable than original image for specific application such as segmentation. Several image enhancement techniques, often elementary or heuristic methods, have been proposed for improving the visual quality of images. Appropriate choice is greatly influenced by the imaging modality, task at hand and viewing conditions [2]. As example, power-law transformations with a fractional exponent can be used to expand the gray scale range of dark images. Log Transformation can be used for enhancing details in darker regions but at the expense of details in higher-level values, i.e. brighter regions. Histogram equalization can be used to stretch the contrast of an image by redistributing the gray-level values uniformly. In section 3 we show that these models suffer also from limitations and do not perform well when addressing complex illumination conditions, such as those illustrated by image of Fig. 1 (d).

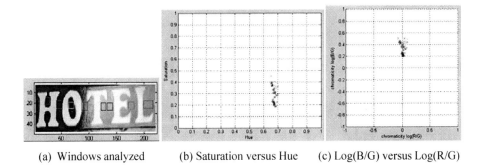

(a) Windows analyzed   (b) Saturation versus Hue   (c) Log(B/G) versus Log(R/G)

Fig. 2. Color space representation of different windows of image (c) in Fig. 1. Colors associated with the points (in (b) and (c)) represent color of corresponding windows (in (a)). Each window is represented by four points which corresponds to the lowest and highest values computed in this window for the two dimensions considered.

Color image segmentation is also a challenging task as solutions have to be effective against image shadows, illumination variations and highlights. Several approaches based on the computation of image invariants that are robust to photometric effects have been proposed in the literature [3-5]. Unfortunately, there are too many color invariant models in the literature, making the selection of the best model and its combination with local image structures (e.g. color derivatives) quite difficult to produce optimal results [6]. In [7], Gevers et al. survey the possible solutions available to the practitioner. In specific applications, shadow, shading, illumination and highlight edges have to be identified and processed separately from geometrical edges such as corners, and T-junctions. To address this issue, Gevers et al. proposed to compute local differential structures and color invariants in a multidimensional feature space to detect salient image structures (i.e. edges) on the basis of their physical nature in [7]. In [8] the authors proposed a classification of edges into five classes, namely object edges, reflectance edges, illumination/shadow edges, specular edges, and occlusion edges to enhance the performance of the segmentation solution utilized. Shadow segmentation is of particular importance in applications such as video object extraction and tracking. Several research proposals have been developed in an attempt to detect a particular class of shadows in video images, namely moving cast shadows, based on the shadow's spectral and geometric properties [9]. The problem is that cast shadow models cannot be effectively used to detect other classes of shadows, such as self shadows or shadows in diffuse penumbra [9] suggesting that existing shadow segmentations solutions could be further improved using invariant color features. The main challenge in color image segmentation is since a decade the fusion of low level image features so that image content would be better described and processed. Several researches provided some solutions to combine color derivatives features and color invariant features, color features and other low level features (e.g. color and texture, color and shape [7]), low-level features and high-level features (e.g. from graph representation [10]). However, none of the proposed solutions appear to provide the expected performance to segment complex color images unlike the human visual system which is able to take into account the semantic contents of images. Of course if some a priori information or knowledge about the segmentation task is incorporated in the process that will optimise the algorithm results.

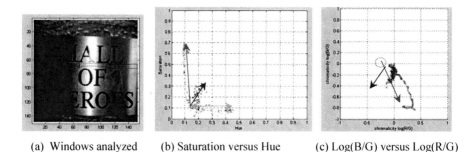

(a) Windows analyzed   (b) Saturation versus Hue   (c) Log(B/G) versus Log(R/G)

Fig. 3. Color space representation of different areas of image of Fig. 1 (d). Colors associated with the points (in (b) and (c)) represent color of corresponding windows (in (a)). Each window is represented by several points computed by sampling of this window. The arrows represent color changes from left to right in the corresponding windows in (a).

Most of existing text segmentation approaches assume that text layers are of uniform color and fail when this is not the case. The background may also be multicolor consequently the assumption according with it is the largest area of (almost) uniform color in the image does not necessarily hold [11]. Lastly, most of existing text segmentation approaches assume that there is a high contrast between text and background in the image this is unfortunately not always the case in real images. Many approaches assume also that in segmenting the highest peak in the lightness histogram we can deduce if text layers are of lower or a higher lightness than the background region, this information may be helpful to segment text layers, but this is once again not always the case in real images.

In this paper we demonstrate that none illuminant-invariant model is sufficiently robust to complex photometric effects to solve the issue of text detection in complex natural scenes. To solve this issue, in a second paper [12], we propose to use another strategy, more robust to photometric effects, based on the computation of the difference of gamma functions to detect text layers in complex scenes.

2   Color Spaces Invariants to Photometric Effects

2.1   Illuminant-Invariant Models

A first approach to compute illuminant-invariant consists to use reflection models (e.g. Lambertian or dichromatic reflectance) but these reflection models are too restricted to model real-world scenes, such as the scene illustrated by Fig. 3, in which different reflectance mechanisms hold simultaneously. Different photometric invariance models based on dichromatic reflection models have been proposed [13-14]. These models are invariant for different types of lighting variations, i.e. light intensity (LI) or light color (LC) change and/or light intensity or light color shift (see Table 1) but are not invariant to strong or complex lighting changes such as those illustrated by image of Fig. 1 (d).

Table 1. Invariance of color models for different types of lighting changes [14]. Invariance is indicated with '+' and lack of invariance with '-'

Color space	LI change	LI shift	LI change and shift	LC change	LC change and shift
Value (V)	-	-	-	-	-
Saturation (S)	-	+	+	-	-
Hue (H)	+	+	+	-	-
log(R/G), log(B/G)	+	+	+	+	+

Fig. 4 and Table 2 show the non-invariance of H, S and log(B/G) color descriptors for a simple real-world scene. These "invariants" fail to attenuate a strong intensity shift due to a smooth specular reflection. Likewise, Fig. 5 and Table 3 show the non-invariance of H, S, log(B/G) and log(B/G) color descriptors for a more complex real-world scene.

In order to attenuate photometric effects for text segmentation in natural images Jim et al. proposed in [15] to decompose the image studied into chromatic and achromatic regions in the HSI color space using a decision function computed in RGB space. Since the HSI space and the decision function used are not invariant to photometric effects this method is not relevant for complex images such as image of Fig. 1 (d). Furthermore, this method is based on the hypothesis that text layers have homogeneous values in the chromaticity image but this is not always the case for complex images, such as in Fig. 6. In Fig. 6 there are two color changes, one from left to center due to a white specular highlight, and a second from center to right due to a second (orange) specular hightlight. Karatzas et al. proposed also to decompose the image studied into chromatic and achromatic regions in the HLS color space using a decision function based on saturation and lightness values. The problem with this strategy is that the exact levels of saturation and lightness for which color should be considered achromatic are not straightforward to set [11]. To simplify the problem either empirical or heuristic methods are generally used.

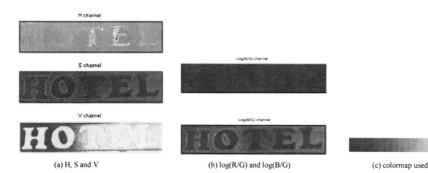

| (a) H, S and V | (b) log(R/G) and log(B/G) | (c) colormap used |

Fig. 4. Representation of H, S, V, log(R/G) and log(B/G) components computed for image of Fig. 1 (c). The V channel shows a LI shift in the background from left to right ($\Delta V_{max2} = 0.71$). On each component, reddish colors and yellowish colors correspond to values closed to 0 and 1, respectively.

Table 2. Invariance of color models / LI change in image (c) of Fig. 1. Color component are normalised in the interval [0, 1]. Invariance is indicated with '+' and lack of invariance with '-'. ΔX_{ext} and ΔX_{max1} represents, respectively, the maximum of difference between two consecutive areas of the background (from left to right) and the maximal difference between two areas of the background, computed from mean values calculated for each letter for color component X. ΔX_{max2} and ΔX_{max3} represents, respectively, the maximum of differences between two consecutive letters (from left to right) and the maximum of differences between two letters, computed from mean values calculated for each letter for color component X.

Color space	Background			Letters		
Saturation (S)	-	$\Delta S_{ext} = 0.16$,	$\Delta S_{max1} = \mathbf{0.61}$	-	$\Delta S_{ci} = 0.04$,	$\Delta S_{max2} = \mathbf{0.12}$
Hue (H)	-	$\Delta H_{ext} = 0.25$,	$\Delta H_{max1} = \mathbf{0.30}$	-	$\Delta H_{max2} = 0.10$,	$\Delta H_{max3} = \mathbf{0.13}$
log(R/G)	+	$\Delta \log(R/G)_{ext} = 0.03$,	$\Delta \log(R/G)_{max1} = \mathbf{0.04}$	+	$\Delta \log(R/G)_{max2} = 0.01$,	$\Delta \log(R/G)_{max3} = \mathbf{0.01}$
log(B/G)	-	$\Delta \log(B/G)_{ext} = 0.19$,	$\Delta \log(B/G)_{max1} = \mathbf{0.20}$	-	$\Delta \log(B/G)_{max2} = 0.01$,	$\Delta \log(B/G)_{max3} = \mathbf{0.16}$

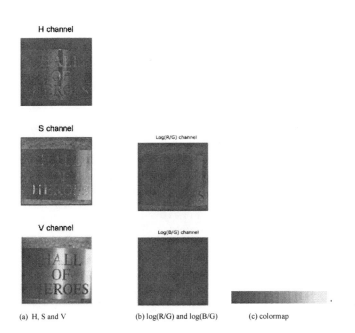

(a) H, S and V   (b) log(R/G) and log(B/G)   (c) colormap

Fig. 5. Representation of H, S, V, log(R/G) and log(B/G) components computed for image (d) of Fig. 1. The V channel shows two LI shifts in the background ($\Delta V_{max2} = 0.94$, 0.92 resp.). The first LI shift (i.e. at center) corresponds also to a LC shit on the H channel meanwhile the second LI shift (i.e. at right) corresponds to a LC shift on the S channel. On each component, reddish colors and yellowish colors correspond to values closed to 0 and 1, respectively.

Table 3. Invariance of color models / LI and LC change and shift in image (d) of Fig. 1. Color component are normalized in the interval [0, 1]. Invariance is indicated with '+' and lack of invariance with '-'. ΔX_{ext} and ΔX_{max1} represents, respectively, the maximum of difference between two consecutive areas of the background (from left to right) and the maximal difference between two areas of the background, computed from mean values calculated for each letter for color component X. ΔX_{max2} and ΔX_{max3} represents, respectively, the maximum of differences between two consecutive letters (from left to right) and the maximum of differences between two letters, computed from mean values calculated for each letter for color component X.

Color space	Background		Letters	
Saturation (S)	- $\Delta S_{ext} = 0.39$,	$\Delta S_{max1} = \mathbf{0.60}$	- $\Delta S_{cl} = 0.36$,	$\Delta S_{max2} = \mathbf{0.55}$
Hue (H)	- $\Delta H_{ext} = 0.25$,	$\Delta H_{max1} = \mathbf{0.32}$	- $\Delta H_{max2} = 0.24$,	$\Delta H_{max3} = \mathbf{0.32}$
log(R/G)	- $\Delta \log(R/G)_{ext} = 0.26$,	$\Delta \log(R/G)_{max1} = \mathbf{0.42}$	- $\Delta \log(R/G)_{max2} = 0.2$,	$\Delta \log(R/G)_{max3} = \mathbf{0.31}$
log(B/G)	- $\Delta \log(B/G)_{ext} = 0.40$,	$\Delta \log(B/G)_{max1} = \mathbf{0.77}$	- $\Delta \log(B/G)_{max2} = 0.49$,	$\Delta \log(B/G)_{max3} = \mathbf{0.87}$

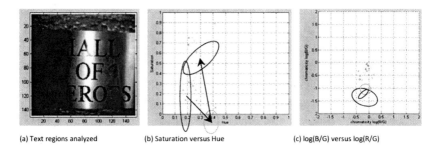

(a) Text regions analyzed   (b) Saturation versus Hue   (c) log(B/G) versus log(R/G)

Fig. 6. Color space representation of several text regions of image (d) in Fig. 1. Colors associated with the points (in (b) and (c)) represent color of corresponding windows (in (a)). Each window is represented by four points which corresponds to the lowest and highest values computed in this window for the two dimensions considered. The color distribution of the blue window (at left on (a)), of the cyan window (at the center) and of the grey window (at right, on the S) are bounded by ellipses in (b) and (c). The arrows represent color changes between these ellipses that is to say from left to center and from center to right in (a).

2.2 Logvinenko's Model

In order to attenuate photometric effects such as shading, shadows, specularities and inter-reflections, as well as change to local variation in the intensity of color of the illumination a new approach has been recently proposed by Logvinenko in 2009 [16]. The main idea of this approach is to consider that the set of possible colors of reflecting objects defines a volume called the object-color solid [17]. The object-color solid depends on the spectral power distribution of the illuminant and the color space being used. Logvinenko has therefore proposed a new object-color space that defines a complete color atlas that is invariant to illumination [16] and describes all colors in the object-color solid under any illuminant. However, Logvinenko's existing implementation for calculating the proposed color descriptors is computationally expensive and does not work for all types of illuminants. Fig. 7 shows the calculated color descriptors for a scene viewed under different lighting sources (images from the Barnard's Database [18]) and illustrates the perceptual correlates of the descriptors ($\alpha\delta\lambda$) as described by Logvinenko. Purity (α) describes the grayness of a color, namely, the relative distance to the gray center. Hence, both black and white have a high purity, so for example the dark areas of the image show as white in Fig. 7 (b). The spectral bandwidth (δ) (see Fig. 7 (c)) correlates with blackness and whiteness, but becomes meaningless for low purities (gray colors). Central wavelength (λ) (see Fig. 7 (d)) is correlated to hue.

A possible application of $\alpha\delta\lambda$ color descriptors is to predict the effect of an illumination change. Since $\alpha\delta\lambda$ coordinates determine a metameric reflectance spectrum, the corresponding sensor response for any given illuminant can be calculated according to Logvinenko's model. Fig. 7 shows the result obtained by calculating the $\alpha\delta\lambda$ color descriptors using different illuminants. Although the $\alpha\delta\lambda$ space is invariant to illumination, the $\alpha\delta\lambda$ color descriptors themselves can change with the illumination, since each $\alpha\delta\lambda$ triplet describes a class of metamers, and metamerism depends on the illuminant. To analyze the effect of each illumination change on $\alpha\delta\lambda$ color descriptors, we have computed the histogram of each component next computed distance histograms (see Tables 4 to 12) based on bin-by-bin dissimilarity metrics such as the χ^2 divergence, the Kullback-Leibner divergence and the Jeffrey divergence [19]. Fig. 8 shows the descriptors for images book3 and Macbeth under different intensities, further illustrating the perceptual correlates (images from the Barnard's Database [18]).

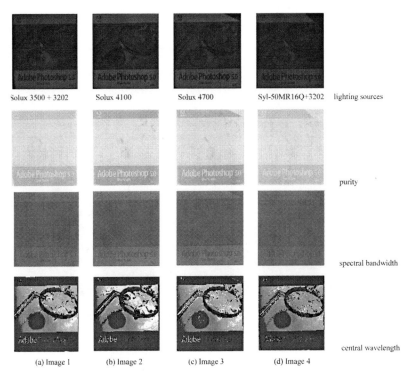

Fig. 7. Image book3 under different lighting sources

Table 4. Dissimilarity distances (Ki2 normalized) computed from histogram of Purity component

Images	Im1	Im2	Im3	Im4	Im5	Im7
Im1		0.60	0.49	0.27	1.33	
Im2			**0.19**	0.62	1.70	
Im3				0.55	1.63	
Im4					1.44	
Im5						
Im6						1.46

Table 6. Dissimilarity distances (Jeffrey) computed from histogram of Purity component

Images	Im1	Im2	Im3	Im4	Im5	Im7
Im1		0.38	0.31	0.16	0.89	
Im2			**0.10**	0.40	1.11	
Im3				0.36	1.07	
Im4					0.96	
Im5						
Im6						0.96

Table 5. Dissimilarity distances (Kullback-Leibler) computed from histogram of Purity component

Images	Im1	Im2	Im3	Im4	Im5	Im7
Im1		0.91	0.78	0.52	**0.07**	
Im2			0.19	**0.10**	0.56	
Im3				0.69	0.31	
Im4					**0.01**	
Im5						
Im6						2.50

Table 7. Dissimilarity distances (Ki2 normalized) computed from histogram of Bandwidth component

Images	Im1	Im2	Im3	Im4	Im5	Im7
Im1		0.53	0.37	0.24	1.13	
Im2			**0.09**	0.61	0.89	
Im3				0.55	0.93	
Im4					1.15	
Im5						
Im6						1.09

Table 8. Dissimilarity distances (Kullback-Leibler) computed from histogram of Bandwidth component

Images	Im1	Im2	Im3	Im4	Im5	Im7
Im1		0.76	0.48	0.81	1.55	
Im2			**0.09**	**0.02**	1.30	
Im3				0.17	1.23	
Im4					1.60	
Im5						
Im6						1.73

Table 9. Dissimilarity distances (Jeffrey) computed from histogram of Bandwidth component

Images	Im1	Im2	Im3	Im4	Im5	Im7
Im1		0.33	0.23	0.16	0.67	
Im2			**0.05**	0.40	0.53	
Im3				0.36	0.54	
Im4					0.69	
Im5						
Im6						0.70

Table 10. Dissimilarity distances (Ki2 normalized) computed from histogram of Central wavelength component

Images	Im1	Im2	Im3	Im4	Im5	Im7
Im1		0.79	0.74	0.66	0.61	
Im2			**0.64**	0.73	0.80	
Im3				**0.14**	**0.51**	
Im4					0.62	
Im5						
Im6						0.76

Table 11. Dissimilarity distances (Kullback-Leibler) computed from histogram of Central wavelength component

Images	Im1	Im2	Im3	Im4	Im5	Im7
Im1		1.63	1.29	1.25	0.72	
Im2			1.15	1.27	1.31	
Im3				**0.15**	0.63	
Im4					0.80	
Im5						
Im6						1.09

Table 12. Dissimilarity distances (Jeffrey) computed from histogram of Central wavelength component

Images	Im1	Im2	Im3	Im4	Im5	Im7
Im1		0.49	0.45	0.41	0.35	
Im2			0.40	0.45	0.49	
Im3				**0.07**	0.28	
Im4					0.35	
Im5						
Im6						0.49

The less images are dissimilar the lower the distance between these histograms is (the three distances considered are bounded by the min value 0). To illustrate our purpose, let us consider images of Fig. 8 and 9. The lowest dissimilarity distances (see Tables 4 to 12) are between images of Fig. 7 (b) and Fig. 7 (c) and between images of

Fig. 7 (c) and Fig. 7 (d). The lowest value for the purity, bandwidth and central wavelength are respectively equal to 0.10, 0.04 and 0.40 for images of Fig. 7 (b) and Fig. 7 (c), and to 0.36, 0.17 and 0.13 for images of Fig. 7 (c) and Fig. 7 (d). These values are not constant. Whatever the set of illuminants considered and the image studied (images of the Barnard's Database [18]) distance between histograms computed are also not constant. This shows that purity, bandwidth and central wavelength components are not invariant to visually perceptible light color changes (see also the first example given in Fig. 7).

Let us now consider images of Fig. 8. The lowest dissimilarity distances (see Tables 4 to 12) between images of Fig. 8 (a) and Fig. 8 (b) and between images of Fig. 8 (c) and Fig. 8 (d) are respectively, for α, δ and λ color descriptors, equal to 0.31, 0.54 and 0.28 for images of Fig. 8 (a) and Fig. 8 (b), and to 0.96, 0.70 and 0.49 for images of Fig. 7 (c) and Fig. 7 (d). These values linked to light intensity changes are not constant and are higher than for illumination changes. Whatever the image studied (images of the Barnard's Database [18]) and light intensity changes, distance between histograms computed are also not constant. This shows that purity, bandwidth and central wavelength components are not invariant to visually perceptible light intensity changes. Our results show that central wavelength (λ) values are less sensitive to light intensity changes than spectral bandwidth (δ) and purity (α), as the former descriptor is correlated to hue meanwhile spectral bandwidth correlates with blackness and whiteness and purity correlates with grayness.

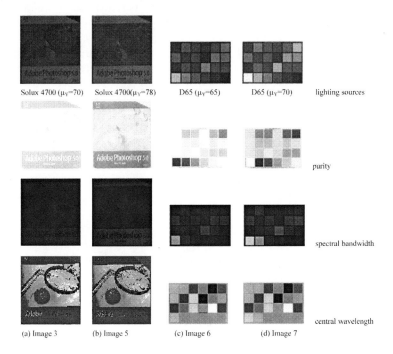

Solux 4700 (μ_Y=70)	Solux 4700(μ_Y=78)	D65 (μ_Y=65)	D65 (μ_Y=70)	lighting sources
				purity
				spectral bandwidth
				central wavelength
(a) Image 3	(b) Image 5	(c) Image 6	(d) Image 7	

Fig. 8. Images book3 and Macbeth under different intensities

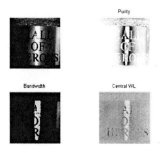

Fig. 9. Representation of α, δ and λ components computed for image (d) in Fig. 1

3   Image Enhancement Methods

3.1   Grey Levels Transformation Methods

In order to better attenuate photometric effects such as shading, shadows, specularities and inter-reflections, as well as change to local variation in the intensity of color of the illumination another approach consists to apply an image enhancement method [20]. The principle objective of image enhancement is to process an image so that results are more suitable than original for specific application [2]. The main task, in our case of study, is to optimize intra-class similarity and inter-class similarity such as every grey-level class (i.e. text regions and background regions) can be well separated.

Different image enhancement algorithms can be used to improve the appearance of an image such as its contrast in order to make the image interpretation, understanding, and analysis easier. Various contrast enhancement algorithms have been developed to modify the appearance of images by highlighting certain features while suppressing others. A widely used approach for contrast enhancement is based on the use of a power law response equation such as follows (see Fig. 10):

$$s = cr^\gamma \tag{1}$$

Generally c and γ are positive constants. r and s represent respectively the input and output intensity levels (see [21]).

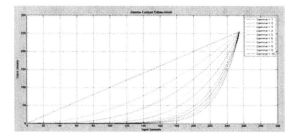

Fig. 10. Influence of the parameter gamma on the contrast of the output image

Another function, the piecewise linear transformation (see Fig. 11) can also be used to modify the distribution of the grey levels of any 1D component such as the saturation or the brightness (see Fig. 12 and 13). In Fig. 12 there are two classes: the background (brighter region) and the text layer (darker regions). The best results that we have experimentally obtained with a piecewise linear transformation are given in Fig. 12 (b). As the most illuminant-invariant components for darker regions (i.e. text layer) are S and log(B/G) components (see Table 2) we apply this transformation on these components. As we can see on Fig. 12 results are not perfect as on the original image (on the most illuminant-invariant components) the inter-class similarity is quite high, e.g. some pixels of the background have the same saturation value than the text layer). In Fig. 13 there are three classes: the background (brighter and darker regions) and the text layer (intermediate regions). The best results that we have experimentally obtained with a piecewise linear transformation are given in Fig. 13 (b). As the most illuminant-invariant components for text regions are V and log(R/G) components (see Table 3) and as the gray scale range of log(R/G) component is too low (see Fig. 5 (b)), we apply this transformation only the V component. As we can see on Fig. 13

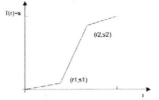

Fig. 11. Example of piecewise linear transformation function used for reducing details in darker regions and brighter regions but at the expense of enhancing details in intermediate regions

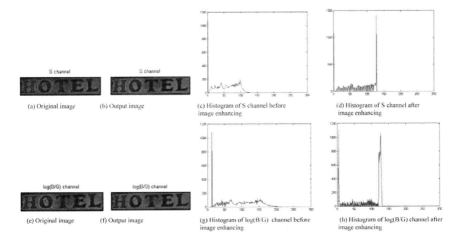

Fig. 12. Examples of image enhancing obtained from a piecewise linear transformation. This transformation is used for enhancing contrast between darker regions (i.e. the text layer) and brighter regions (i.e. the background) without enhancing too much details in intermediate regions. For S we have used the values (r1=15, s1=5) and (r2=75, s2=120) and for log(B/G) the values (r1=90, s1=120) and (r2=110, s2=130).

results are not very good as on the original image the inter-class similarity is too high as some pixels of the background have the same V value than the text). We can note also on Fig. 6 that for darker regions and brighter regions the intra-class similarity is higher on log(R/G) and H components than for log(B/G) and S components for text regions, but as the inter-class similarity of the background and text regions (see Fig. 3) is lower than the intra-class similarity of each of these two classes we cannot attenuate as desired photometric effects.

3.2 Morphological Reconstruction Based on Geodesic Transform

In order to suppress lighter objects (e.g. text layers) than their surroundings and connected to border of the image, another strategy consists to use a morphological reconstruction transform based on geodesic dilation.

According to Soille [22] geodesic dilation of a bounded image always converges after a finite number of iterations (i.e. until the proliferation or shrinking of the marker image is totally impeded by the mask image). For this reason geodesic dilation is considered as a powerful morphological reconstruction scheme. The reconstruction by dilation $R_g^{\partial}(f)$ of a mask image (g) form a marker image (f) is defined as the geodesic dilation of (f) with respect to (g) iterated until stability as follows (see Fig. 14):

$$R_g^{\partial}(f) = \partial_g^{(i)}(f) \qquad (2)$$

The stability is reached at the iteration i when: $\partial_g^{(i)}(f) = \partial_g^{(i+1)}(f)$. This reconstruction is constrained by the following conditions that both (f) and (g) images must have

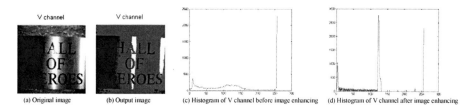

| (a) Original image | (b) Output image | (c) Histogram of V channel before image enhancing | (d) Histogram of V channel after image enhancing |

Fig. 13. Examples of image enhancing obtained from a piecewise linear transformation. This transformation is used for enhancing contrast between intermediate regions (i.e. the text) and darker and brighter regions (i.e. the background) without enhancing too much details in background regions. In this example (r1=15, s1=5), (r2=75, s2=120), (r3=240, s3=130) for V.

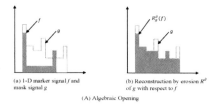

(a) 1-D marker signal *f* and   (b) Reconstruction by erosion R^{∂}
mask signal *g*   of g with respect to *f*

(A) Algebraic Opening

Fig. 14. Algebraic opening for a 1-D signal

the same definition domain (i.e. $D_f = D_g$) and $f \leq g$. This reconstruction transform presents several properties: it is increasing ($g_1 \leq g_2 \Rightarrow R^{\partial}_{g1}(f) \leq R^{\partial}_{g2}(f)$), anti-extensive ($R^{\partial}_g(f) \leq g$), and idem-potent $R^{\partial}_g(R^{\partial}_g(f)) = R^{\partial}_g(f)$). This reconstruction transform corresponds to an algebraic closing of the mask image. The connected opening transformation, $\gamma_x (g)$ of a mask image (g) can be defined as:

$$\gamma_x (g) = R^{\partial}_g(f_x) \tag{3}$$

where the marker image f_x equals to zero everywhere except as x which has a value equal to that of the image (g) at the same position.

According to Soille [22] the connected opening transformation can be used to extract connected image objects having higher intensity values than their surrounding when we chose the mask image zero everywhere, except for the point x which has a value equal to that of the image (g) at the same position (see Fig. 15).

In order to suppress lighter objects than their surroundings and connected to border of the image, we choose the marker image zero everywhere except the border of the image. At the border of the image we chose the pixel value of marker the same as mask pixel value at the same position. Once we get the connectivity information with the help of morphological reconstruction based on geodesic transform, we suppress these lighter objects connected to image border. After this preprocess step most of the non-text regions are reduced and kept only most probable text layer candidates which leads us to emphasize more on region of interest of the image (see Fig. 15 (b)). Especially in our experiments we have seen that this process reduce the background intensity variations and enhance the text layers of the image.

(a) Original image   (b) Connected opening   (c) Original image   (d) Connected opening (the border of image was first set to 0)   (e) Connected opening (without changing the border of the image)

Fig. 15. (b) Connected image objects having higher intensity values than their surrounding can be extracted by the connected opening transform. (d) Connected image objects having darker intensity values than their surrounding can be extracted by the connected closing transform.

In order to suppress darker objects (e.g. text layers) than their surroundings and connected to border of the image the connected closing transformation can be used. The first shortcoming of this morphological transformation and of the former (i.e. closing and opening) is that we must first estimate if the background is lighter or darker than the text layers, i.e. we must first extract the background of the image. The second shortcoming of these two transformations is that they work quite fine when text layers are only darker or whiter than the background but do not perform well when text layers are darker and whiter than their surrounding local background in the image. Lastly, these transforms do not work well when the border of the image has the same intensity than text layers, such as in image (d) in Fig. 1. That why, to enhance this image we set its borders to zero before applying the connected closing transform (see Fig. 15 (d)) otherwise this transform is inefficient (see Fig. 15 (e)).

4 Conclusion

In this paper we have shown that even if illuminant-invariant models greatly attenuate most of photometric effects these models suffer from limitations when addressing complex illumination conditions. We have also shown that even if most of image enhancement methods can greatly attenuate most of photometric effects these methods suffer from limitations which makes them inoperative when addressing complex illumination conditions. To face this issue we propose to use an image enhancement method based on morphological reconstruction through geodesic transform. This method is used to remove objects connected to borders which are lighter than their surroundings. The idea behind this method is that in images/videos of natural-scenes, the most interesting information area at the center of the image not at its periphery. In this context, we consider as noise any region which does not belong to text layers and which are lighter than their surroundings. In other words, noise corresponds to regions which do not belong to the background region and which are not necessarily connected to image borders. Thanks to the proposed method most of the noise in the image is removed which facilitates further processing steps.

Another approach used in several studies consists firstly to use Gaussian mixture models (GMMs) with spatial connectivity information to model color distributions of text layers and background regions [23], next to reduce local variations in the corresponding regions. We do not believe that the GMMs are effective to model complex images, such as that illustrated by image (d) in Fig. 1. For complex backgrounds there may be several classes that overlap, i.e. when the intra-class variances are high and the inter-class variances are low as in Fig. 3. Furthermore, there may be an overlap between classes, i.e. between the background and the text layers, such as in image (d) in Fig. 1 where the color of the background is very close in the left part of the figure to that of text layers. In such cases, characters may not be segmented as separate objects of background. Such a strategy is equivalent to segment the image first.

To solve the issue of shadowing, reflection and uneven illumination, we have shown in another paper (see [12]) that the Generalized Extreme Value Distribution (GEVD) is a very relevant model to approximate differences of gamma functions. Indeed GEVD is capable of finding proper extreme values based on image statistics allowing us to deal with extreme conditions like shadows, high illuminations and reflections. To solve the problem of low contrast between text and background, we have shown in paper [12] that the difference of gamma functions is a very relevant model to enhance contrast between text layers and background regions while reducing noise, using substantially lesser complex processes than other well-known approaches. Lastly, we have also demonstrated that the propose method is robust to photometric effects.

References

1. Finlayson, G.D., Hordley, S.D., Lu, C., Drew, M.S.: On the Removal of Shadows From Images. IEEE Pattern Analysis and Machine Intelligence (PAMI) 28(1), 59–68 (2006)
2. Maini, R., Aggarwal, H.: A Comprehensive Review of Image Enhancement Techniques. Journal of Computing 2(3), 8–13 (2010)

3. van de Weijer, J., Gevers, T., Geusebroek, J.M.: Edge and corner detection by photometric quasi-invariants. IEEE Trans. on Pattern Analysis and Machine Intelligence 27(4), 625–630 (2005)
4. Li, B., Xue, X., Fan, J.: A robust incremental learning framework for accurate skin region segmentation in color images. Pattern Recognition 40(12), 3621–3632 (2007)
5. Moreno-Noguer, F., Sanfeliu, A., Samaras, D.: Integration of deformable contours and a multiple hypotheses Fischer color model for robust tracking in varying illuminant environments. Image and Vision Computing 25, 285–296 (2007)
6. Trémeau, A., Tominaga, S., Plataniotis, K.: Color in Image and Video Processing: most recent trends and future research directions. EURASIP Journal on Image and Video Processing 2008, article ID 581371, 26 pages (2008)
7. Gevers, T.: Chapter 9: Color feature detection. In: Color Image Processing: Methods and Applications Book, pp. 203–226. CRC Press, Boca Raton (2007)
8. Koschan, A., Abidi, M.: Detection and classification of edges in color images. IEEE Signal Processing Magazine, 64–73 (2005)
9. Salvador, E., Cavallaro, A., Ebrahimi, T.: Cast shadow segmentation using invariant color features. Computer Vision and Image Understanding 95, 238–259 (2004)
10. Dong, G., Xie, M.: Color clustering and learning for image segmentation based on neural networks. IEEE Trans. on Neural Networks 16, 925–936 (2005)
11. Karatzas, D., Antonacopoulos, A.: Colour text segmentation in web images based on human perception. Image and Vision Computing 25, 564–577 (2007)
12. Trémeau, A., Fernando, B., Karaoglu, S., Muselet, D.: Detecting text in natural scenes based on a reduction of photometric effects: problem of text detection. In: Proceedings of CCIW 2011. LNCS, vol. 6626, pp. 217–233. Springer, Heidelberg (2011)
13. van de Sande, K.E.A., Gevers, T., Snoek, C.G.M.: Evaluation of color descriptors for object and scene recognition. In: Proceedings of the IEEE Conference on Computer Vision and Pattern Recognition (CVPR), pp. 453–464 (2008)
14. Álvarez, J.M., Gevers, T., López, A.M.: Learning Photometric Invariance for Object Detection. Int. J. Comput. Vis. 90, 45–61 (2010)
15. Lim, J., Park, J., Medioni, G.G.: Text segmentation in color images using tensor voting. Image and Vision Computing 25, 671–685 (2007)
16. Logvinenko, A.D.: An object-color space. J. Vis. 9(11), 1–23 (2009)
17. Wyszecki, G., Stiles, W.S.: Color Science: Concepts and Methods, Quantitative Data and Formulae, 2nd edn. Wiley-Interscience, Hoboken (August 2000)
18. Barnard, K.: Practical Colour Constancy, Phd thesis, Simon Fraser University, School of Computing (1999),
    http://kobus.ca/research/data/objects_under_different_lights/index.html
19. Rubner, Y., Puzicha, J., Tomasi, C., Buhmann, J.M.: Empirical Evaluation of Dissimilarity Measures for Color and Texture. In: International Conference on Computer Vision, vol. 2, p. 1165 (1999)
20. Chen, S., Beghdadi, A.: Natural enhancement of color image. Eurasip Journal on Image and Video Processing, 19 pages (2010), doi:10.1155/2010/175203
21. Gonzalez, R.C., Woods, R.E.: Digital Image Processing, 2nd edn. Pearson Education, London (2008) ISBN-13: 978-0135052679
22. Soille, P.: Morphological Image Analysis: Principles and Applications, pp. 182–198. Springer, Heidelberg (2003)
23. Ye, Q., Gao, W., Huang, Q.: Automatic text segmentation from complex background. In: IEEE Int. Conf. on Image Processing, vol. 5, pp. 2905–2908 (2004)

Detecting Text in Natural Scenes Based on a Reduction of Photometric Effects: Problem of Text Detection

Alain Trémeau[1], Basura Fernando[2], Sezer Karaoglu[2], and Damien Muselet[1]

[1] Laboratoire Hubert Curien, Batiment E, 18 rue Benoit Lauras, University Jean Monnet,
42000 Saint Etienne, France
{alain.tremeau,daminen.muselet}@univ-st-etienne
[2] Erasmus Mundus CIMET Master, University Jean Monnet, Batiment B,
18 rue Benoit Lauras, 42000 Saint Etienne, France

Abstract. In this paper, we propose a novel method for detecting and segmenting text layers in complex images. This method is robust against degradations such as shadows, non-uniform illumination, low-contrast, large signal-dependent noise, smear and strain. The proposed method first uses a geodesic transform based on a morphological reconstruction technique to remove dark/light structures connected to the borders of the image and to emphasize on objects in center of the image. Next uses a method based on difference of gamma functions approximated by the Generalized Extreme Value Distribution (GEVD) to find a correct threshold for binarization. The main function of this GEVD is to find the optimum threshold value for image binarization relatively to a significance level. The significance levels are defined in function of the background complexity. In this paper, we show that this method is much simpler than other methods for text binarization and produces better text extraction results on degraded documents and natural scene images.

Keywords: Text binarization, Contrast enhancement, Gamma function, Photometric invariants, Color invariants.

1 Introduction

One of the most challenging tasks for color image segmentation is to be effective against image shadows, illumination variations and highlights. Several approaches based on the computation of image invariants that are robust to photometric effects have been proposed in the literature [1-3]. Unfortunately, there are too many color invariant models in the literature, making the selection of the best model and its combination with local image structures (e.g. color derivatives) quite difficult to produce optimal results [4]. In [5], Gevers et al. survey the possible solutions available to the practitioner. In specific applications, shadow, shading, illumination and highlight edges have to be identified and processed separately from geometrical edges such as corners, and T-junctions. To address the issue, Gevers et al. proposed to compute local differential structures and color invariants in a multidimensional feature space to detect salient image structures (i.e. edges) on the basis of their physical nature in [5]. In [6] the authors proposed a classification of edges into five classes, namely object

R. Schettini, S. Tominaga, and A. Trémeau (Eds.): CCIW 2011, LNCS 6626, pp. 230–244, 2011.

edges, reflectance edges, illumination/shadow edges, specular edges, and occlusion edges to enhance the performance of the segmentation solution utilized. Shadow segmentation is of particular importance in applications such as video object extraction and tracking. Several research proposals have been developed in an attempt to detect a particular class of shadows in video images, namely moving cast shadows, based on the shadow's spectral and geometric properties [7]. The problem is that cast shadow models cannot be effectively used to detect other classes of shadows, such as self shadows or shadows in diffuse penumbra [7] suggesting that existing shadow segmentations solutions could be further improved using invariant color features. The main challenge in color image segmentation is since a decade the fusion of low level image features so that image content would be better described and processed. Several researches provided some solutions to combine color derivatives features and color invariant features, color features and other low level features (e.g. color and texture, color and shape [5]), low-level features and high-level features (e.g. from graph representation [8]). However, none of the proposed solutions appear to provide the expected performance to segment complex color images unlike the human visual system which is able to take into account the semantic contents of images. Of course if some a priori information or knowledge about the segmentation task is incorporated in the process that will optimise the algorithm results. In section 2.1 we show that former solutions suffer from limitations and are useless when addressing complex illumination conditions, such as those illustrated by image (d) of Fig. 1.

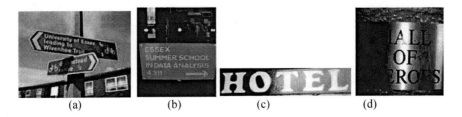

Fig. 1. Color changes due to shading (a), local variation in the intensity of the illumination (b), specularities (c), and specularities and inter-reflections (d)

In a first paper (see [9]) we have demonstrated that none illuminant-invariant model is sufficiently robust to complex photometric effects to solve the issue of text detection in complex natural scenes. To solve this issue, in this paper we propose to use another strategy, more robust to photometric effects, based on the computation of the difference of gamma functions to detect text layers in complex scenes.

Most of existing text segmentation approaches assume that text layers are of uniform color and fail when this is not the case. Furthermore, the background may also be multicolor consequently the assumption according with it is the largest area of (almost) uniform color in the image does not necessarily hold [10]. Lastly, most of existing text segmentation approaches assume that there is a high contrast between text and background in the image this is unfortunately not always the case in real images. Furthermore, many approaches assume that in segmenting the highest peak in the lightness histogram we can deduce if text layers are of lower or a higher lightness than the background region, this information may be helpful to segment text layers, but this is once again not always the case in real images.

In this paper we propose to use a new text segmentation method robust to photometric effects. The proposed method, introduced in [11-12] (see flowchart in Fig. 2), first uses a geodesic transform based morphological reconstruction technique to remove dark/light structures connected to the borders of the image and to emphasize on objects in center of the image. Next uses a method based on difference of gamma functions approximated by the Generalized Extreme Value Distribution (GEVD) to find a correct threshold for binarization. The main function of this GEVD is to find the optimum threshold value for image binarization relatively to a significance level. The significance levels can be optimized using relative background complexity of the image. This approach is based on a new concept of difference of gamma functions used to emphasize certain regions in function of to their intensity distribution. The novel thresholding algorithm is presented in sections 2.3 and 2.4. Next, experimental results are given in section 3. In order to assess text detection methods we use two datasets (ICDAR 2003 and DIBCO 2009) used for competitions [13-15]. Lastly a conclusion is drawn in section 4.

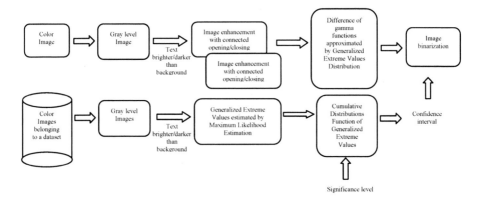

Fig. 2. Flow Chart of the method proposed

2   Text Segmentation

2.1 Image Enhancement Methods

Existing text segmentation approaches are broadly divided under two main strategies: thresholding based, and grouping based. Thresholding based methods use global or local threshold(s) to separate text from background [16]. Commonly used methods are histogram based thresholding and adaptive thresholding. Adaptive or local binarization methods use several thresholds for each study areas of the images instead of one. The most widely used adaptive thresholding algorithms had been proposed by Niblack [17] and Sauvola [18].These methods are more robust against uneven illumination and varying colors than global ones but suffer regarding to dependency of parametric values. Trier and Taxt presented an evaluation of binarization methods for document images in [19]. Most of existing text segmentation approaches assume that text layers and background regions are of uniform color and that there is a high contrast between text layers and background regions in the image this is unfortunately not always the case in real images. For example Karatzas proposed in [10] a text segmentation method which first splits the image in regions that are perceptually different in color next merges connected components having the highest overlapping degree. The splitting process in based on histogram analysis. Peaks are identified by locating minima and maxima on lightness histogram next on hue histogram then a tree structure of layers is created. This method is based on the hypothesis that the intra-class variances are low and the inter-class variances are high but this is not always the case for complex images.

Region based grouping methods are mainly based on spatial-domain region growing, or on splitting and merging. They are commonly used in the field of image segmentation but these techniques are in general not well adapted to segment features such as text. To get more efficient results these methods are generally combined with scale-space approaches based on top-down cascades (high resolution to low resolution) or bottom-up cascades (low resolution to high resolution). The problem of these methods is that they depend on several parameters such as seed values; homogeneity criterion (i.e. threshold values) and initial step (i.e. start point). They are therefore not versatile and cannot produce robust results for complex natural scenes. In addition, in terms of computation time, region based grouping methods are not efficient. However, they use spatial information which groups text pixels efficiently. Clustering based grouping methods are based on classification of intensity or color values in function of a homogeneity criterion. Two main categories of clustering algorithms are histogram based and density based. Multi dimensional histogram thresholding can be used to pre-segment color images from the probability distribution of colors but 3-D histogram must be computed. These methods are not well-adapted for complex natural scenes such as urban scenes with complex background. To be effective these methods require that the intra-class variances are low and the inter-class variances are high. The K-means algorithm and the fuzzy-cmeans algorithm were until recently two of the main techniques used for clustering based grouping. Recently, several studies have also shown that the mean-shift algorithm based density estimation outperforms K-means algorithm [20]. That is, the K-means algorithm is commonly considered as a simple way to classify color pixels through a priori fixed number of clusters. The main idea is to define k centroids, next to perform an iterative process till all pixels belong to a cluster whose centroid is the nearest one.

Even if many approaches have been specifically developed for text layers segmentation based on image binarization most of these approaches fail when image is complex such as in natural scene images. The aim of this work is to present a new strategy to segment text layers in complex images. The main objective is to be robust against photometric effects such as shadows, highlights, specular reflection, non-uniform illumination, complex background, varying text size, colors and styles. The second objective is to reduce noise while enhancing contrast between text layers and background regions using substantially lesser complex processes than other well-known approaches. Noise removal is essential not only for text segmentation but also for other processes such as Optical Character Recognition (OCR).

2.2 Morphological Reconstruction Based on Geodesic Transform

In order to suppress lighter objects (e.g. text layers) than their surroundings and connected to border of the image, another strategy consists to use a morphological reconstruction transform based on geodesic dilation.

According to Soille [21] geodesic dilation of a bounded image always converges after a finite number of iterations (i.e. until the proliferation or shrinking of the marker image is totally impeded by the mask image). For this reason geodesic dilation is considered as a powerful morphological reconstruction scheme. The reconstruction by dilation $R_g^\partial(f)$ of a mask image (g) form a marker image (f) is defined as the geodesic dilation of (f) with respect to (g) iterated until stability as follows (see Fig. 3):

$$R_g^\partial(f) = \partial_g^{(i)}(f) \qquad (1)$$

The stability is reached at the iteration i when: $\partial_g^{(i)}(f) = \partial_g^{(i+1)}(f)$. This reconstruction is constrained by the following conditions that both (f) and (g) images must have the same definition domain (i.e. $D_f = D_g$) and $f \le g$. This reconstruction transform presents several properties: it is increasing ($g_1 \le g_2 \Rightarrow R_{g1}^\partial(f) \le R_{g2}^\partial(f)$), anti-extensive ($R_g^\partial(f) \le g$), and idem-potent $R_g^\partial(R_g^\partial(f)) = R_g^\partial(f)$). This reconstruction transform corresponds to an algebraic closing of the mask image. The connected opening transformation, γ_x (g) of a mask image (g) can be defined as:

$$\gamma_x (g) = R_g^\partial(f_x) \qquad (2)$$

where the marker image f_x equals to zero everywhere except as x which has a value equal to that of the image (g) at the same position.

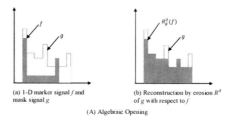

(a) 1-D marker signal f and   (b) Reconstruction by erosion R^∂
mask signal g of g with respect to f

(A) Algebraic Opening

Fig. 3. Algebraic opening for a 1-D signal

According to Soille [21] the connected opening transformation can be used to extract connected image objects having higher intensity values than their surrounding when we chose the mask image zero everywhere, except for the point x which has a value equal to that of the image (g) at the same position (see Fig. 4). In order to suppress lighter objects than their surroundings and connected to border of the image, we choose the marker image zero everywhere except the border of the image. At the border of the image we chose the pixel value of marker the same as mask pixel value at the same position. Once we get the connectivity information with the help of morphological reconstruction based on geodesic transform, we suppress these lighter objects connected to image border. After this preprocess step most of the non-text regions are reduced and kept only most probable text layer candidates which leads us to emphasize more on region of interest of the image (see Fig. 4 (b)). Especially in our experiments we have seen that this process reduce the background intensity variations and enhance the text layers of the image.

In order to suppress darker objects (e.g. text layers) than their surroundings and connected to border of the image the connected closing transformation can be used. The first shortcoming of this morphological transformation and of the former (i.e. closing and opening) is that we must first estimate if the background is lighter or darker than the text layers, i.e. we must first extract the background of the image. The second shortcoming of these two transformations is that they work quite fine when text layers are only darker or whiter than the background but do not perform well when text layers are darker and whiter than their surrounding local background in the image. Lastly, these transforms do not work well when the border of the image has the same intensity than text layers, such as in image (d) of Fig. 1. That why, to enhance this image we set its borders to zero before applying the connected closing transform (see Fig. 4 (d)) otherwise this transform is inefficient (see Fig. 4 (e)).

(a) Original image   (b) Connected opening   (c) Original image   (d) Connected opening (the border of image was first set to 0)   (e) Connected opening (without changing the border of the image)

Fig. 4. (b) Connected image objects having higher intensity values than their surrounding can be extracted by the connected opening transform. (d) Connected image objects having darker intensity values than their surrounding can be extracted by the connected closing transform.

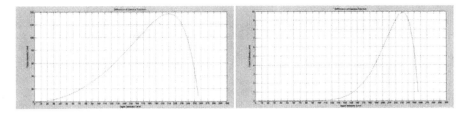

Fig. 5. (a) Difference of gamma functions for ($\gamma 1 = 2$, $\gamma 2 = 4$). (b) Difference of gamma functions for ($\gamma 1 = 9$, $\gamma 2 = 10$).

2.3   Background Estimation Based on Difference of Gamma Functions

In order to classify pixels belonging to the foreground (e.g. text layers) of those belonging to the background, we propose here an additional step based on the computation of the difference of gamma functions.

Let us now consider two gamma contrast enhancement functions defined as follows:

$$g_1(r){=}c_1 r^{\gamma_1}; g_2(r){=}c_2 r^{\gamma_2} \qquad (3)$$

where r represents the input intensity levels, $g_1(r)$ and $g_2(r)$ represent the output intensity levels for gamma values $\gamma 1, \gamma 2$ ($\gamma 1 < \gamma 2$). M is the maximum intensity value (i.e. $0 \le r \le M$, e.g. with a 8-bit image M = 255). The constant c is defined by $c = M^{(1-\gamma)}$.

The two functions defined by eq. (4) can be applied to image $f(x, y)$ to obtain two enhanced images $f_1(x, y)$ and $f_2(x, y)$. Then, we can compute the difference of gamma functions as follows (see Fig. 5):

$$\text{diff}_{f1,f2}(x,y){=}\left| f_1(x,y){-}f_2(x,y) \right| \qquad (4)$$

Then, in order to classify pixels belonging to the foreground (e.g. text layers) of those belonging to the background (see Fig. 6), we propose to apply the following rule.

$$\forall\ (x,y){\in}f(x,y)\ \text{if diff}_{f1,f2}(x,y){>}T \implies (x,y) \in \text{foreground} \qquad (5)$$

$$\text{otherwise } (x,y) \in \text{background}$$

where $\text{diff}_{f1,f2}(x, y)$ is the image corresponding to the difference of gamma functions.

Fig. 6. (a) Original Images. (b) Gamma correction applied to connected opening (resp. closing) enhanced image. (c) Gamma correction applied to connected opening (resp. closing) enhanced image. (d) Difference between gamma corrected images. (e) Thresholded image.

The above rule makes sense only if, in the enhanced image $\text{diff}_{f1,f2}(x, y)$, higher values correspond to text layers and lower values correspond to background regions. As it can be seen in Fig.5, the choice of gamma values affects the suppression of some intensity ranges on the resulting image, so they play a major role in the classification process. As example, the gamma values used in Fig. 6 (b1) and (c1) yield to the suppression of low intensity ranges in Fig. 6 (d1) (see Eq. (6)).

As the background is always either darker or lighter than the surround we consider that there is always a contrast issue between them. When the background is lighter than the foreground, such as in Fig. 6 (a2), rather than using two power law functions (i.e. two negative gamma coefficients) we propose to apply the above difference of gamma functions on the inverse of the image. In the following we consider that the background is darker than the foreground.

When $\gamma_1 < \gamma_2$ the second gamma function $f_2(x, y)$ suppresses more background intensities and enhances more contrasts of foreground intensities than the first $f_1(x, y)$. Unlike other binarization techniques which generate noise artifacts, especially in relatively homogeneous areas such as the background, when we take the difference between two gamma-corrected images we do not generate noisy artifacts in the background. The function $diff_{f1,f2}(x, y)$ presents two main advantages; firstly it better contrasts middle range intensity values, secondly it suppresses lower and higher intensities (see Fig. 5).

By thresholding the resulting image by a value very close to zero, we obtain a perfect separation of foreground and background (see Fig. 6 (e)). As mentioned earlier, different gamma values for γ_1 and γ_2 yields suppression of different intensity ranges. Depending on gamma values γ_1, γ_2 and threshold value T we obtain different binarization results. In order to improve the classification process of foreground pixels and background pixels, we propose now to use a non-supervised process whose objective is to optimize the choice of gamma values for γ_1, γ_2 and of threshold parameter T. Fig.5 shows that the suppression of some intensity ranges depends on the value of γ_1 and γ_2. In the following we use the following notations to define the difference of gamma functions:

$$\Delta f_{\gamma_1, \gamma_2}(x) = M^{(1-\gamma_1)}x^{\gamma_1} - M^{(1-\gamma_2)}x^{\gamma_2} \tag{6}$$

It can be seen on Fig. 5 that $\Delta f_{2,4}$ has a lower power of suppression of intensity ranges compared to $\Delta f_{9,10}$. Let us now consider an arbitrary threshold corresponding to an output value of 2, then for $\Delta f_{2,4}$ the suppression concerns a range of intensity values less than 10, meanwhile for $\Delta f_{9,10}$ the suppression concerns a range of intensity values 10 times larger. When we use the function $\Delta f_{9,10}$ with a threshold value $T = 2$ then the corresponding threshold is 100 for the input image. When we use the function $\Delta f_{2,4}$ with a threshold value $T = 2$ then the corresponding threshold is 10 for the input image.

2.4 Background Estimation Based on Generalized Extreme value Distribution

As discussed in the introduction, the main problem of text extraction is to find correct thresholds to remove background in order to separate text layers from background. The main problem we have to face here is to find appropriate gamma values and threshold value to obtain a relevant binarization. Fig. 5 shows clearly that depending on the gamma values, the suppression of intensity ranges by function $\Delta f_{\gamma_1, \gamma_2}$ varies significantly. How to find appropriate gamma values without a prior knowledge of the image studied?

To solve this issue we propose to compute image statistics from a dataset of text images and to use these statistics to model the distribution of intensities of text images. This proposal is justified by the fact that in natural scene images most of pixels belonging to text layers reside in the middle range of the distribution of pixel intensities. We propose to use the Generalized Extreme Value Distribution (GEVD) model [22] to find the best thresholds (i.e. the optimized ones) to separate text layers from background. Extreme value theory is a well-known statistical tool that deals with extreme events. This theory is based on the assumption that three types of distributions are necessary to model the maximum and the minimum values of a collection of random observations from a unique distribution. These three distributions are called Gumbel, Fréchet, and Weibull distributions [22]. Extreme value theory is an excellent tool to deal with the modeling of sparse data. It is a useful tool to face the thresholding problem in the field of image binarizartion.

Generalized Extreme Value Distribution can be written as:

$$\text{For } k \neq 0 \qquad f(x) = \left\{ \frac{1}{\sigma} \exp^{\left(-(1+kz)^{-1/k}\right)} \cdot (1+kz)^{-1-(1/k)} \right. \tag{7}$$

$$\text{For } k = 0 \qquad f(x) = \left\{ \frac{1}{\sigma} \exp^{\left(-z - \exp(-z)\right)} \right. \tag{8}$$

where $z = \frac{x-\mu}{\sigma}$, x is the variable under study (e.g. the intensity), k is a shape parameter which is 1 for our case (Gumbel), σ is a scale parameter and μ is a location parameter.

We propose to use the Maximum Likelihood Estimation (MLE) method to estimate the function f(x). To find parameters of the GEVD using MLE, different methods can be used, such as [23-24]. Pickands showed in [25] that if X is a random variable and F (x) is its Probability Distribution Function (PDF) then under certain conditions, F (x | u) = P(X ≤ u + x | X > u) can be approximated by a Generalized Pareto Distribution (GPD) [26]. In other words, GPD can be used to find the thresholds of an identical distribution. Let X = {$X_1, X_2, X_3, ... X_n$} be independent random variables with identical distribution F. Next, suppose that D_n = max(X), then it can be shown that for a large value of n:

$$P(D_n < x) \approx f(x) \tag{9}$$

here f(x) corresponds to the Generalized Extreme Value Distribution (GEVD) and u represents the threshold over which the observations {X} exceed. Then, u can be modeled by GPD.

We propose here to use the Cumulative Distributions Function (CDF) of the GEV to define the significance levels which best describe the distributions studied. Next, we propose to compute these significance levels to find proper thresholds for binarization. From our experimentations, we have empirically considered that a significance level of 10% is sufficient to detect simple backgrounds; (see Fig. 7 and 8) meanwhile a significance level of 35-40% is necessary to detect complex backgrounds in natural scenes (see Fig. 9 (a) and (c)).

(a)   (b)

Fig. 7. (a) Input Image with simple background. (b) Threshold image (nb. a significance level of 10% corresponds here to an input intensity value of 146).

To remove both background and over exposed regions we have to define a confidence interval. We assume that foreground intensities lie in a given range:

$$Pr(U_{t1} < X < U_{t2})$$ (10)

here U_{t1} and U_{t2} are, respectively, the lower and the upper thresholds of this interval.

To find t_1 and t_2, we propose to compute for U_{t1} the cumulative probability of P_1 and for U_{t2} the cumulative probability of P_2, in function of the significance level desired. According to our experiments done from 500 images belonging to the ICDAR 2003 dataset [13] and DIBCO 2009 dataset [15], the GEV cumulative probabilities $P_1 = 0.7$ and $P_2 = 0.99$ are sufficient to remove most of overexposed regions and backgrounds [12]. As example, see Fig. 9 (c) and (d).

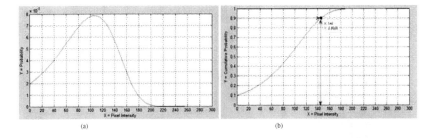

Fig. 8. (a) PDF of the GEVD of the image of Fig. 6 (a). (b) CDF of the GEVD of Fig. 6 (a).

Fig. 9. (a) Input image with a complex background. (b) Threshold image. (c) Input image with over exposed background. (d) Threshold image.

3   Experimental Results

Fig.7 and 10, and Table 1 illustrate some experimental results that we get with the DIBCO2009 dataset [15]. The main interest of the DIBCO2009 dataset is that the ground truth of the binarization of each image is provided and that evaluation performance measures are also provided. Let us note that most of the images belonging to this database are not overexposed nor subjected to shadows, in other words their background is moderately complex (see Fig. 10). Consequently, to binarize these images we have used a significance level of 10%. For each of these images we have computed the Precision (PR), recall (RC), F-measure (FM) and peak signal to noise ratio (PSNR) values relatively to the ground truths provided. To analyze the performance of our binarization method we have compared the results that we get with those obtained by Niblack [17], Sauvola [18] and Otsu [27] algorithms.

The results of the DIBCO2009 competition can be found in [15]. All performance calculations based on DIBCO dataset have been computed according to the definitions provided for DIBCO2009 competition. The comparison of results computed from the DIBCO dataset is done in Table 1. As it can be seen the proposed method has the best F measure (value equal to 88.49) and the higher PSNR (value equal to 17.20). Niblack has a very poor PSNR value because it generates noisy artifacts. Sauvola has a very low recall while Otsu has a very low precision.

Fig. 9, 11 and 12 illustrate some experimental results that we get with the ICDAR 2003 dataset [13]. These images are highly complex, subject to shadows or overexposed (see Fig. 11 (a) and 12 (a)). For these images a significance level of 35% is used for binarization. As shown in Fig. 11 (d) and Fig. 12 (b), our results do not suffer from noise and are robust to uneven illumination and shadows. Niblack suffers from a lot of noise and takes a long time to perform binarization. Our algorithm seems to be more robust for text extraction and segmentation.

Fig. 10. Output images corresponding to three handwritten images (with moderately complex background) belonging to the DIBCO2009 dataset [15]

Furthermore, we can see on Fig. 11 (d2) that our algorithm does not suffer from uneven hue variation changes. Both Sauvola and Niblack suffer from hue variations and specular reflections, such as those shown in Fig. 11 (a2). Lastly, in Fig. 12, we have selected some of the most difficult images of ICDAR 2003 dataset. As it can be seen from Fig. 12 (b), the proposed algorithm is robust against uneven illumination; shadowing and specular reflections. Unfortunately, no ground truth has been provided for the ICDAR 2003 dataset for thresholding evaluation. As a result we cannot provide any evaluation performance measures for the images belonging to this dataset to assess the robustness of our binarization algorithm.

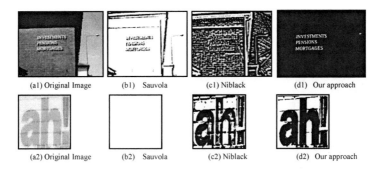

| (a1) Original Image | (b1) Sauvola | (c1) Niblack | (d1) Our approach |
| (a2) Original Image | (b2) Sauvola | (c2) Niblack | (d2) Our approach |

Fig. 11. Output images corresponding to two outdoor images (with complex background and uneven illumination) belonging to the ICDAR 2003 dataset [13]

Table 1. Summary of experimental results

Method	RC	PR	FM	PSNR
Niblack	0.94	0.31	43.75	6.50
Sauvola	0.58	0.98	69.54	14.73
Otsu	0.96	0.16	78.48	15.17
Our Method	0.88	0.89	88.49	17.20

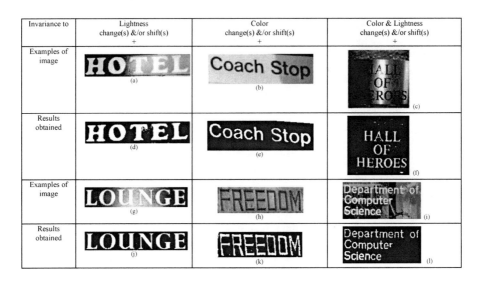

Fig. 12. Output images corresponding to images with uneven illumination, hue variations, specular reflections. Images (a), (b), (g) and (h) belongs to the ICDAR 2003 dataset [13]. Invariance to lightness &/or color change(s) &/or shift(s) is indicated with '+' and lack of invariance with '-'.

Lastly, Fig. 12 shows the color invariance of the proposed algorithm to different types of lighting changes [28, 9].

(a) view 1   (b) view 2   (c) view 3

(d) view 4   (e) view 5   (f) view 6

Fig. 13. According to the angle of observation some letter are hidden by highlights

4 Conclusion

From the results we obtained from ICDAR 2003 and DIBCO 2009 datasets we can conclude that the binarization algorithm proposed in this paper performs well on images with shadows, non-uniform illumination, low-contrast, large signal-dependent noise, smear and strain. Several examples have been given in this paper to show this invariance. In comparison to other methods mentioned in DIBCO 2009 and in H-DIBCO 2010 [29], the proposed method is much simpler. Moreover, the F-measure (FM) results are very close to the best results reported in 2009 meanwhile PSNR values are higher. Lack of noise in the threshold image, good and robust performance results (as recall, precision), and low complexity time are of paramount importance when performing optical character recognition (OCR) in degraded documents and text extraction from natural scenes applications. The experimental results that we have obtained show that the proposed method enables to reach this objective to greater extent.

The proposed methodology is based on the computation of the difference of gamma functions and on an approximation of these differences by image statistics. The main advantage of this novel algorithm is that it is not necessary to provide external parameters to tune the image results. Users have only to indicate if the image is a complex image or a moderately complex image, in the former case the significance level is put to 35%, otherwise to 10%. Rather than asking to the user if the image is complex or not, it would be desirable to use an automatic process, but how to differentiate a complex image of a moderately complex image? We have shown in this study that this seems very complicated given the different photometric effects and cases of study that may exist in natural images.

To solve the issue of shadowing, reflection and uneven illumination, we have shown that the Generalized Extreme Value Distribution (GEVD) is a very relevant model to approximate differences of gamma functions. Indeed GEVD is capable of finding proper extreme values based on image statistics allowing us to deal with extreme conditions like shadows, high illuminations and reflections. To solve the problem of low contrast between text and background, we have shown that the difference of gamma functions is a very relevant model to enhance contrast between text layers and background regions while reducing noise, using substantially lesser complex processes than other well-known approaches. Furthermore, this tool is robust to photometric effects. In the proposed paper, users have to indicate if the text is darker or lighter than the background. Different methods could be used to automatically estimate the intensity level of the background, but we have shown in this study that without any prior knowledge it is very complicated to characterize complex backgrounds in natural image. Lastly, the proposed algorithm is very fast and easy to implement.

In the future, we aim to address the challenging problem of text detection and segmentation with multi-view images. The idea will be to combine the text information extracted from different views, as example see Fig. 13. We aim also to address the challenging problem of text detection and segmentation in video sequences. The idea will be to take into account the evolution of text information over time under the hypothesis that the camera moves in the scene, in other words that the angles of observation changes during the video and then local photometric effects can be temporally compensated. The interest of exploiting temporal redundancy is that it can increase the probability of detecting text layers since the same text may appear under varying lighting conditions from frame to frame [16]. Consequently, missed texts in individual frames can be interpolated. It can also remove false alarms in individual frames since they are usually not stable over time.

References

1. van de Weijer, J., Gevers, T., Geusebroek, J.M.: Edge and corner detection by photometric quasi-invariants. IEEE Trans. on Pattern Analysis and Machine Intelligence 27(4), 625–630 (2005)
2. Li, B., Xue, X., Fan, J.: A robust incremental learning framework for accurate skin region segmentation in color images. Pattern Recognition 40(12), 3621–3632 (2007)
3. Moreno-Noguer, F., Sanfeliu, A., Samaras, D.: Integration of deformable contours and a multiple hypotheses Fischer color model for robust tracking in varying illuminant environments. Image and Vision Computing 25, 285–296 (2007)
4. Trémeau, A., Tominaga, S., Plataniotis, K.: Color in Image and Video Processing: most recent trends and future research directions. EURASIP Journal on Image and Video Processing 2008, article ID 581371, 26 p. (2008)
5. Gevers, T., van de Weijer, J., Stokman, H.: Color feature detection. In: Color Image Processing: Methods and Applications Book, ch. 9, pp. 203–226. CRC press, Boca Raton (2007)
6. Koschan, A., Abidi, M.: Detection and classification of edges in color images. IEEE Signal Processing Magazine, 64–73 (January 2005)
7. Salvador, E., Cavallaro, A., Ebrahimi, T.: Cast shadow segmentation using invariant color features. Computer Vision and Image Understanding 95, 238–259 (2004)
8. Dong, G., Xie, M.: Color clustering and learning for image segmentation based on neural networks. IEEE Trans. on Neural Networks 16, 925–936 (2005)
9. Trémeau, A., Godau, C., Karaoglu, S., Muselet, D.: Detecting text in natural scenes based on a reduction of photometric effects: problem of color invariance. In: Schettini, R., Tominaga, S., Trémeau, A. (eds.) CCIW 2011. LNCS, vol. 6626, pp. 234–248. Springer, Heidelberg (2011)
10. Karatzas, D., Antonacopoulos, A.: Colour text segmentation in web images based on human perception. Image and Vision Computing 25, 564–577 (2007)
11. Fernando, B., Karaoglu, S., Trémeau, A.: Extreme value theory based text binarization in documents and natural scenes. In: Proceedings of IEEE, ICMV, Hong-Kong (to be published)
12. Karaoglu, S., Fernando, B., Trémeau, A.: A Novel Algorithm for Text Detection and Localization in Natural Scene Images. In: Proceedings of IEEE, DICTA 2010, Sydney, Australia, December 1-3 (2010) (to be published)

13. ICDAR 2003 robust reading competitions. In: Proc. of 7th Intl. Conf. on Document Analysis and Recognition, pp. 682–687 (2003)
14. ICDAR 2003 text locating competition results. In: Proc. of 8th Intl. Conf. on Document Analysis and Recognition, pp. 80–84(1) (2005)
15. Document Image Binarization Contest (DIBCO 2009) in the framework of ICDAR2009. In: Proc. of 10th Intl. Conf. on Document Analysis and Recognition, pp. 1375–1382 (2009)
16. Lienhart, R., Wernickle, A.: Localizing and segmenting text in images and videos. IEEE Trans. on Circuits and Systems for Video Technology 12(4), 256–268 (2002)
17. Niblack, W.: An Introduction to Image Processing, pp. 115–116. Prentice-Hall, Englewood Cliffs (1986)
18. Sauvola, J., Pietaksinen, M.: Adaptive document image binarization. Pattern Recogn. 33, 225–236 (2000)
19. Trier, O.D., Taxt, T.: Evaluation of binarization methods for document images. IEEE Trans. Pattern Anal. Machine Intell. 17, 312–315 (1995)
20. Lim, J., Park, J., Medioni, G.G.: Text segmentation in color images using tensor voting. Image and Vision Computing 25, 671–685 (2007)
21. Soille, P.: Morphological Image Analysis: Principles and Applications, pp. 182–198. Springer, Heidelberg (2003)
22. Coles, S.: An Introduction to Statistical Modeling of Extreme Values, pp. 45–50, 75-78. Springer, Heidelberg (2001) ISBN 1-85233-459-2,
23. Lawless, J.F.: Statistical Models and Methods for Lifetime Data, pp. 211–255. Wiley, New York (1982)
24. Prescott, P.: Parameter estimation for the generalized extreme value distribution. Journal of Statistical Computation and Simulation 16(3&4), 241–250 (1983)
25. Pickands, J.: Statistical inference using extreme order statistics. The Annals of Statistics 3, 119–131 (1975)
26. Behrens, C.N., Lopes, H.F., Gamerman, D.: Bayesian Analysis of Extreme Events with Threshold Estimation. Statistical Modeling 4(3), 227–244 (2004)
27. Otsu, N.: A threshold selection method from graylevel histograms. IEEE Trans. Systems Man Cybernet. 9(1), 62–66 (1979)
28. Álvarez, J.M., Gevers, T., López, A.M.: Learning Photometric Invariance for Object Detection. Int. J. Comput. Vis. 90, 45–61 (2010)
29. Pratikakis, I., Gatos, B., Ntirogiannis, K.: H-DIBCO 2010 - Handwritten Document Image Binarization Competition. In: Proceedings of the 12th International Conference on Frontiers in Handwriting Recognition, pp. 727–732 (2010)

Color Target Localization under Varying Illumination Conditions

Simone Bianco and Claudio Cusano

DISCo (Dipartimento di Informatica, Sistemistica e Comunicazione),
Università degli Studi di Milano-Bicocca, Viale Sarca 336, 20126 Milano, Italy
{bianco,cusano}@disco.unimib.it

Abstract. In this work we have investigated the use of color descriptors to automatically locate the color target in the scene. Three different local descriptors have been tested. These descriptors are then used to return multiple localization hypotheses and a geometrical and appearance validation are introduced to select the most feasible pose. The experimental results on a public dataset of RAW images containing the Macbeth ColorChecker CC target and acquired in uncontrolled environments, showed that all the descriptors considered benefited from the hypothesis validation introduced.

1 Introduction

Color targets are widely used in imaging applications. There are two approaches in the field of input device colorimetric characterization: the spectral sensitivity based approach and the color target based approach. In the former approach, the input device spectral sensitivity needs to be measured using expensive specialized apparatus [1]. In the latter approach only a known target is required, making it more practical [2,3]. In the field of multispectral imaging the color targets are also crucial [4]: in fact, for the system characterization a color target with known reflectances is needed. Common practice in the computational color constancy field is to place a known color target in the scene to measure the ground truth illuminant and to assess the performance of the computational color constancy algorithms [5]. Color targets are also used to measure the physical properties of the devices, such as the dynamic range, the noise levels and the optical resolution.

Different color targets are commercially available, each one specifically designed for a different class of devices and for the property to assess (see Figure 1 for some examples). Moreover, custom targets can be used for specific applications: for example Smoyer et al. [6] used a custom made Gamblin oil paint target to assess the reproduction quality of museum digital camera systems; Marguier et al. [7] used a custom made color target to assess human skin color from uncalibrated images.

The color targets placed in the scene are usually manually localized to extract the required information. When dealing with large image datasets, as for example those used for computational color constancy, the target localization can

R. Schettini, S. Tominaga, and A. Trémeau (Eds.): CCIW 2011, LNCS 6626, pp. 245–255, 2011.
© Springer-Verlag Berlin Heidelberg 2011

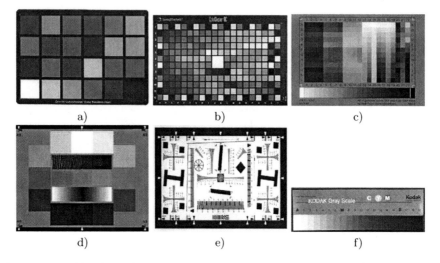

Fig. 1. Examples of standard targets used in imaging applications: a) Macbeth ColorChecher CC; b) Macbeth ColorChecker DC; c) Agfa IT8; d) ISO 15739 noise test chart; e) ISO 12233 resolution test chart; f) Kodak grey scale

be lengthy and tedious. To overcame this problem, we designed a method, based on local color descriptors, to automatically locate the color target in the scene. Three different local descriptors have been tested for the localization task of the Macbeth ColorChecker CC (MCC) in a dataset of 568 RAW images acquired in uncontrolled environments [5]. These descriptors are then used to return multiple localization hypotheses which are then validated on the basis of geometrical and appearance criteria which select the most feasible pose. Appearance validation has been specifically designed to be robust with respect to variations in illumination conditions.

The paper is organized as follows. In Section 2 the general approaches for object localization are described. In Section 3 the proposed approach is described. In Section 4 the experimental results are reported. Finally, in Section 5, conclusions are drawn.

2   Object Localization Methods

Object detection consists in finding instances of a given class of objects in digital images and videos. Object localization is a simplified scenario where it is assumed that exactly one instance is present in the scene. In many cases the class of objects of interest is simply defined by a single image showing a reference instance of the objects to be found. Template matching techniques represent a simple approach to object detection and localization. While very effective for certain environments where object pose and illumination are carefully controlled, template matching becomes infeasible when significant variations in scale, illumination, and 3D pose are allowed. This approach is even more problematic when the object is partially occluded, or placed in a cluttered scene. An alternative approach is to consider only particularly distinctive parts of the image which can be easily matched. This approach usually consists of three major steps [8]: i) a set of distinctive keypoints is selected, ii) the patches surrounding each detected keypoint are described, iii) the set of descriptors extracted from the target and from the template image are compared and matched. Corner detectors (such as the Harris corner detector [9]) are a common choice for keypoint extraction. They identify those locations corresponding to peaks in local image variation which can be reliably and accurately identified in different images. A common problem of early corner detectors is that they examine an image at a single scale: different keypoints are detected when the scale changes significantly. To overcome this problem a multi-scale detector is needed. For instance, Lowe developed the Scale Invariant Features Transform (SIFT) [10], which analyzes the differences of Gaussians at multiple scales. The resulting extrema in the scale-space are selected and labeled with the corresponding scale, and with an orientation computed on the basis of local gradient directions. For each keypoint a neighborhood is selected on the basis of the location, scale and orientation and is described by a feature vector. In order to allow a robust matching, these descriptors should be invariant with respect to changes in illumination and viewpoint. The local descriptors considered in this work are illustrated in the following section. In order to perform object detection, the keypoints and the descriptors found on both the target and the template image must be matched. The approach considered here is similar to the one originally proposed by Lowe [10]. For each keypoint of the template, the best match in the target image is computed by comparing all the extracted descriptors. In case of ambiguity (high similarity for multiple target descriptors, or low similarity for all the target descriptors) the pair is ignored. An affine transform is determined to geometrically match the template and the target keypoints of each pair of matching descriptors. To do so, the Hough transform is used to identify clusters of matching pairs, and each cluster is then verified by a least-squares fitting of the best affine projection parameters relating the template image to the target image. In our approach, the largest clusters are further validated by considering geometric and appearance criteria. The most suitable hypothesis (i.e. the cluster which matches best those criteria) is finally selected.

3 The Proposed Approach

The proposed approach involves the following steps:

1. Detection of scale-space extrema using a difference-of-Gaussian function to identify potential interest points that are invariant to scale and orientation.
2. A detailed model is fit to determine location and scale at each candidate location. Only stable keypoints are retained.

3. On the basis of the local image gradient directions one or more orientations are assigned to each keypoint location.
4. Taking into account the keypoint scale and orientation, each of the descriptors considered is used to describe the region around each keypoint.
5. Once all the keypoints of the color target and of the image in which we want to locate it are described, they are matched to find corresponding keypoints.
6. A Hough transform is used to identify the largest clusters of keypoints belonging to a single object.
7. For each of the identified clusters a verification step is computed through least-squares solution to find consistent pose parameters.
8. Pose parameters are verified to ensure that they correspond to admissible position and orientation.
9. Color descriptors, extracted from the template and the region identified by the pose parameters, are compared.
10. The region which maximizes the similarity with the template is finally selected.

The whole procedure, with the exception of the last three steps, is general purpose and could be applied to various object detection/localization problems. The main difference with the standard approach is that in step (6) the Hough transform is not used to identify a single cluster of keypoints, but it is used to identify multiple clusters. This means that we generate multiple hypotheses about the target pose and we need an hypothesis validation step to select the best hypothesis. Hypothesis validation is performed by the last three steps, which have been specifically designed for the target localization problem by taking into account the following considerations: i) the color target must be placed in such a way that it is entirely contained in the image, and must be oriented in such a way that it is clearly visible; ii) the color target can be easily characterized in terms of its color distribution; iii) a color correction method should be applied to make the color descriptor robust with respect to changes in illumination.

3.1 Local Descriptors Considered

The color descriptors considered belong to the class of gradient-based descriptors. The first one is the Scale Invariant Feature Transform (SIFT): The SIFT descriptor has been proposed by Lowe [10] and describes the local shape of a region using edge orientation histograms. The region is described using a 4×4 array of histograms with 8 orientation bins in each, giving a descriptor with length $4 \times 4 \times 8 = 128$. The second and third descriptors considered are extensions of the SIFT: they are the Opponent-SIFT and the rg-SIFT. The Opponent-SIFT has been included as it is suggested in [11] for its ability to cope with unknown data. The rg-SIFT has been included as it performed best in a previous target localization task [12].

The Opponent-SIFT descriptor computes the SIFT descriptors for all the three color channels of the $O_1O_2O_3$ opponent color space, which is defined as:

$$\begin{bmatrix} O_1 \\ O_2 \\ O_3 \end{bmatrix} = \begin{bmatrix} \dfrac{R-G}{\sqrt{2}} \\ \dfrac{R+G-2B}{\sqrt{6}} \\ \dfrac{R+G+B}{\sqrt{3}} \end{bmatrix}. \tag{1}$$

The final descriptor length is thus 3x128=384.

The rg-SIFT descriptor computes the SIFT descriptor of the r and g chromaticity components of the normalized RGB color space, i.e.:

$$\begin{bmatrix} r \\ g \end{bmatrix} = \begin{bmatrix} \dfrac{R}{R+G+B} \\ \dfrac{G}{R+G+B} \end{bmatrix}, \tag{2}$$

and concatenates them with the original SIFT descriptor. The descriptor length is thus $3 \times 128 = 384$.

3.2 Hypothesis Validation

The hypothesis validation is divided into two different step: a geometric validation and appearance validation. In the geometric validation, the affine transformation A determined in step (7) is decomposed using QR-decomposition: $A = QR$, where Q is an orthogonal matrix ($Q^T Q = I$) and R is an upper triangular matrix:

$$A = \begin{bmatrix} a_{11} \ a_{12} \ a_{13} \\ a_{21} \ a_{22} \ a_{23} \\ 0 \ \ 0 \ \ 1 \end{bmatrix} = \begin{bmatrix} \cos(\theta) \ -\sin(\theta) \ 0 \\ \sin(\theta) \ \ \cos(\theta) \ \ 0 \\ 0 \qquad 0 \qquad 1 \end{bmatrix} \cdot \begin{bmatrix} s_x \ s_h \ t_x \\ 0 \ s_y \ t_y \\ 0 \ 0 \ 1 \end{bmatrix} = Q \cdot R. \tag{3}$$

The Q matrix gives information about the rotation angle θ. Since we do not pose any constraint about the admissible range of rotation, no validation is done on Q. On the other hand the matrix R gives information about scale, shear and shift. The geometric validation acts on R to exclude unfeasible transformations: first of all the shifts t_x and t_y must be in an admissible range (related to the image size) in order to be sure that the center of mass of the target is inside the image. The scales s_x and s_y cannot be too large, too small and too different from each other. The shear s_h cannot be to large. These conditions are given as thresholds: if an affine transformation passes all these conditions, then the appearance validation is performed.

In the appearance validation step the visual characteristics of the object we want to find are exploited. Since we know that the MCC is composed by 24 different colored patches and that the last row is composed of neutral patches, first of all the matrix A is inverted and applied to the image to obtain a normalized view of the object (i.e. the object aligned with the given template). The average values of the R,G,B channels of the image at the expected patches position are extracted. The average values extracted from the last row are used to white balance the object. Then a 24-bins color histogram is extracted and compared with the one of the object template. The histogram is defined by a nearest neighbor quantization which uses as centroids the average RGB values of the 24 patches of the template.

The object pose with the most similar color histogram to the one of the template is then selected. The histograms are compared using the χ_2^2 similarity measure, which for two $d-$dimensional histograms H and H' is defined as

$$\chi_2^2(H, H') = \sum_{i=1}^{d} \frac{(H(i) - H'(i))^2}{H(i) + H'(i)}. \tag{4}$$

The whole hypothesis validation is synthesized in Figure 2.

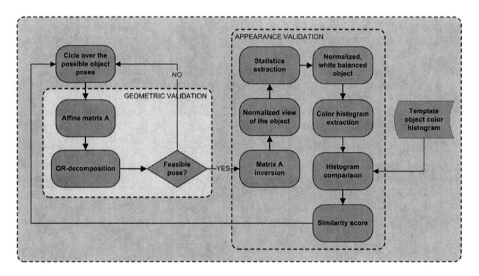

Fig. 2. Block diagram of the hypothesis validation. The two steps in which it is divided are clearly visible: the geometric validation and the appearance validation. In the geometric validation the localizations with a unfeasible target pose are discarded. In the appearance validation the object pose with the most visually similar object to the template is selected.

4   Experimental Results

To test the performance of the descriptor considered, a standard dataset of RAW camera images having a known color target has been used [5]. This dataset is captured using a high-quality digital SLR camera in RAW format, and is therefore free of any color correction. Using a freely available software (dcRAW, http://www.cybercom.net/~dcoffin/dcraw/) we have then demosaiced and converted the images within the dataset into uncompressed linear 16-bit files, paying particular attention to convert the images always using the same multiplicative gains in order to bypass the camera Automatic White Balance (AWB) estimation. The dataset consists of a total of 568 images. The Macbeth ColorChecker (MCC) chart is included in every scene acquired and the task of the descriptors considered is to locate it. The performance measure used to identify the correctly located MCC color target is the same used for the detection task in the PASCAL Visual Object Class Challenge [13]. We consider a correct localization if the area of overlap a_o between the predicted bounding box B_p and the ground truth bounding box B_{gt} exceeds the threshold of 50%, where the area of overlap is computed as:

$$a_o = \frac{\text{area}(B_p \cap B_{gt})}{\text{area}(B_p \cup B_{gt})}. \tag{5}$$

The ratios of correct target localizations given by the descriptors considered are reported in Table 1. The most performing descriptor for the given task is the

Table 1. Ratios of correct localizations given by the descriptors considered

Descriptor name	Validation	Descriptor length	Correct localizations ($a_o > 50\%$)
SIFT	no	128	79.58%
Opponent-SIFT	no	$3 \times 128 = 384$	90.85%
rg-SIFT	no	$3 \times 128 = 384$	94.01%
SIFT	yes	128	89.79%
Opponent-SIFT	yes	$3 \times 128 = 384$	96.30%
rg-SIFT	yes	$3 \times 128 = 384$	96.30%

rg-SIFT with 94.01% of correct localizations. The hypothesis validation introduced was able to improve the ratio of correct localizations of all the descriptors considered: SIFT passed from 79.58% to 89.79%, opponent-SIFT from 90.85% to 96.30% and rg-SIFT from 94.01% to 96.30%.

In Figure 3 are reported the plots of the rates of correct target localizations as a function of the area of overlap a_o for the descriptors considered, both with and without the hypothesis validation.

In Figure 4 an example of the proposed approach is reported. In the first row the image in which we want to locate the color target and the multiple localizations extracted are reported. The second and third row contain two different localizations. From left to right, the first image is the normalized view of the localized area. The second one is the white balanced version of it. The third one is the 24-bin histogram extracted from the localized area and the last one is the 24-bin histogram of the reference target.

Examples of correct target localization using the rg-SIFT descriptor followed by the hypothesis validation are reported in Figure 5. Analyzing the localization

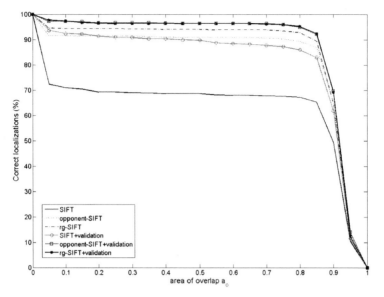

Fig. 3. Plot of the rates of correct target localization as a function of the area of overlap a_o for the descriptors considered, both with and without the hypothesis validation

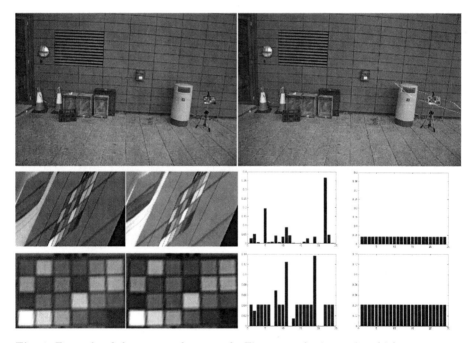

Fig. 4. Example of the proposed approach. First row: the image in which we want to locate the color target and the multiple localizations extracted. Second and third row: two different localizations. From left to right: normalized view of the localized area; white balanced version of it; 24-bin histogram extracted from the localized area; 24-bin histogram of the reference target.

Fig. 5. Examples of correct target localization using the rg-SIFT descriptor followed by hypothesis validation

Fig. 6. Examples of images on which all the descriptors failed the target localization. The area of overlap a_o of the SIFT, opponent-SIFT and rg-SIFT, all followed by the hypothesis validation are (left to right, top to bottom): [0.07% 0% 0%], [9.84% 9.84% 0.16%], [0% 0% 0%], [0.24% 0.24% 0%], [3.15% 0% 0.58%], [8.93% 0.57% 0.57%]

results we noticed that among the images in the dataset there are 18 of them on which all the descriptors failed the target localization (considering an area of overlap $a_o > 50\%$). Examples of failed localizations are reported in Figure 6.

5   Conclusions

Given the importance of color targets in imaging applications and the need to use large datasets, in this work we have investigated the use of color descriptors to automatically locate the color target in the scene. Three different gradient-based descriptors have been tested. These descriptors are then used to return multiple localization hypotheses and a geometrical and appearance validation are introduced to select the most feasible pose. The experimental results on a public dataset of RAW images containing the Macbeth ColorChecker CC target and acquired in uncontrolled environments, showed that the most performing descriptor for the given task is the rg-SIFT. The hypothesis validation introduced was able to improve the ratio of correct localizations of all the descriptors considered: a localization rate of more than 96% has been achieved with Opponent-SIFT and rg-SIFT descriptors.

Most of the missed targets were over or underexposed. As a future development, we plan to deal with these cases by performing a contrast enhancement before the appearance validation of candidate regions.

References

1. Martinez-Verdú, F., Pujol, J., Capilla, P.: Calculation of the Color Matching Functions of Digital Cameras from Their Complete Spectral Sensitivities. Journal of Imaging Science and Technology 46, 15–25 (2002)
2. Bianco, S., Gasparini, F., Russo, A., Schettini, R.: A new method for RGB to XYZ transformation based on pattern search optimization. IEEE Transactions on Consumer Electronics 53, 1020–1028 (2007)
3. Bianco, S., Gasparini, F., Schettini, R., Vanneschi, L.: Polynomial modeling and optimization for colorimetric characterization of scanners. Journal of Electronic Imaging 17(4), 043002-1– 043002-13 (2008)
4. Hardeberg, J.Y., Schmitt, F., Brettel, H.: Multispectral color image capture using a liquid crystal tunable filter. Optical Engineering 41(10), 2532–2548 (2002)
5. Gehler, P.V., Rother, C., Blake, A., Minka, T., Sharp, T.: Bayesian Color Constancy Revisited. In: Proceedings of the IEEE Computer Society Conference on Computer Vision and Pattern Recognition (CVPR 2008), pp. 1–8 (2008)
6. Smoyer, E.P.M., Taplin, L.A., Berns, R.S.: Experimental evaluation of museum case study digital camera systems. In: Proceedings of the IS&T's 2005 Archiving Conference, vol. 2, pp. 85–90 (2005)
7. Marguier, J., Bhatti, N., Baker, H., Harville, M., Süsstrunk, S.: Assessing human skin color from uncalibrated images. International Journal of Imaging, Systems and Technology, special issue on Applied Color Image Processing 17(3), 143–151 (2007)
8. Lowe, D.G.: Object recognition from local scale-invariant features. In: Seventh International Conference on Computer Vision (ICCV 1999), vol. 2, pp. 1150–1157 (1999)
9. Harris, C., Stephens, M.: A combined corner and edge detector. In: Proceedings of the 4th Alvey Vision Conference, pp. 147–151 (1988)
10. Lowe, D.G.: Distinctive image features from scale-invariant keypoints. International Journal of Computer Vision 60(2), 91–110 (2004)

11. van de Sande, K.E.A., Gevers, T., Snoek, C.G.M.: Evaluation of color descriptors for object and scene recognition. IEEE Transactions on Pattern Analysis and Machine Intelligence (2009) (in press), doi:10.1109/TPAMI.2009.154
12. Bianco, S., Cusano, C.: Color target localizations using local descriptors. Colore e Colorimetria: contributi multidisciplinari (2010) (in press)
13. Everingham, M., Van Gool, L., Williams, C.K.I., Winn, J., Zisserman, A.: The PASCAL Visual Object Classes Challenge (VOC 2009) Results (2009), http://www.pascal-network.org/challenges/VOC/voc2009/workshop/index.html

Author Index